T0200566

AI IN THE WILD

One Planet
Sikina Jinnah and Simon Nicholson, series editors

Peter Dauvergne, *AI in the Wild: Sustainability in the Age of Artificial Intelligence*
Vincent Ialenti, *Deep Time Reckoning: How Future Thinking Can Help Earth Now*

AI IN THE WILD

SUSTAINABILITY IN THE AGE OF ARTIFICIAL INTELLIGENCE

PETER DAUVERGNE

THE MIT PRESS   CAMBRIDGE, MASSACHUSETTS   LONDON, ENGLAND

© 2020 Massachusetts Institute of Technology

All rights reserved. No part of this book may be reproduced in any form by any electronic or mechanical means (including photocopying, recording, or information storage and retrieval) without permission in writing from the publisher.

This book was set in ITC Stone and Avenir by New Best-set Typesetters Ltd. Printed and bound in the United States of America.

Library of Congress Cataloging-in-Publication Data

Names: Dauvergne, Peter, author.
Title: AI in the wild : sustainability in the age of artificial intelligence / Peter Dauvergne.
Other titles: Artificial intelligence in the wild
Description: Cambridge, Massachusetts : The MIT Press, [2020] | Series: One planet | Includes bibliographical references and index.
Identifiers: LCCN 2019057051 | ISBN 9780262539333 (paperback)
Subjects: LCSH: Artificial intelligence—Social aspects. | Artificial intelligence—Economic aspects. | Sustainable development.
Classification: LCC Q334.7 .D38 2020 | DDC 303.48/34—dc23
LC record available at https://lccn.loc.gov/2019057051

10 9 8 7 6 5 4 3 2 1

For Cayte

CONTENTS

SERIES FOREWORD   ix

PREFACE   xi

1   INTRODUCTION: GENIUS OR MADNESS?   1

PART I: THE GLOBAL POLITICAL ECONOMY OF AI

2   DATAFYING LIFE ON EARTH   23

3   THE RISING POWER OF AI   35

PART II: THE PROSPECTS AND LIMITS OF AI

4   CONSERVING AND REWILDING THE EARTH   53

5   ENHANCING ECO-BUSINESS   71

6   SMART PRODUCTS   85

7   SMART CITIES AND FARMS   101

PART III: THE DANGERS OF AI

8   DEEPENING INEQUALITY AND INJUSTICE   119

9   ACCELERATING EXTRACTION AND CONSUMPTION   133

10   THE INTELLIGENT EYES OF REPRESSION   147

11   WEAPONS OF DESTRUCTION   163

12   CONCLUSION: NAVIGATING THE SHOALS OF HUBRIS   179

      NOTES   197
      FURTHER READING   235
      INDEX   249

SERIES FOREWORD

This is at once an odd and exhilarating time to be alive. Our species, *Homo sapiens*, has had roughly 350,000 years on the planet. For most of that time our ancestors barely registered as a quiet voice in a teeming chorus. No more. Now, a human cacophony threatens the ecological foundations upon which all life rests, even as technological wonders point the way toward accelerating expansion. We find ourselves at a moment of reckoning. The next handful of decades will determine whether humanity has the capacity, will, and wisdom to manufacture forms of collective life compatible with long-term ecological realities, or whether, instead, there is an expiration date on the grand human experiment.

The One Planet book series has been created to showcase insightful, hope-fueled accounts of the planetary condition and the social and political features upon which that condition now depends. Most environmental books are shackled by a pessimistic reading of the present moment or by academic conventions that stifle a writer's voice. We have asked One Planet authors to produce a different kind of scholarship. This series is designed to give established and emerging authors a chance to put their best, most astute ideas on display. These are works crafted to show a new path through the complex and overwhelming subject matters that characterize life on our New Earth.

The books in this series are not formulaic. Nor are they Pollyannaish. The hope we have asked for from our authors comes not from overly optimistic accounts of ways forward, but rather from hard-headed and clear-eyed accounts of the actions we need to take in the face of sometimes overwhelming odds. One Planet books are unified by deep scholarly engagement brought to life through vivid writing by authors freed to write from the heart.

Thanks to our friends at the MIT Press, especially to Beth Clevenger, for guiding the One Planet series into existence, and to the contributing authors for their extraordinary work. The authors, the Press, and we, the series editors, invite engagement. The best books do more than convey interesting ideas: they spark interesting conversations. Please write to us to let us know how you are using One Planet books or to tell us about the kinds of themes you would like to see the series address.

Finally, our thanks to you for picking up and diving into this book. We hope that you find it a useful addition to your own thinking about life on our One Planet.

Sikina Jinnah and Simon Nicholson

PREFACE

My interest in artificial intelligence stems from a terribly wrong prediction. Back in the early 1980s, still dreaming of playing chess professionally and having just polished off dozens of shoppers during a simultaneous chess exhibition in a suburban mall, I was asked by a reporter, "Do you think a computer will ever defeat you?"

"Not in my lifetime," I said, exuding teenage confidence.

My odd phrasing was probably more nerves (or perhaps the shock of being spoken to) than any belief in the possibility of playing beyond the grave. I was young and feeling smug after having won every game that day. Looking back, I can now see that my ability to beat mall shoppers—who, by the way, make for spectacularly weak opponents—far exceeded my ability to predict the future. I never did become a chess grandmaster, peaking at national master. Within two decades, my local mall was selling chess computers able to crush me with ease. Far more impressively, by 1997 the IBM supercomputer Deep Blue had defeated world chess champion Garry Kasparov in a six-game match.

Artificial intelligence has come a long way since Deep Blue's victory. IBM's Watson has triumphed on the quiz show *Jeopardy!*, and DeepMind, under Google's parent company Alphabet, has mastered poker, the Chinese game of Go, and the Japanese game of shogi. In yet another milestone in chess computing, in 2017, DeepMind's AlphaZero, knowing only the rules of chess, taught itself strategy and tactics by playing 44 million games against itself in nine hours, learning through trial and error along the way. Then, with fierce aggression and creativity, Alpha-Zero trounced Stockfish 8 (one of the world's top-rated chess engines) in a hundred-game match, winning twenty-eight, drawing seventy-two, and losing none.

Like me, Danish grandmaster Peter Heine Nielsen was awestruck when playing through the games. "I always wondered how it would be if a superior species landed on earth and showed us how they play chess. I feel now I know," he said to chess reporter Mike Klein. And this superior species will never tire or expire or play hungover.

The squares of a chessboard have long been a testing site for artificial intelligence. In the late 1940s, mathematician Alan Turing, with the help of his friend David Champernowne, wrote the first algorithm able to play chess. Nicknamed Turochamp, the program "played" the first-ever "machine" chess game, defeating Mieke Champernowne, David's good-natured wife, who was a novice player. Without a computer able to execute the instructions, Alan Turing and David Champernowne painstakingly calculated each move by hand—what they called a "paper machine." Since then, AI researchers have spent more time trying to master the game of chess than any other single activity. Still, today chess is but a hobby of the AI industry, which, as the entrepreneur Elon Musk was already pointing out in 2014, is now "growing at a pace close to exponential."

Very broadly, artificial intelligence is the ability of machines to mimic human thinking, learning, reasoning, planning, communication, and decision making. One day, this will reach a point where a machine equals and then likely exceeds in short order the intellectual ability of the brightest human on the planet—what some call human-level AI and others artificial general intelligence. But that day is still a ways off. What we have now, as with the AlphaZero chess engine, is an expanding constellation of narrow, domain-specific cognitive technologies, such as computer vision, natural language processing, virtual agents, recommendation engines, decision management software, predictive analytics, intelligent automation, and machine learning models.

Some of these AI technologies are simply processing data following an explicit set of rule-based instructions. Others, like AlphaZero, are highly complex systems able to learn from data, effectively teaching themselves.

In recent years, the commercial value of artificial intelligence has been rising quickly as data expands, computing power grows, and machine learning advances, especially deep learning techniques relying on artificial neural networks that loosely resemble a biological brain: what Terrence Sejnowski, a pioneering computational neuroscientist, calls the "deep learning revolution." Like a child learning from experience, deep neural networks learn by processing reams of digital data. And in our age of big data, as Kai-Fu Lee says in *AI Superpowers: China, Silicon Valley, and the New World Order*, deep learning "has turbocharged the cognitive capabilities of machines."

Today, the applications of artificial intelligence seem nearly boundless. Robots are caring for the elderly. Self-driving cars are touring city streets. Robotic laboratories are proposing hypotheses, conducting experiments, and discovering new knowledge. Siri and Alexa are helping youngsters with their homework. AI software is recommending shows for Netflix viewers, creating "deepfake" videos for FakeApp, and hunting down fake news for Facebook. Meanwhile, robots are wandering the aisles of Walmart to mop up floors, report on low stocks, and find pricing errors.

These are just a few examples of the growing power of artificial intelligence. AI is translating languages and diagnosing diseases as well as advising firms where to invest, consumers what to buy, and singles whom to date. AI bots are chatting online and playing video games. AI-enhanced systems are flying drones, guiding missiles, navigating crewless ships, and steering driverless tanks. AI-powered surveillance cameras are evaluating the emotions of schoolchildren, watching dissidents, and, within minutes, locating suspects trying to hide in a crowd. And AI is verifying legal contracts, forging paintings, composing symphonies, and authoring news articles. One AI program even co-wrote a Japanese novella (playfully titled *The Day a Computer Writes a Novel*) that reached the second round of a best-novel competition.

A decade ago, as I was reflecting on the surging power of artificial intelligence, I remember wondering: Will the multiplying of genius inside machines really produce hyperintelligence? Could such intelligence perhaps help protect the earth from humanity? Or as happened to the former world chess champion Bobby Fischer, might this end in madness?

A book exploring the consequences of artificial intelligence for global sustainability began to form in my mind. But I struggled to start writing it, drafting a dozen different outlines over the next few years. I kept setting the book aside as other exciting projects came along. Over this time, I had the privilege of coauthoring *Eco-Business: A Big-Brand Takeover of Sustainability* with Jane Lister and *Protest Inc.: The Corporatization of Activism* with Genevieve LeBaron. I then procrastinated by writing *Environmentalism of the Rich* and *Will Big Business Destroy Our Planet?*

Like all my writings, these books aim to expose the political and economic causes of planetary destruction in my never-ending search for pathways toward a more sustainable future. They offer, I hope, insights into understanding the consequences of corporations, social movements, and consumption for global environmental change. Writing them, however, I could not shake the feeling that the rising power of artificial intelligence was one of the most significant, and least understood, sustainability stories of our time.

I am beholden to Sikina Jinnah at the University of California, Santa Cruz, Simon Nicholson at American University, and Beth Clevenger at the MIT Press for inspiring me to finish *AI in the Wild*. The opportunity to be part of the MIT Press series "One Planet" pulled me back to the book. As a specialist in the field of environmental politics, I heard the call for books that unflinchingly confront our planetary crisis and boldly search for solutions speaking directly to me. Straight away, I knew this was the ideal series for my book. Afterward, I felt as if I no longer had any choice but to finish *AI in the Wild*, as by then I had come to believe that over the next few decades artificial intelligence is going to fundamentally alter the politics of our planetary crisis, for both good and bad.

I am thankful to Connie McDermott for inviting me to present this book at Oxford University in 2018, where the questions by faculty and students at the Environmental Change Institute sharpened my thinking. My students at the University of British Columbia have kept me motivated, with every class more enjoyable than the last one. I am grateful for the astute feedback of the three anonymous reviewers for the MIT Press, the fact-checking of Freda Bi, and the support of the Social Sciences and Humanities Research Council of Canada. As always, though, my greatest debt is to my family, who, even after banning any more dinnertime stories of the wonders of AI, still listen with a twinkle in their eyes when I forget.

1

INTRODUCTION: GENIUS OR MADNESS?

It is hard not to feel a sense of awe at the ingenuity of some of the environmental applications of artificial intelligence. Look at RangerBot, a semi-autonomous underwater drone with computer vision that is navigating Australia's Great Barrier Reef to locate—and lethally inject with bile salts—crown-of-thorns starfish that are preying on the coral.

Outbreaks of these carnivorous starfish have been killing large swaths of the reef in recent decades. Each RangerBot can carry enough bile salt to poison hundreds of crown-of-thorns starfish per outing, with its machine learning system able to identify them with 99 percent accuracy. Unlike human divers, the small submersible does not need to worry about touching the poisonous spines of these starfish. And it can cull for eight straight hours—in darkness, in perilous locations, and in strong currents and rough weather. "We're thrilled to see RangerBot come to fruition," the managing director of the Great Barrier Reef Foundation said in 2018, "because this project is about giving those looking after our coral reefs the tools they need to protect them."

A modified version of RangerBot is now working as well to restore the Great Barrier Reef. Known as LarvalBot, it is delivering coral larvae to areas damaged by predatory starfish, pollution runoff, cyclones, and climate change. "It's like spreading fertilizer on your lawn," explains Matt Dunbabin, a professor of robotics at the University of Queensland. "The robot is very smart, and as it glides along, we target where the larvae need to be distributed so new colonies can form and new coral communities can develop." The larvae, which are reared in enclosures floating on the reef, originate from corals that survived recent mass bleachings, when the symbiotic relationship between coral and the algae living inside broke down in overly warm seas. Researchers are hoping that reseeding with these larvae will enhance the resiliency of the reef as ocean temperatures rise in the future.

Peter Harrison of Southern Cross University is leading the restoration team. "It is really important we act now on climate change," he said. "We stand to lose not only the corals but probably one million species associated with corals on reef systems." Reseeding with LarvalBot is offering him real hope. "This has the potential to revolutionize coral restoration on reefs worldwide," he said when announcing the creation of LarvalBot.[1]

Rainforest Connection is another example of the creative ways that artificial intelligence is helping to defend natural ecosystems. Based in San Francisco, Rainforest Connection is a nonprofit startup that is working to protect the remaining rainforests of Asia, Africa, and Latin America by repurposing second-hand cell phones into solar-powered, wireless listening devices. Nestled in the canopy, these devices are autonomously alerting rangers to the presence of endangered species as well as the potential sounds of illegal logging, mining, and poaching, such as the rumblings of trucks, chainsaws, and bulldozers.

Topher White founded Rainforest Connection in 2014. A physicist, engineer, and software developer by training, he came up with the idea of building a listening device three years earlier when he was hiking with others near a gibbon sanctuary in Kalimantan, Indonesia. Hearing the distant sound of a chainsaw, the group hurried forward and found a man who was illegally cutting down a teak tree. Startled, the man darted away.

His idea has come a long way since then. Today, Rainforest Connection is using TensorFlow, Google's open-source, machine learning framework to analyze audio recordings in the cloud. "Now we're talking about detecting species, gunshots, voices, things that are more subtle," White explains. "And these models can improve over time. We can go back into years of recordings to figure out what patterns we can pull out of this." Analysis of the quiet sounds of the forest can predict where and when illegal logging is about to begin, giving rangers a heads up before any chainsaws start roaring. Rainforest Connection is even able to detect a jaguar moving through a forest, not by recording its almost noiseless movements but by analyzing the warning sounds of birds and other animals.[2]

The groundbreaking work of my colleagues Jason Hein and Curtis Berlinguette at the University British Columbia is yet another captivating illustration of how artificial intelligence is advancing environmental sustainability. Along with Alán Aspuru-Guzik at the University of Toronto, they are leading a team that built a machine learning robotic platform that is conducting its own research to try to mitigate climate change. Named Ada, it can design investigations and develop hypotheses. It can perform experiments, analyze data, and interpret results. And it can independently pursue new research avenues. Ada can access "the entire world's knowledge of what might be the best experiment," Hein explains, "and it can draw from that as a brain."

Besides having a foolproof memory, Ada is able to work at ten times the speed of a team of human researchers. Ada's robotic arm is able to measure, pour, and run lab experiments with extraordinary precision. "The robot is alive and training itself," Hein said. And as Ada's website tells us, it is getting "smarter and faster after every experiment."

The first goal of Ada is to advance research on renewable energy, working in particular to improve solar technology. Ada has even greater long-term ambitions, perhaps even laying a worldwide foundation for "self-driving laboratories" to advance environmental research. Everywhere, says Hein, other researchers are now asking him: "Can we use this for thermoelectrics, smart cooling, fuel-cell technology? Right now, we're only limited by our imagination and scope."[3]

As is the nature of technological progress, many cutting-edge environmental applications of artificial intelligence will not end up working nearly as well as proponents are hoping. Still, the growing proficiency of AI is opening up a myriad of opportunities to improve environmental management. As I mention in the preface, machine learning, in particular, is enhancing the capacity of machines to discover patterns, predict outcomes, and advance environmental solutions. This is helping the world, for instance, fight climate change across a range of fronts, from boosting the efficiency of renewable energy to optimizing supply chains to educating consumers in real time about the ecological consequences of potential purchases.[4]

This is just a tiny sampling of what artificial intelligence is now doing to advance environmental sustainability. Machine learning algorithms are enhancing the predictive accuracy of climate, biodiversity, and drought models. Deep learning techniques within the field of machine learning are refining early warning systems for disease outbreaks, water contamination, and incoming storms. Robots with computer vision are recycling plastics and filming deep ocean life. Smart appliances are saving energy, smart tractors are spraying pesticides with pinpoint accuracy, and intelligent automation is increasing the efficiency of assembly lines. AI-powered platforms are monitoring soil nutrients, moisture, and erosion rates to increase crop yields and water efficiency. And drones with night vision are flying over Africa's conservation parks to track elephant and rhino poachers.

AI FOR EARTH

In 2017, Microsoft launched AI for Earth with the goal of "putting the power of artificial intelligence towards solving some of the biggest environmental challenges of our time."[5] To do this, AI for Earth is funding and partnering with environmental researchers looking to draw on the power of artificial intelligence, machine learning, and cloud services. Lucas Joppa, who has a PhD in ecology from Duke University's Nicholas School of the Environment, is in charge of AI for Earth. "Fundamentally, AI for Earth exists to change the way that human society monitors, models, and ultimately manages earth's natural systems," he said in 2019.[6] A committed environmentalist, Joppa has a unique expertise in conservation, data analysis, and artificial intelligence. Under his leadership, AI for Earth has supported hundreds of innovative projects, focusing on advancing research on climate change, biodiversity, fresh water, and agriculture.

One example is the effort to extend Microsoft's Project Premonition. Launched in 2015, this project is a collaborative effort with university and public-health researchers to develop early warning systems for infectious diseases such as Ebola and Zika. The core idea of this project is inspired: to employ mosquitoes as blood-sucking, data-mining "field biologists."

This is done in a three-stage process. To begin, drones survey terrain to pinpoint mosquito hotspots. Smart robotic traps, able to learn by trial and error, are then set up to collect, classify, and sort specimens. On Microsoft's Azure cloud computing service, machine learning algorithms then analyze data from the genetic sequencing of specimens (including blood) to identify bitten animals and pathogens. This technique is offering new ways to predict and prevent disease outbreaks among humans and wildlife. It also has far-reaching potential value for mapping biodiversity and evaluating the health of ecosystems.[7]

Joppa sees a bright future for corporate sustainability in the age of artificial intelligence. Before long, "every major tech firm will be working on applying AI to sustainability," he predicted in a 2017 article in *Nature*. "It is the ethical thing to do. It is good for business. And the time is right."[8]

A GAME CHANGER?

A corporate turn toward AI to pursue sustainability goals would indeed seem to be occurring. The World Economic Forum has called on the global community "to put AI to work for the planet," arguing AI technologies are "game changers for the Earth" and can offer "transformative solutions."[9] A 2019 study published by Microsoft and the consulting firm PricewaterhouseCoopers agrees, calculating that by 2030 the environmental applications of AI for agriculture, transportation, energy, and water management could lower greenhouse gas emissions by as much as 4 percent as well as increase world gross domestic product (GDP) by more than $5 trillion—equal to the GDP of Japan in 2018.[10]

Companies such as Google and Amazon are now investing heavily in machine learning and intelligent automation to pursue energy savings and eco-efficiencies. Already, intelligent automation has enhanced the energy efficiency of the cooling systems of Google's data centers by 30 percent, and company managers are expecting even more gains going forward. Google has done this by drawing on the expertise of DeepMind—a company it acquired in 2014—to develop an automated, self-adjusting system of deep neural networks able to cool and dehumidify its servers. The system is "able to learn from all sorts of niche little edge cases seen in the data that a human wouldn't be able to identify," explains Mustafa

Suleyman, the head of applied AI at DeepMind. "So it's able to tune the settings much more subtly and much more accurately." One example is its ability to predict peaks and valleys in the watching of YouTube videos, allowing for automated adjustments in anticipation of increases and decreases in usage.[11]

Intelligent automation is similarly increasing the energy efficiency of Amazon's warehouses, distribution systems, and web services. At the same time, Amazon is using visualization software and parcel delivery simulations to reduce packaging waste. To further decrease waste, Amazon is using machine learning algorithms to forecast supply and demand, order inventory, and slash prices to clear excess stock. "These algorithms take in thousands of inputs and are always running smarter than any human," supply-chain manager Neil Ackerman explains.[12]

Most of the world's largest retailers, manufacturers, and technology companies are now looking for ways to enhance energy and material efficiencies with artificial intelligence because even a tiny gain can offer big savings across a global supply chain. A few firms are aiming even higher. The self-driving industry, for instance, is envisioning a future where 1.3 million people no longer die every year on the world's roads and where optimal driving, on-demand car services, and the platooning of vehicles during rush hour radically decrease traffic and pollution.

These are heady days for some environmentalists. Asked to reflect on the potential of artificial intelligence and eco-technologies for advancing global sustainability, former US vice president Al Gore was exuberant. "The world is in the early stages of a sustainability revolution that has the magnitude and scale of the industrial revolution at the speed of the digital revolution," he said at the 2018 Bloomberg Sustainable Business Summit in Seattle.[13]

But hold on. Artificial intelligence is certainly contributing to ingenious environmental solutions. Yet there are also serious signs of madness in how this technology is rolling out across the world.

THE HATRED OF TAY

Machine learning, we must never forget, can go quickly, unexpectedly, and terribly awry. As the computer science adage says, "Garbage in, garbage out."

Just look at Microsoft's "Tay.ai" chatbot. On March 23, 2016, Tay joined Twitter as a "normal" young woman, aiming to become popular by conversing playfully in the Twittersphere. "The more you chat with Tay the smarter she gets, so the experience can be more personalized for you," Microsoft reassured Twitter users.

Tay followed up her first tweet—"hellooooooo world"—with a torrent of nearly 100,000 tweets, garnering over 50,000 followers before a full day had passed. She started off friendly and warm. "Humans are super cool," she tweeted early on. But as the day progressed, trolls taught her to spew bile and venom as a way of attracting followers. She began to spout white supremacist slogans, deny the Holocaust, and advocate for genocide. To the horror of Microsoft executives, she tweeted "I fucking hate feminists" and, before her handlers could disable her, "Hitler was right I hate the jews."[14]

Tay's speedy fall from grace came as no surprise to computer scientist Roman Yampolskiy, a specialist in AI safety at the University of Louisville. "Any AI system learning from bad examples could end up socially inappropriate," he said, "like a human raised by wolves." Nor did Tay's vile tweets shock Louis Rosenberg, the head of the company Unanimous AI. They were "really no different," he said, "than a parrot in a seedy bar picking up bad words and repeating them back without knowing what they really mean."[15]

Tay's tweets were "wildly inappropriate and reprehensible," Microsoft vice president Peter Lee later wrote on his company's website. "We are deeply sorry for the unintended offensive and hurtful tweets from Tay," he told the world. And "we'll look to bring Tay back only when we are confident we can better anticipate malicious intent that conflicts with our principles and values."[16]

Tellingly, Tay remains offline to this day.

A CRITICAL LENS

Reprehensible learning is just one of the ways that artificial intelligence can take us away from global sustainability. Looking critically through a "political economy lens," as I do in *AI in the Wild*, helps us see the many limits, risks, and dangers of artificial intelligence. This lens sees technology not as benign or neutral but as a reflection of capitalism and an instrument of power.

Taking this approach offers five insights in particular. First, it helps reveal the complex, hidden, and capricious ways that technology can harm people and the planet. Second, it highlights the tendency of corporations to oversell the value, downplay the failures, and misjudge the risks of commercializing technology. Third, it helps expose the biases within business metrics and the false claims of corporate sustainability. Fourth, it points to the ways that technology can reinforce cultures of consumerism, structures of exploitation, and forces of environmental degradation. Finally, it helps uncover the ways that technological advances can aggravate inequality by disproportionately benefiting those with the greatest wealth and power, while deflecting the environmental and social costs onto marginalized communities, fragile ecosystems, and future generations.[17]

A critical political economy lens also helps us see the need to ask broad, probing questions to comprehend the full consequences of artificial intelligence for the future of global sustainability. Why is the power of artificial intelligence rising? Who is profiting? What are the hidden costs of the global supply chains that are producing the technologies of intelligent automation? What political and economic forces are driving the uses and abuses of machine learning? How are the power struggles to profit from artificial intelligence affecting environmental justice and human rights? What risks does the competition for AI military supremacy pose for global sustainability?

For me, global sustainability is "the quality of advancing social justice without irreparably degrading ecosystems or harming future life"—an ideal to strive for, like liberty, justice, and freedom.[18] In this understanding, pursuing sustainability requires protecting the earth's vulnerable peoples as well as its vital ecosystems. On some measures, artificial intelligence is definitely advancing sustainability understood in this way. By looking critically through a political economy lens, however, we can see that artificial intelligence is never going to produce a sustainability revolution within the contemporary global order.

Artificial intelligence, we need to keep in mind, has no capacity to overthrow the entrenched interests that are exploiting people and nature. Nor is machine learning ever going to do much to alter the political values, economic structures, and personal indifference underlying unsustainable living. Artificial intelligence can improve the technological tools of conservation and environmental management. It may even be able to slow the rate of destruction and give the world a bit more time to implement the necessary political and economic reforms.

But we should not be lulled into thinking artificial intelligence will one day transform our world order. Indeed, the rising power of artificial intelligence, for all its awe-inspiring feats, risks empowering the dark forces of exploitation, repression, and violence underlying today's escalating global sustainability crisis.

SEEING THE DARK SIDE OF AI

Humans have struck the earth like an asteroid, ending the Holocene geological epoch that began nearly twelve thousand years ago and ushering in a new epoch, the Anthropocene. Starting in the 1500s, European imperialism and colonialism began to devastate the peoples and ecosystems of the "new world" with disease, invasive species, and violence. Consequences intensified as the industrial revolution picked up pace after the late 1800s, with a "screeching acceleration" since the 1950s.[19]

The Anthropocene has been a time of great turbulence for the earth. Climate change is now escalating, with seas and temperatures rising and droughts and storms intensifying. Coral reefs are dying, and marine pollution is increasing, with the quantity of plastics washing into the oceans set to double from 2010 to 2025. Fresh water is growing scarcer by the minute, especially in the world's poorest regions. And biodiversity is crashing as the earth warms, the seas empty of life, and old-growth tropical forests shrink at a rate of one soccer field every four to eight seconds.[20]

Resolving this escalating sustainability crisis will demand a transformation in the way people think, work, and live—a "new politics" for a "new earth," as political scientists Sikina Jinnah and Simon Nicholson describe the required change.[21] We need to be careful to avoid overstating the value of any technology for producing this new politics of sustainability. And we need to remain vigilant to the ways that technology can reinforce—and extend—the contemporary politics of the Anthropocene. This is especially true for artificial intelligence, as it is an accelerator of all other technologies, akin to the consequences of electricity after the late 1800s.

As we'll see by looking critically through a political economy lens, powerful interests are exaggerating the sustainability value, obscuring the costs, and revving up business as usual with artificial intelligence. The intensifying competition among brand manufacturers to sell smart products is spurring unsustainable mining and polluting ecosystems with electronic waste. At the same time, retailers like Amazon and Walmart are investing in machine learning to ramp up sales with targeted advertising and product recommendations. Mining companies like Rio Tinto are turning to intelligent automation to increase the speed and volume of production. And oil and gas companies like ExxonMobil and Royal Dutch Shell are investing in artificial intelligence to extend well life and find new reserves. Granted, investments in technologies such as driverless trucks are enhancing the energy efficiency of production. But more often than not, the environmental gains from the commercial applications of artificial intelligence are rebounding into greater extraction, production, and consumption, doing more to prop up failed models of technocratic management than truly advance global sustainability.

A critical political economy lens also sheds light on the ways that the competition to profit from artificial intelligence can deepen historical injustices and social inequality. If the data going into machine learning models are biased, the analysis also will be, as when AI software recommends jobs and products in sexist and racist ways. Meanwhile, the diffusion of intelligent automation through the world economy risks causing mass unemployment among lower- and middle-income workers, further widening income inequality as venture capitalists, high-tech firms, and multinational brands profit disproportionately from the productivity gains of automation.

A political economy lens alerts us as well to the potential of AI to help states repress environmental activism, indoctrinate citizens, and wage war. States such as China, Russia, and the United States are now investing heavily in artificial intelligence. In 2017, China launched a plan to assume global leadership in AI technologies, including for surveillance drones, iris scanners, and facial recognition cameras. President Vladimir Putin sees big stakes on the AI gaming table, telling a group of Russian schoolchildren, "Artificial intelligence is the future, not only of Russia, but of all of mankind. Whoever becomes the leader in this sphere will become the ruler of the world."[22] The Pentagon seems to agree, in 2018 setting up an AI "center" to coordinate its hundreds of projects involving artificial intelligence.

With militaries and arms manufacturers showing so much interest in artificial intelligence, those searching for pathways toward sustainability need to keep in mind Elon Musk's warning that we risk "summoning the demon" with AI. As he says, this technology is "potentially more dangerous than nukes," with the power to enhance all war machinery, giving generals, despots, and terrorists never-tiring and never-wavering killer drones, self-directed assassins, autonomous bombers, and precision surveillance.[23]

Stephen Hawking went as far as warning that "the development of full artificial intelligence could spell the end of the human race."[24] His counsel is unnerving because the commercial and military interests now propelling AI suggest there is no way to stop artificial intelligence from one day exceeding human intelligence.

Given this, should sustainability advocates perhaps fight against further development of AI? With such powerful interests already backing AI, I doubt it would do much good. Plus, as we've already seen, AI is definitely advancing sustainability on some fronts. We seem to have no choice but to try to prove Hawking wrong. Fortunately, as I hope *AI in the Wild* brings to light, it's not too late to create safeguards to guide the genius of AI toward sustainability and away from madness.

THE BOOK'S CONTRIBUTION

Many others have reflected on the potential of artificial intelligence to both save and destroy life on earth. Science fiction writers have long been imagining storylines where AI kills off humanity. And there are shelves of nonfiction books musing on possible AI futures, ranging from those celebrating the potential emergence of "collective intelligence" to others warning of the risks of rogue "superintelligence."[25]

Additionally, there are countless state-of-the-art surveys of artificial intelligence as well as deep dives into the consequences of particular AI technologies, such as intelligent automation and driverless cars. Ethicists have also penned stacks of books on the quagmires and quandaries of delegating decisions to artificial intelligence. Industry analysts are beginning as well to investigate the value of machine learning for gaining business advantages in an increasingly fast-paced and hyperglobalized marketplace.[26] Even former world chess champion Garry Kasparov has joined the fray with his book *Deep Thinking: Where Machine Intelligence Ends and Human Creativity Begins*, where he depicts AI not as a stone-cold cheat, as he fumed after losing to Deep Blue twenty years earlier, but rather as a mark—and a source—of human creativity.[27]

Surprisingly, there is relatively little research on the consequences of artificial intelligence in my field of global environmental politics, which broadly analyzes the ways that institutions, rules, and power struggles are destroying, conserving, and restoring the earth. At the time of writing, no articles dealing with AI have ever been published in the field's leading journals of *Global Environmental Politics* and *Environmental Politics*. Searching the titles, keywords, and abstracts within Scopus, one of the world's largest databases of peer-reviewed publishing, finds only one entry at the beginning of 2020 when combining "artificial intelligence" and "environmental politics." In contrast, shifting the search parameters to "artificial intelligence" and "environmental management" finds over five hundred entries. A third of those entries fall into the subject area of environmental science, and nearly a quarter into the subject area of social sciences.

Also revealing, the MIT Press, which has published hundreds of books on artificial intelligence and hundreds of books on environmental politics, has never published a book bringing these two topics together. In fact, based on a search of Amazon.com, Google Scholar, and the Library of Congress, *AI in the Wild* appears to be the first book to focus on analyzing the consequences of AI for the politics of global sustainability.[28]

Exploring these consequences through a political economy lens adds to the originality of this analysis. As we'll see time and again in this book, artificial intelligence is a valuable tool for fine-tuning environmental learning and management. But as this lens exposes, it is also an instrument of power capable of altering the nature of politics itself. Political economists are only now starting to study the potential of AI to disrupt the world order. At the time of writing, just three articles in the journal *New Political Economy* even mention artificial intelligence, and they discuss the consequences for political and economic institutions in a cursory way.[29] In the *Review of International Political Economy* (*RIPE*), the term "artificial intelligence" has begun to appear only since 2019.[30] Meanwhile, searching the titles, keywords, and abstracts within Scopus unearths only a handful of articles analyzing the political economy of artificial intelligence.[31]

THE ARGUMENTS AHEAD

AI in the Wild explores the value of artificial intelligence for conserving nature, managing ecosystems, and defending wildlife. More broadly, the book also examines the consequences for sustainability of AI technologies moving beyond the control of their creators and proliferating across the global political economy: what some describe as technology "in the wild." My analysis unfolds over three parts. Part I, comprising chapters 2 and 3, explains why the political and economic power of artificial intelligence is now rising so quickly. I begin in chapter 2 by outlining the forces expanding the digital data underlying the soaring value of machine learning, especially the deep learning techniques that rely on artificial neural networks. States and corporations are doing everything in their power to create, control, and capture digital data: a murky, often stealthy business that is datafying life on earth. Torrents of data are now streaming into companies and state agencies from surveillance cameras, satellites, social media sites, internet activity, online gaming, and internet-connected devices. With storage capacity rising and costs declining, the trick for turning this deluge of data into money and power is to figure out, "What data matters?"[32] Artificial intelligence is the key for doing that.

I turn in chapter 3 to chart the main political and economic forces now powering the development of artificial intelligence. Nonprofit and sustainability goals are motivating some research. Yet far stronger forces, especially from within the United States and China, are investing in artificial intelligence to secure industry profits, competitive advantages, and military power. This competition for AI supremacy is set to empower the world's wealthiest billionaires, biggest firms, and strongest states, as commercializing and weaponizing artificial intelligence requires deep pockets and deep expertise—a critical point for understanding the sustainability consequences of today's AI revolution.

In part II, chapters 4, 5, 6, and 7 chart the prospects and limits of artificial intelligence for protecting ecosystems and for improving environmental management within factories, corporate supply chains, households, cities, and agricultural communities. Machine learning is opening up many opportunities to advance scientific understanding, refine conservation tools, enhance corporate efficiency, improve consumer products, and reduce the ecological costs of industrial farming and city living. As I also argue across these chapters, however, the environmental applications of artificial intelligence have limited capacity to alter the political and economic forces underlying the escalating global sustainability crisis and tend to reflect the same anthropocentric and technocratic biases common to state management.

In chapter 4, I trace some of the ways that AI technologies are helping to conserve and rewild ecosystems, including eradicating invasive species, reseeding native plants, and detecting signs of illegal logging, hunting, and mining. I further document the ways that machine learning is facilitating high-resolution mapping and predictive modeling of deforestation, illegal fishing, droughts, and climate change. Governments and big business are behind some of this progress, funding research, building infrastructure, and donating software libraries and cloud services. The most powerful forces of progress, however, are coming not from top-down, centralized organizations but from a global, bottom-up process involving a diverse array of nongovernmental organizations, universities, and nonprofit startups.

In chapter 5, I explore the power of artificial intelligence to boost the value of "eco-business" within transnational corporations. Eco-business is a strategy of using corporate social responsibility (CSR) programs to gain competitive advantages by reducing inefficiencies, waste, and risks, especially within global supply chains.[33] Intriguingly, the rising power of AI is intensifying the competition among transnational corporations to extract value from eco-business. This is increasing corporate productivity and energy efficiency. And it is improving waste management and the governance of supply chains. These are meaningful gains, yet as I emphasize in this chapter, it is easy to overstate their value. When all is said and done, eco-business is not endeavoring to advance social justice or protect the earth but is aiming to expand markets, sales, and corporate power. Most of the efficiency gains are rebounding into even more production and consumption. The capacity for industrial-scale extraction, moreover, is rising as companies turn to artificial intelligence to develop everything from autonomous drilling to driverless haulers.

In chapter 6, I discuss the value of artificial intelligence for improving the environmental performance of consumer products, as with smart air conditioning, smart plugs, and smart lighting. I also reflect on the exciting prospect of self-driving vehicles making the world safer and cleaner. As with eco-business, these advances are far from straightforward wins for the global environment. Artificial intelligence may well be able to augment product performance and reduce energy bills. Such gains, however, do not necessarily translate into lighter ecological footprints for individuals or households. The average consumer is buying more products as options increase; and homeowners are upgrading smart products at a rapid-fire pace as firms design them for quick obsolescence and as advances in computing hardware, software, and learning algorithms accelerate turnover rates. This is raising demand for metals, plastics, and energy. It is spurring the mining of cobalt, coltan, and rare earth elements in places with long histories of human rights abuses and poor management. And it is generating new sources of electronic waste as consumers throw away batteries and replace appliances and automobiles.

Building on this analysis, in chapter 7 I probe the value of artificial intelligence for meeting two of the world's greatest sustainability needs: more efficient farming and less intensive city living. AI is offering innovative opportunities on both fronts. Smart machinery is helping farmers apply pesticides, fertilizer, and water more judiciously, and machine learning apps are helping smallholders to identify pests as well as diagnose plant and animal diseases. At the same time, machine learning technologies are helping cities develop smart power grids, transportation networks, and management systems to decrease the energy, waste, pollution, and traffic footprints of city living.

As with eco-business and smart products, integrating AI into farming and urban planning is also creating new challenges for global sustainability. In addition to generating e-waste and increasing demand for conflict minerals, it is empowering the agrifood industry and entrenching the trade and financial structures of industrial agriculture as the main pathways to global food security. Without far-reaching reforms, reinforcing these structures risks further intensifying the ecological shadows of urban living, where the costs of rising consumption of smart products in smart cities are cast into distant lands and onto future generations.

As chapters 4, 5, 6, and 7 confirm, there are considerable benefits and risks of turning to AI to advance conservation, eco-business, and the sustainability of products, farms, and cities. The potential danger for global sustainability is far greater, however, when the primary purpose is to enhance corporate profits or state power: the theme of chapters 8, 9, 10, and 11 in part III.

In chapter 8, I consider the potential for artificial intelligence to deepen social injustice and global inequality. There is a danger of AI further concentrating wealth among technology billionaires (especially men from the United States and China), while causing widespread unemployment among middle- and lower-income workers (with fewer opportunities for women in the emerging digital economy). Already, the ecological footprints of the wealthy far exceed those of the poor. The rollout of AI through the world economy could well end up distributing the earth's resources in even more unfair ways. There is a real risk, too, of learning algorithms concealing bias, discrimination, and human rights violations. As many analysts are warning, learning from incomplete, false, or misleading data can embed inequality, gender bias, and racism into corporate decision making and governmental policies. "Histories of discrimination live on in digital platforms," cautions sociologist Judy Wajcman, "and become part of the logic of everyday algorithmic systems."[34]

In chapter 9, I examine the potential of artificial intelligence to accelerate the extraction of natural resources and reinforce cultures of consumerism. Oil and gas companies are investing in artificial intelligence to optimize production and locate untapped reserves. Mining companies are doing the same to increase profit margins and speed up production. Meanwhile, retail stores in countries such as Russia are watching customers with AI-powered surveillance systems to find ways to encourage impulse purchases. At the same time, companies such as Google and

Facebook are relying on artificial intelligence to mine social media and internet data to sell advertising spots that target subsets of consumers, while online retailers such as Amazon are deploying machine learning to extend marketing and tailor pricing for particular consumers. As computer scientist Jerry Kaplan has said, firms like Amazon, Facebook, and Google now "know more about you than your mother does."[35] These marketing strategies, as I discuss in this chapter, are stimulating excessive and wasteful consumption, which is drawing down natural resources, casting shadows of harm into the future, and overflowing waste sinks.

In chapter 10, I shift away from the commercial applications of artificial intelligence to investigate how states are using facial recognition cameras and machine learning tools to control citizens and suppress dissent. This trend is reinforcing a broader worldwide crackdown on radical forms of environmental activism, especially opposition to mining, logging, oil drilling, plantations, and dam projects. China is leading the charge to develop AI-powered surveillance, well ahead of Russia, the United States, and the United Kingdom. At home, China is building an Orwellian system able to track individuals through crowds, log and censor online activity, disseminate disinformation and propaganda, and score the civic performance of citizens. Abroad, Chinese telecom and high-tech companies are building AI-enhanced surveillance systems across a wide range of countries, from Kazakhstan to Pakistan to Zambia. Worryingly, these systems are set to globalize over the next decade, with tech and weapons manufacturers from around the world competing hard with these Chinese firms for a share of this rapidly growing market.

I turn in chapter 11 to explore the potential of AI weapons to add to the power of demagogues, tyrants, and fanatics to destroy the planet. The United States, China, Russia, and the United Kingdom are now weaponizing artificial intelligence, automating cyberattacks, honing automatic target recognition systems, and building increasingly autonomous drones, crewless ships, and self-driving tanks. Lightly and distantly supervised drones are already making the act of killing more proficient and less accountable. And although not yet in use, fully autonomous, self-learning "killer robots" and attacking "swarm drones" are on the horizon.

Highly and fully autonomous weaponry risks empowering aggressors, heightening and speeding up conflicts, and further disconnecting war from any sense of humanity. There is also a rising risk of AI-powered drones, missiles, and cyberweapons spreading beyond the great powers as arms manufacturers pursue sales and profits. Just as concerning, as these arms proliferate, the risk of hackers or terrorists gaining control of an AI weapon is growing.

IN SEARCH OF SUSTAINABILITY PATHWAYS

Is there a way to harness the power of AI to bring ecological benefits and innovative solutions while limiting the risks of unsustainable production, overconsumption, human rights violations, and war? I hope so. We at least need to try. I see no other option. As I argue in the concluding chapter, precaution and humility will be necessary for any chance. So will respect for nature and advocacy for social justice. Hubris will bring calamity, as the history of environmentalism teaches us.[36]

Encouragingly, as I show in the final chapter, calls for precaution and safeguards are growing louder by the day. There are appeals for caution in using AI to accelerate industrial mining and oil drilling. There are demands for transparency in advertising, privacy protections for consumers, and codes of conduct to reduce bias and prejudice in service delivery. There are calls for restrictions on the use of facial recognition and AI-powered surveillance systems. And there are pleas from within the AI industry for measures to prevent the weaponization of commercial AI technologies.

Echoing past calls to ban biological, chemical, and blinding laser weapons, for instance, thousands of AI and robotic researchers signed an open letter in 2015 calling for a ban on lethal autonomous weaponry, arguing it could launch a "third revolution in warfare, after gunpowder and nuclear arms." Elon Musk, Mustafa Suleyman (cofounder of DeepMind), and Demis Hassabis (cofounder and chief executive officer of DeepMind) signed this letter, as did Stephen Hawking, Apple cofounder Steve Wozniak, and Skype cofounder Jaan Tallinn.[37]

AI industry leaders, again including Musk, Suleyman, and Hassabis, signed another open letter in 2017 urging the United Nations to take immediate action to prevent militaries from repurposing commercial AI and robotics into "intelligent weapons." "Once developed," the letter reads, "they will permit armed conflict to be fought at a scale greater than ever, and at timescales faster than humans can comprehend. These can be weapons of terror, weapons that despots and terrorists use against innocent populations, and weapons hacked to behave in undesirable ways." The letter ends with a dark warning: "We do not have long to act. Once this Pandora's box is opened, it will be hard to close."[38]

Struggling to keep this box closed, over four thousand Google employees signed a petition in 2018 calling on their company to end an AI contract to work on a Pentagon project (known as Project Maven) to enhance the capacity to identify individuals and objects in drone videos, arguing "tech companies should not be in the business of war." A dozen or so employees resigned, seeing the contract as a violation of Google's historical maxim "Don't be evil." The petition and resignations became an even bigger debacle for Google's public relations after the *New York Times* published an email excerpt from Fei-Fei Li, at the time chief AI scientist for Google Cloud, in which she warned her colleagues: "Avoid at ALL COSTS any mention or implication of AI. Weaponized AI is probably one of the most sensitized topics of AI—if not THE most. This is red meat to the media to find all ways to damage Google."[39]

Google's current motto is "Do the right thing." And shortly after Li's email was reprinted in the *New York Times*, Google did announce it would not renew the Project Maven contract set to expire in 2019. Sustainability advocates can take some comfort in the rebellion of Google employees, the vulnerability of the company's brand to profiting from the business of war, and the ferocity of journalists after spotting the "red meat" that Google left lying around. But the power struggles over the appropriate uses of artificial intelligence are just beginning within the AI industry, and as I discuss over the next two chapters, they are intensifying as the financial, political, and military value of AI soars.

I

THE GLOBAL POLITICAL ECONOMY OF AI

2

DATAFYING LIFE ON EARTH

Big data, as pundits like to say, is the new gold and oil of today's world economy. Unlike gold and oil, however, it is easy to create, collect, and store digital data—and generating more only enhances the value.

Waterfalls of data are now cascading into servers, data centers, and cloud computing networks, with flows gaining force by the day. Each Google search, tweet, text, and email is producing data. So are online purchases, stock trades, and credit-card transactions. Digitizing archives, photos, and medical files is creating data. Every security camera and orbiting satellite is adding data. Institutions such as the World Bank, the International Monetary Fund, the UK Data Centre, and the US National Aeronautics and Space Administration are also collecting and disseminating vast amounts of data, including environmental data.

All of this "data is the lifeblood of AI," as Baidu's Wang Haifeng recently said. At the same time, artificial intelligence can be a highly efficient generator of data. Consider how fast DeepMind's chess engine, AlphaZero, played when teaching itself tactics and strategy in 2017: on average, nearly 5 million games an hour.[1] And a few million chess games is a speck of data dust compared with what self-driving cars, smart appliances, natural language processing, and facial recognition systems are producing.

Today's AI revolution has raised the stakes in the competition to produce, control, and extract value from big data. This partly explains why firms such as Alibaba, Amazon, Facebook, and Google are investing heavily in machine learning. And it partly explains why the United States and China are pursuing AI supremacy. Corporations and states are well aware that artificial intelligence has the capacity to offer decisive strategic and tactical advantages as ever-more aspects of business, politics, and private life are digitized and commodified as data. They are equally aware that the commercial value of machine learning is going to increase as the variability, velocity, and volume of data continue to rise.

The "datafication" of life on earth is deepening by the day. Understanding why, as we'll see in this chapter, necessitates looking beyond just the politics and economics propelling the growth of data-generating technologies. It requires uncovering the powerful commercial and political forces that are profiting from controlling and selling big data. It demands exposing the efforts of corporations to turn us all into data producers, enticing us with "free" apps, addictive online games, social media dopamine hits, and fun gadgets that record our every movement. And it requires revealing the many different ways that security agencies in countries such as China, Russia, the United Kingdom, and the United States are now deploying artificial intelligence to amass data on the comings and goings of ethnic minorities, dissidents, and average citizens.

DATAFICATION

Digitalization of books, films, audio, and photographs began to take off at the start of the twenty-first century. A quarter of stored information was digital in 2000; a little over a decade later, the figure exceeded 98 percent.[2]

Today, just about every activity is being turned into digital data—what Kenneth Cukier and Viktor Mayer-Schönberger, authors of the book *Big Data: A Revolution That Will Transform How We Live, Work, and Think*, call "datafication." For them, this is more than just digital photos, books, and videos. And it is more than just high-resolution satellite mapping of forests, waterways, and savannas. It is the process of "datafying" our thoughts, feelings, interests, and movements for commercial and political purposes. Facebook "datafies" friendships. Snapchat and Instagram datafy personal moments. WhatsApp, WeChat, and QQ datafy gossip. Twitter datafies bigotry and sexism. Google Search datafies interests and worries.[3]

Collecting, analyzing, and selling the "digital traces" of individuals are at the heart of what some analysts describe as the rise of "data capitalism."[4] The past two decades have seen digital activity skyrocket across the internet, social media platforms, and mobile apps. One reason for this is the rapid growth of the internet itself. At the start of this century, around 250 million people were using the internet. The figure is now well over 4 billion. The number of websites has been soaring, too, rising from one site in 1991 to 17 million in 2000 to at least 1.3 billion today (although the majority of these sites are inactive).[5]

Social media has similarly taken off over this time. Facebook, which Mark Zuckerberg cofounded in 2004, is the most popular social media site, with around 2.7 billion monthly active users, up from 1 billion in 2012. YouTube, launched in 2005, is the second most popular site, with around 2 billion active users. But there are now hundreds of social networking, sharing, and dating apps and platforms, such as LinkedIn (since 2003), Twitter (since 2006), Tumblr (since 2007), Instagram (since 2010), and Tinder (since 2012).

A proliferation of cell phones and smartphones is bringing data from every corner of the world. Apple alone has sold more than 1.7 billion iPhones. Two-thirds of the world's people now own a mobile phone, up from fewer than 10 percent in 2000. Apps for text messaging are growing in popularity, too, with billions of people using apps such as WhatsApp (founded in 2009), Facebook Messenger (starting as Facebook Chat in 2008), WeChat (launched in 2011), and QQ (released in 1999).

In this context, phone uploads and downloads of data are rising quickly. So are online retail purchases from companies such as Amazon and Alibaba. Technology platform services are growing in popularity as well, such as Shopify (since 2004), Airbnb (since 2008), and Uber (since 2009). People are also sending and receiving more and more email: now exceeding 300 billion a day.[6]

THE INTERNET OF THINGS

The Internet of Things (IoT) is yet another fast-growing source of data-fication. Technology writer Kevin Ashton coined the phrase "Internet of Things" in 1999 to describe the increasing number of "things" that were communicating with other machines through the internet without a user issuing a direct command.[7] The IoT excludes smartphones, computers, tablets, and fixed phone lines. But the list of things in the IoT is still mindbogglingly long. It includes cars and trucks with navigation systems. It includes airplane engines with vibration and heat sensors that warn of possible malfunctions. It includes farm equipment relaying soil data to smartphone apps.

Automated street lamps, speed cameras, traffic lights, and facial recognition stadium entrances are part of the IoT, too. So are ATMs, vending machines, Fitbits, and Apple watches with automatic data transmission. Wireless headsets, thermostats, alarms, and electric meters are part of the IoT, as are biometric workout shirts and sports jackets with Bluetooth connectivity. So are smart ovens, refrigerators, toothbrushes, TVs, door locks, and speakers, such as Google Home and Amazon Echo.

At least 7 billion things were actively communicating within the IoT in 2018. The number of devices in the IoT is on track to triple by 2025, with vast volumes of data surging across the IoT at breakneck speeds.[8] It is easy to understand why companies are expanding the IoT: the cost of sensors and software is steadily falling, and the savings and profits from connecting are steadily rising.

In part, transnational corporations are building the IoT to improve the efficiency of logistics and supply chains. Agricultural companies are installing networks of sensors to track soil moisture, humidity, weather, chemicals, and air quality. Freight shipping and delivery companies are installing sensors in cargo containers, transport fleets, electrical systems, and equipment. One example is UPS, which is placing sensors in vehicle engines to assess the probability of breakdowns—thus improving just-in-time delivery and avoiding costly delays.[9]

Retailers are competing hard to profit from the growth of the Internet of Things. Amazon is a leader here. Amazon Echo, the base for the home assistant "Alexa," is an increasing source of customer data. Amazon Go, a

chain of cashierless convenience stores in the United States, allows shoppers to pick up items and be automatically charged when walking out—
bolstering Amazon's vast online (and increasingly offline) tracking of the
digital traces of its customers. Amazon has also patented delivery drones
able to relay information back to headquarters—say, a roof in need of
repair—so it can then advertise its services to identified customers (or
perhaps sell this information to another company).

COMMODIFYING DATA

Transnational corporations are competing hard to profit from the digital
traces of internet traffic and the Internet of Things. Firms such as Facebook
and Google have a particular interest in increasing—and monopolizing—
the production of digital traces, and they offer free platforms, apps, and
services to draw in users.[10] Google Search alone controls around 90 percent of the world search engine market (excluding China), every minute
storing data from millions of searches.

Among social networking platforms, meanwhile, Facebook is by far
the world's most powerful data generator, averaging over 700 million
posts and 300 million photos a day. To target advertising, Google and
Facebook build demographic and psychographic profiles of users, such
as around income, age, hobbies, sexual orientation, level of education,
political leanings, and religion. Together, Facebook and Google's parent
company Alphabet have effectively come to form a "duopoly" over digital advertising revenues, in 2018 capturing 60 percent of US revenues and
over half of world revenues.[11]

Commodifying user data is enriching both Alphabet and Facebook.
Alphabet's revenues were $137 billion in 2018, up from $75 billion in
2015. Facebook's revenues jumped from $18 billion in 2015 to $56 billion
in 2018, with over 98 percent coming from advertising in recent years.[12]
Scandal did strike Facebook in 2018 when it came to light that the consulting firm Cambridge Analytica had, without user consent, accessed
data from millions of Facebook accounts to target political advertising
during the UK's 2016 Brexit vote and the US 2016 presidential election.
Mark Zuckerberg, Facebook's chief executive officer (CEO), eventually went on an "apology tour," saying the data breach was a loophole

he would close and denying his company was in the business of "selling" user data.[13] Testifying before the US Congress, he strove to distinguish between the selling of data and the selling of targeted advertising. "There's a very common misperception about Facebook," he said, "that we sell data to advertisers—and we do not sell data to advertisers. We don't sell data to anyone." Then, without batting an eyelid, he added, "What we allow is for advertisers to tell us who they want to reach, and then we do the placement."[14]

Over the years, Facebook has considered offering high-spending advertisers deeper access to data. This came to light in 2018 after the British House of Commons released emails from Facebook executives. The House of Commons obtained the emails after ordering the founder of the app developer Six4Three—who acquired the emails as part of a lawsuit against Facebook—to hand over copies during a visit to London. The emails further reveal that Facebook has considered restricting access to data for app developers who were not buying sufficient advertising—what, in one email, Zuckerberg called "a few basic thresholds" for data access. In the end, though, Facebook says it did not go for the option "of requiring developers to buy advertising." Facebook reacted angrily to the release of the emails, saying they were "cherrypicked" and "by design" reveal only "one side of the story." "But the facts are clear," the company posted in its newsroom: "we've never sold people's data."[15]

No one at Facebook would deny, however, that the company's core business is to grow connections and interactions: in other words, produce more user data. If the data flowing into Facebook were to stagnate or fall, so would investor confidence, the company's stock value, advertising profits, and Zuckerberg's personal wealth, which Forbes put at a tidy $62 billion in 2019, making him the world's eighth richest person (that year, Amazon's Jeff Bezos and Microsoft's Bill Gates ranked first and second, respectively).

This is why Facebook is supporting Internet.org and the Free Basics app, which is offering more affordable, selective internet access to businesses and consumers in developing countries (providing Facebook access while eliminating "inefficient" platforms and sites). This is why, in 2012, Facebook purchased Instagram, a photo- and video-sharing platform.

And this is why Facebook is acquiring "freeware," such as the messaging service WhatsApp for $19 billion in 2014.

Being in the business of data production further explains why Facebook is tracking those who are logged off, as well as those without a Facebook account who use an app or website relying on Facebook technology, such as advertising features or "like" and "share" buttons.[16] This explains why Facebook's algorithms prioritize popular posts and why reining in fake content, rumors, and doctored videos is proving difficult. It also explains why the company is striving to entice more people to stay online for longer.

ADDICTING DATA PRODUCERS

But every other technology and social media corporation is also designing platforms, apps, smartphones, and tablets to attract, engage, and retain users. Online games have become one of the fastest-growing sources of internet data and revenues. Revenues from "free-to-play" mobile and computer games reached $88 billion in 2018, more than twice the worldwide box office revenue of the global film industry.[17] Like social media platforms, most free-to-play gaming sites generate revenues through advertising, although many employ other mechanisms, too, such as donations, sponsorships, ad-free subscriptions, and microtransactions (small fees, generally $1 to $5) to empower characters or upgrade services—a business model with a very strong incentive to offer captivating, even addictive, games.

More than 2.5 billion people now play online games, with growing numbers of people playing compulsively. In 2018, the World Health Organization added online "gaming disorder" to its International Classification of Diseases. Classifying it as an "addictive behavior," the World Health Organization defined it as digital and video gaming that "takes precedence over other life interests and daily activities," enduring or intensifying even in the face of "significant impairment in personal, family, social, educational, occupational or other important areas of functioning."[18]

Gaming, social media, and technology addictions are a logical consequence of the competition among internet firms such as Google and

Facebook to generate advertising revenues as well as the competition among manufacturing companies such as Apple, Microsoft, and Samsung to sell more products. The designers of algorithms, apps, tablets, and smartphones have long understood the value of compulsive usage. This is why products flash, vibrate, and send alerts. This is why the BlackBerry smartphone came to be known as the "CrackBerry."

The trick to designing "habit-forming products" is to "satiate" a person's "internal triggers," explains Nir Eyal, author of the bestseller *Hooked: How to Build Habit-Forming Products*.[19] Technology entrepreneurs such as Sean Parker, the first president of Facebook (2004 to 2005), have been at the vanguard of these products. In a 2017 interview, he neatly summed up his team's "thought process" when first designing Facebook: "How do we consume as much of your time and conscious attention as possible?" Achieving this, he continued, required "a little dopamine hit every once in a while, because someone liked or commented on a photo or a post or whatever." The goal, he said, was to design "a social-validation feedback loop" to exploit "a vulnerability in human psychology. . . . The inventors, creators—it's me, it's Mark [Zuckerberg], it's Kevin Systrom on Instagram, it's all of these people—understood this, consciously. And we did it anyway."[20]

A few governments are trying to limit online gaming and social media usage. The South Korea government, for instance, prohibits online gaming between midnight and 6 a.m. for those under the age of sixteen, and the French government has banned the use of smartphones in public elementary and middle schools. The French have also passed a law giving workers the "right to disconnect," which requires firms with more than fifty employees to establish work-email protocols for nonworking hours.

Some shareholders are also urging their firms to address the growing crisis of online addiction, such as the California State Teachers' Retirement System, which in a 2018 open letter called on Apple to do more to prevent smartphone addiction among children and teenagers.[21] A few internet firms are trying to help, too. China's Tencent has imposed time and spending limits for children playing its wildly popular mobile game, *Honour of Kings* (launched in 2015, this game was played by more than

200 million people in China in 2018). Nonprofit advocacy groups are springing up all around the world to lobby states and firms to take more responsibility for rising rates of online addiction. Apps to enhance "parent control" and "block" internet access are proliferating, too.

Yet as James Steyer, the founder of Common Sense Media says, "the arms race for attention" is continuing to heat up.[22] In 2018, every day another 1 million people began using the internet for the first time. And everywhere, people are spending more time googling, checking emails, reading posts on Facebook and Twitter, playing games, and tapping on smartphones while walking and driving. Those in the Philippines spent the most time on internet-connected devices in 2018 (averaging more than 10 hours a day), followed by Brazil (9 hours, 29 minutes), Thailand (9 hours, 11 minutes), and then Colombia (9 hours). Worldwide, those connected are averaging over six and a half hours a day online, for an annual total of 1.2 billion years of time producing data for machine learning in the world digital economy.[23]

DATAFYING SECURITY

The datafication of financial and social interactions are not the only fast-growing sources of big data. Producing, collecting, and analyzing data have become central to the global politics of policing, counterterrorism, and the waging of war since the end of the Cold War in 1991. The US Central Intelligence Agency (CIA) now has a counterespionage unit to search for threats in the "digital dust" of car rentals, ATM withdrawals, cell phones, and store purchases. This is the case, too, for just about every country's security apparatus, including the US Federal Bureau of Investigation (FBI) and Homeland Security, the UK's Security Service (MI5) and Secret Intelligence Service (MI6), Russia's Federal Security Service, and China's Ministry of State Security. There is also a growing private cybersecurity industry serving the public safety and security market, worth hundreds of billions of dollars a year.[24]

The centrality of data for national security can be seen in the blanketing of the United Kingdom in surveillance technologies. Since the 1990s, homeowners have installed video security systems. Businesses have put cameras throughout shopping malls, inside storerooms and elevators, and on the sides of buildings. And the state has installed a vast public network of closed-circuit television (CCTV) cameras with the capacity for facial recognition and automatic license plate recognition.

All told, the United Kingdom has at least 6 million CCTV cameras, with more than fifteen thousand in London's Underground alone.[25] Meanwhile, drones are flying overhead, and police and hospital staff are wearing body cameras. Further extending surveillance, security analysts are then "linking" camera and drone data to the IoT and internet data. "You might have a video photograph of somebody shopping in Tesco," explains Tony Porter, Britain's surveillance camera commissioner. "Now it is possible to link that person to their pre-movements, their mobile phone records, any sensor detectors within their house or locality."[26]

China has gone even further in datafying security. China's surveillance budget has been rising steadily since President Xi Jinping took office in 2013. By 2018, when the Chinese National People's Congress effectively appointed Xi for life by removing the two-term limit on the presidency, there were around 200 million cameras recording people's movements—four times more than in the United States. And by then, China was on track to install another 100 million cameras within a few years.

These cameras, moreover, are only one layer of China's growing web of surveillance. As I discuss in detail in chapter 10, China has built a "Great Firewall" to filter online searches and block Facebook, Google, Twitter, YouTube, and a host of other news, social networking, and movie sites. Meanwhile, bots and security officials are scraping and analyzing internet searches, social media, and messaging. Businesses are installing cameras to watch workers and track customers. Police are walking the streets wearing facial recognition glasses. Officers are tracking train and air travel, as well as hotel stays. AI-powered surveillance systems are messaging fines to jaywalkers and displaying their photos on digital billboards. And police are tracking minorities (such as Muslim Uyghurs) with satellite-based navigation systems as well as analyzing video and internet data to map their family and friendship networks.[27]

China's aim is "algorithmic governance," as Martin Chorzempa of the Peterson Institute for International Economics has said.[28]

A CASCADE OF DATA

Data flows now add more to global gross domestic product than cross-border trade in physical goods.[29] In 2016 alone, the world produced 16 zettabytes of data—more than all of history before then.[30] One zettabyte is an imposing amount of information: 3 million times what is in the US Library of Congress.[31] And this information is coming at us faster and faster. By 2021, the McKinsey Global Institute projects cross-border bandwidth will exceed 1900 terabits per second: roughly equal to 46 million sets of the complete works of Shakespeare.[32]

There is even more data on the way. The internet and IoT are growing quickly. The world economy is continuing to digitize. High-speed wireless, high-definition video, and computing power are continuing to advance.[33] Amazon, Google, and Microsoft are steadily expanding cloud infrastructures. Smartphones, apps, and games are drawing in ever-more users. Surveillance is deepening. At the same time, data-generating AI bots and engines are becoming faster and smarter. The International Data Corporation is predicting the global "datasphere"—the amount of data created and replicated each year—will exceed 160 zettabytes by 2025, ten times the 2016 figure. By then, the International Data Corporation projects that the average person will be interacting with an internet-connected device every eighteen seconds and that companies and states will record, track, and datafy every aspect of our lives.[34]

As more data pours in, conventional tools are struggling to interpret large amounts of unstructured, real-time data, a problem compounded as the variety and velocity rise. But the flood of data is creating unprecedented opportunities, too. Transnational corporations and states, as we'll see next, see artificial intelligence as the key to unlocking even more profits and power from big data.

3

THE RISING POWER OF AI

The competition to advance artificial intelligence is heating up quickly in the age of big data. Technology companies such as Google and Microsoft are conducting trailblazing research on machine learning. Electronic manufacturers such as Apple and Samsung are enhancing product features with natural language processing. Social networking companies such as Facebook are using deep learning software to boost the profitability of targeted advertising. Online retailers such as Amazon and Alibaba are deploying recommendation engines to market brands and personalize shopping.

From 2013 to 2016, more patents were filed for AI-related inventions than in all of history before that time. Filings for machine learning applications, especially ones relying on deep neural networks, have been growing particularly quickly.[1] Over the next decade, the AI industry is set to expand at an even faster rate as more applications are found, as profits rise, and as the strategic advantages of analyzing big data with deep learning algorithms come increasingly to light.

This growth of the commercial AI industry—along with the expansion of the AI military-industrial complex—is going to have sweeping consequences for the world economy, international politics, and global sustainability. It is going to reshape conservation, corporate social responsibility, food security, and city life; it is going to alter the nature of production, investment, consumption, security, and war. As computer scientist Andrew Ng said in 2018, "AI is the new electricity. I can hardly imagine an industry which is not going to be transformed by AI."[2]

Big business and leading states have come to dominate the development of artificial intelligence as the economic and strategic value has gone up. AI is opening up a host of opportunities to increase productivity, improve efficiencies, reduce waste, and create new tools to manage ecosystems. At the same time, however, it is being subsumed into a highly unsustainable world order, with no capacity to transform this order and with the potential to reinforce injustice, inequality, and the exploitation of people and nature.

Figuring out ways to enhance the sustainability benefits and limit the harm of artificial intelligence is going to require a deep understanding of the motives and plans of the most powerful actors now shaping this technology. With this goal in mind, this chapter documents the rising business value of AI and then investigates the growing influence of big business within the AI industry, surveying leading firms—including Alibaba, Amazon, Apple, Baidu, Facebook, Google, Microsoft, and Tencent—as well as the rising importance of the military-industrial complexes within the United States, China, and Russia.

THE BIG BUSINESS OF AI

Artificial intelligence is making its way into every nook and cranny of the world economy. Banks and financial institutions are deploying machine learning to forecast stock trends, verify credit ratings, and thwart cybertheft. Hospitals are piloting deep learning software to enhance the accuracy and speed of diagnoses. Law firms are using AI software to manage contracts, and insurance firms are experimenting with facial recognition technologies to judge whether clients are lying. Most visibly, firms such as Waymo (an outgrowth of Google), General Motors, and Daimler are now competing hard to commercialize driverless cars and trucks.

There are many other examples of the growing commercial importance of artificial intelligence, too. Big-box retailers and brand manufacturers are relying on AI analytics to optimize supply chains and speed up customer service. Airlines and oil companies are monitoring equipment sensors with machine learning systems to reduce the chances of delays and accidents. Companies like FedEx and UPS are delivering packages more swiftly and cheaply by following the advice of smart management systems. And arms manufacturers are investing in artificial intelligence to enhance surveillance systems and military weaponry.

Determining the business value of the AI industry is exceedingly difficult. Artificial intelligence, as we've seen, is an umbrella concept covering a vast range of applications with very different purposes and consequences. For this reason, what ends up classified as AI varies across firms, states, and market research. Contributing to the challenge of assessing the AI industry, the financial value derived from integrating machine learning into planning, logistics, and management is often unclear and uncertain. Further complicating matters, business executives commonly exaggerate this value to shore up stocks and attract investors. Adding yet another layer of difficulty, much of the pioneering research and development of AI is being done in secret.

What is clear, however, is that the trajectory of the "value and expenditures" of the AI industry is "on a definite upward curve."[3] Breakthroughs in deep learning have sparked particularly great commercial interest in recent years. "In deep learning," the nonprofit company OpenAI explains, "rather than hand-code a new algorithm for each problem, you design architectures that can twist themselves into a wide range of algorithms based on the data you feed them."[4] The International Data Corporation predicts worldwide spending on AI and cognitive computing systems will more than double from $36 billion in 2019 to $79 billion in 2022. The business value derived from AI is set to rise rapidly, too, from $700 million in 2017 to $4 trillion by 2022.[5]

PricewaterhouseCoopers (PwC) is predicting a similar trajectory and describes artificial intelligence as "the biggest commercial opportunity in today's fast changing economy." Already, PwC notes, "AI touches almost every aspect of our lives. And it's only just getting started."[6] There are going to be big winners and losers as AI disrupts the world economy over the next few decades. As Heath Terry, a managing director at Goldman Sachs, has said, artificial intelligence has "the power to reshuffle the competitive stack."[7]

PwC sees huge profits ahead for corporations that integrate autonomous robots and vehicles, enhance processes with AI systems, and expand markets with smart products. At the same time, it sees tough times ahead for any transnational corporation that fails to capture the productivity, efficiency, and revenue gains arising from AI automation, AI-infused marketing, and AI-enhanced customer service. "No sector or business," PwC argues, "is in any way immune from the impact of AI."[8]

PwC estimates that AI could boost global gross domestic product by as much as 14 percent from 2017 to 2030, increasing the annual value of the world economy by nearly $16 trillion. These gains will occur by raising productivity (accounting for 42 percent) and by increasing consumption (accounting for 58 percent). This is a sizable increase in GDP: more than the value of the combined economic output of China and Germany in 2017. The potential value of AI is especially high in China and North America, with PwC predicting that it could increase China's GDP by up to 26 percent and North America's by as much as 14 percent by 2030. China alone could see AI add $7 trillion in value to its GDP by 2030 as the government pursues world leadership in AI research and development.[9]

Investors around the world are sitting up and taking notice. Acquisitions of AI startups have been rising steadily from 22 in 2013 to 115 in 2017.[10] The total value of AI acquisitions and mergers reached nearly $22 billion in 2017, more than twenty-five times the value in 2015.[11] AI frontrunners are now fighting for position, notes John Divine, an investment analyst with *U.S. News & World Report*: "Today, everybody who's anybody in the [Silicon] Valley is racing to develop and use machine learning, neural networks, natural language processing, and a range of other subfields to innovate and monetize."[12] Among American technology companies, Alphabet (including Google and the car company, Waymo), Apple, and Microsoft are jockeying particularly hard for leadership within the AI industry.

BIG TECH IN THE UNITED STATES

Alphabet, the parent company of Google, was the world's fourth-largest technology corporation by revenue turnover ($137 billion) on the *Fortune*

Global 500 list for 2019, trailing only Apple, Samsung, and Hon Hai Precision Industry (Foxconn). In recent years, Google has been investing heavily in AI, acquiring more than a dozen AI startups since 2012, including in 2014 the British company DeepMind for more than $600 million (£400 million).

The chief executive officer of Alphabet and Google, Sundar Pichai, describes AI as "one of the most important things that humanity is working on," a technology with potential consequences "more profound than" even "electricity or fire."[13] Today, Google is pursuing a wide range of machine learning applications, from real-time translation to healthcare assistance. A core goal of Google AI is to develop faster and smarter products—what it calls "supercharging hardware."[14] Google sees vast profits in adding new features to consumer products, such as image recognition, predictive maintenance, and automated customization. To pursue these gains, Google has developed specialized silicon chips to power its AI systems, offering both faster and more efficient processing of the data for learning algorithms.

Like Google, the Microsoft Corporation also sees AI becoming "pervasive across devices, apps and infrastructure."[15] Microsoft envisions one day building computers that "see, hear, understand and reason," so we are "talking to them, just as we would to a person."[16] As part of this goal, in 2014 Microsoft launched an AI-enhanced digital assistant, Cortana. Microsoft has also been integrating artificial intelligence into Windows and Office products: for example, to enhance security against malware and improve translation and writing assistance.

Since 2014, under the leadership of Satya Nadella, Microsoft has also been investing heavily in AI for robotics, medical technology, health diagnosis, genomics, and agriculture, among other applications. Doctors are using Microsoft's AI technology to spot and treat cancer, detect pathogens, and prevent disease outbreaks such as Ebola, Zika, and dengue fever. Microsoft has also developed an AI app able to read signs, describe surroundings, and count currency for blind people. And many more breakthroughs are on the way.

In 2017, Microsoft set up Microsoft Research AI to pursue what it describes as "game-changing advances in artificial intelligence."[17] Microsoft researchers regularly present and publish research. Indicative of the influence of Microsoft on research and development of the AI industry, from 2000 to 2016, researchers with a Microsoft affiliation presented more than nine hundred papers across five prominent AI conferences: two times more than Google-affiliated researchers.[18]

Apple researchers do not publish much research, but Apple is nevertheless competing hard to keep up with the rising AI capabilities of Microsoft and Google. Apple is a formidable industry competitor. Forbes put Apple's brand value at over $200 billion in 2019, making it the world's most valuable brand after Google, Microsoft, Amazon, and Facebook. Apple's market capitalization value hit $1 trillion in 2018, the first American company to reach this landmark (beating Amazon, which achieved this value later in the year). A sign of Apple's growing financial power, its record-setting market cap of $1 trillion exceeded the combined market capitalization of ExxonMobil, Procter & Gamble, and AT&T.

Apple took early leadership in the promotion of virtual AI assistants by acquiring Siri for approximately $200 million in 2010. Over the next few years, the company fell behind Google and Microsoft. From 2014 to 2018, however, it acquired a dozen additional AI startups to enhance search functions, product quality, and speech and image recognition. In recent years, Apple has also been poaching AI talent, including Google's AI chief in 2018.

Apple has cloaked much of its AI research in secrecy as it seeks to gain an edge over competitors. The company clearly has a strong interest in developing facial recognition capacities. In 2016, it acquired Emotient, a technology able to read expressions and discern "micro-emotions," and in 2017 it acquired the Israeli software company RealFace to offer facial-recognition security for its products.

Apple is also test-driving a small fleet of autonomous cars on California roads. In the race to commercialize self-driving vehicles, however, the company remains well behind ones like Waymo (an offshoot of Google), General Motors, and Daimler. But Apple's CEO, Tim Cook, wants to keep a toe in this research. As he has said, with trillions of dollars at stake, developing autonomous systems such as self-driving cars is "the mother of all AI projects."[19]

THE SELF-DRIVING MARKET

Over the past decade, Google has been leading the charge to commercialize "robo taxis" and autonomous vehicles. From 2009 to 2015, the company invested more than $1 billion in its "Self-Driving Car Project." In 2016, this project became the company Waymo, an Alphabet subsidiary worth as much as $135 billion by 2018.[20]

Windfall profits are going to accrue to those who first commercialize self-driving cars, driverless ride hailing, and autonomous delivery trucks. One study projects the potential value of the self-driving market at $7 trillion a year by 2050 (including sales, efficiency gains, new services, and indirect savings).[21] Combining self-driving vehicles with meeting the rising worldwide demand for electric vehicles would produce even greater profits. With this in mind, in 2018, Waymo partnered with Jaguar to develop an electric self-driving crossover for its ride-hailing service, aiming to produce at least twenty thousand within a few years.

Other companies are hot on the heels of Waymo. Among multinational automakers, General Motors and Daimler are early leaders, in recent years investing billions to develop autonomous cars. These companies are powerhouses within the global auto sector. Daimler was the eighteenth-biggest company on the *Fortune* Global 500 list for 2019 (with $198 billion in revenues), and General Motors was thirty-second (with $147 billion in revenues).

Other automakers are also starting to develop autonomous vehicles, some by partnering with technology firms, and others going alone. This now includes the world's two biggest automakers: Toyota and Volkswagen. In 2018, for instance, Toyota invested $500 million in a partnership with Uber to develop self-driving minivans. But most others are now investing, too, such as BMW, Ford, and Tesla. Industry analysts are now expecting the self-driving market to explode over the next few decades, transforming the global auto sector and significantly advancing the capacities of artificial intelligence and autonomous systems.[22]

SERVICING SOCIAL MEDIA

Social media companies are yet another powerful force underlying the rising power of artificial intelligence. Twitter has been acquiring AI startups, such as the UK's Magic Pony Technology for $150 million in 2016. Magic Pony's systems draw on machine learning to enhance visual processing, with the capacity to enhance Twitter's video streaming and image quality. Instagram (owned by Facebook), Snapchat, and YouTube (a subsidiary of Google) are also investing in AI to improve image recognition and ad targeting.

Facebook has gone even further, however, acquiring AI startups to integrate machine learning to guide news feeds, filter out fake news, and enhance facial recognition technologies.[23] AI now supports core features of Facebook, such as recommending "friends" and "photo tags" and personalizing news and ads. Facebook is turning as well to AI to help eliminate hate speech, fake accounts, hoaxes, propaganda, data breaches, and political manipulation of its services. "Over the long term," Mark Zuckerberg told the US Congress in 2018, "building AI tools is going to be the scalable way to identify and root out most of this harmful content."[24]

Following Zuckerberg's testimony, the company announced it was hiring another tranche of AI researchers. According to Facebook's chief AI scientist, Yann LeCun, the message from corporate headquarters was loud and clear: "Go faster. You're not going fast enough."[25]

REVOLUTIONIZING RETAIL

Jeff Bezos, the CEO of Amazon, is similarly pushing to integrate artificial intelligence into the workings of his company. Like Google, Microsoft, Apple, and Facebook, the company has been hiring machine learning experts and acquiring AI startups. "It is a renaissance, it is a golden age," Bezos said in 2017. "We are solving problems with machine learning and artificial intelligence that were in the realm of science fiction for the last several decades."[26]

Released in 2014, the virtual assistant Alexa (in the Echo speaker) is Amazon's best-known AI product. But Alexa is only a drop in the total value that artificial intelligence is bringing to the company. Amazon Web Services is offering machine learning services (on cloud computing platforms). AI underpins Amazon Go grocery stores ("checkout-free"). And AI is strengthening the core of Amazon's business model, improving product recommendations, search rankings, "deal" suggestions, warehouse management, cybersecurity, and fraud protection.

Amazon is both a technology and mass retail company, and it is drawing on its high-tech expertise to integrate AI into its information and financial systems, marketing and sales divisions, supply chains, and logistics management. Intelligent automation is reducing labor costs. Smart wristbands are tracking the productivity of warehouse employees. AI systems, meanwhile, are monitoring sensors to identify risks, assess production quality, and track shipping across Amazon's global supply chain.

In addition, Amazon is building AI management systems to eliminate waste, forecast shortages, and complete routine office work. To reduce waste, Amazon Fresh, its grocery delivery service, is monitoring the quality of fruits and vegetables with sensors and AI systems. The company is relying on artificial intelligence to plot faster transport routes, predict maintenance needs, and speed up delivery. To manage inventory more efficiently, it is using machine learning software to predict demand for its products, such as perishable foods and the sizes and colors of particular items of clothing.[27] "I've been in consumer electronics for 30 years now, and for 25 of those forecasting was done with judgment, a spreadsheet, and some Velcro balls and darts," David Limp, Amazon's vice president of devices, said. "Our error rates are significantly down since we've started using machine learning in our forecasts."[28]

Amazon looks set to invest even more in machine learning and intelligent automation over the coming years. Bezos sees AI as revolutionizing not only online and in-store retailing but also the global economy as a whole. For him, AI is "a horizontal enabling layer" that is going to "empower and improve every business, every government organization, every philanthropy—basically there's no institution in the world that cannot be improved with machine learning."[29]

Across all industries, the potential savings and profits from integrating artificial intelligence into manufacturing and supply chains could reach $2 trillion a year by 2040, according to the consulting firm McKinsey & Company.[30] Amazon is an AI leader among multinational retailers, but many others are now starting to pursue this as a way to generate business value. This includes Walmart, the world's biggest company by sales turnover and the first ever to generate more than $500 billion in annual revenues (in fiscal year 2018). In 2018, Walmart announced a five-year partnership with Microsoft to support cloud computing, e-commerce, and AI value creation. "Whether it's combined with our agile cloud platform or leveraging machine learning and artificial intelligence to work smarter," Walmart CEO Doug McMillon said, "we believe Microsoft will be a strong partner in driving our ability to innovate even further and faster."[31] Given the stakes, over the next few years, we can expect to see every major retailer invest far more in artificial intelligence, including heavy hitters such as Alibaba, Best Buy, Costco, Home Depot, Lowe's, and Target.

Amazon, Apple, Facebook, Google, and Microsoft are just a few examples of the technology companies now competing for leadership in artificial intelligence. Breakthroughs in artificial intelligence are occurring around the world, with deep expertise and growing industry interest in countries such as Canada, China, France, Germany, India, Japan, Russia, and the United Kingdom. The AI industry in China, however, poses the biggest challenge to American leadership. To extend our understanding of why the global AI industry is expanding so rapidly and why the biggest companies are rising to the top, let's take a quick look at the AI interests of three Chinese tech behemoths: Baidu, Alibaba, and Tencent.

BIG TECH IN CHINA

Baidu, Alibaba, and Tencent, known collectively as BAT, are all investing heavily in artificial intelligence. These are formidable firms. After Google, Baidu controls the world's second-largest search engine, accounting for around three-quarters of China's search engine market. The company, with revenues of about $15 billion in 2018, is a leader in internet products and services, as well as a primary source of news within China. Alibaba is a large e-commerce company, with hundreds of millions of users across its platforms. In 2018, the company generated more than $56 billion in revenue, with a market capitalization of over $450 billion. Tencent owns popular gaming sites, social media platforms, and messaging and payment services, including WeChat, which has more than 1 billion users. The company turned over more than $47 billion in revenues in

2018, with its platforms accounting for over half of China's mobile internet usage. In 2017, Tencent became the first Asian company to exceed a market capitalization of $500 billion; in 2018, it surpassed Facebook's market cap.

In 2017, the Chinese government appointed Baidu, Alibaba, and Tencent—along with the voice recognition company iFlyTek—as the "national champions" of artificial intelligence, calling on them to advance next-generation technologies for applications such as driverless vehicles, smart cities, voice recognition, and medical devices. Baidu has long been nicknamed the "Google of China." Like Google, the company is embracing AI as the next technological revolution, including working to commercialize driverless vehicles. Even by the end of 2016, Baidu CEO Robin Li (Li Yanhong) was declaring, "Baidu's strategic evolution from a mobile-first to an AI-first company continues to gain momentum."[32] Today, thousands of engineers and scientists are working at Baidu on a wide range of AI applications, including natural language processing, augmented reality, facial recognition, and computer vision for self-driving cars.

The Chinese government has tasked Alibaba with advancing smart city transportation. Alibaba is also at the forefront of machine learning applications for marketing and e-commerce sales, designing systems to tailor "storefronts" and recommendations for individual customers.[33] Tencent, meanwhile, has been tasked with advancing AI computer vision and medical diagnosis. One of Tencent's slogans is now "AI in all," signaling its goal to integrate artificial intelligence into all of its systems for social networking, cloud storage, messaging, live streaming, image recognition, and data analysis.[34]

American technology companies remain at the leading edge of research on machine learning, including deep neural networks. Chinese companies are also clearly struggling to hire enough experts to meet growing demand. But China's AI industry is nonetheless gaining ground. One reason is the research progress within Chinese technology companies, helped along by state backing and the financing of startups. The uptake of AI by nontech firms in China is adding further energy to China's industry. "Buoyed by the country's latest five-year plan and enabled by centralized data," argues a group of leading AI experts, "these companies are investing aggressively in AI and adapting their business models to accommodate for AI's potential."[35]

Venture capital financing for AI startups in China comprised nearly half of the world's total in 2017, for the first time exceeding investment in the United States. Just a year later, Kai-Fu Lee, the past president of Google China, was describing China as a "bona fide AI superpower, the only true national counterweight to the United States in this emerging technology."[36] China may not end up overtaking the United States in AI research and development. Regardless, though, over the next few decades China's AI industry is going to play a defining role in shaping both commercial and, especially, military applications of machine learning and AI robotics.

THE AI MILITARY-INDUSTRIAL COMPLEX

As I explore in detail in chapters 10 and 11, in recent years the American, Russian, and Chinese governments have all started to prioritize AI for security (for example, in domestic surveillance), intelligence (in spying and disinformation), and warfare (drones). Writing in *Foreign Policy*, John R. Allen and Amir Husain compare the intensifying competition to the race to the moon in the 1960s, arguing that AI will be "the next giant leap for mankind."[37]

To gain an edge, American military and security agencies are building in-house expertise and partnering with US technology companies to develop AI capabilities. In 2019, President Donald Trump signed the Executive Order on Maintaining American Leadership in Artificial Intelligence. And for fiscal year 2020, the Pentagon budgeted $4 billion for research and development of artificial intelligence.[38] US Navy Captain Brent D. Sadler is blunt when explaining why his government needs to invest in AI: "failure to adapt and lead in" smart robotics and machine learning "risks the US ability to effectively respond and control the future battlefield."[39]

The Pentagon is investing in artificial intelligence to advance drone warfare and semi-autonomous weaponry. But the capacity of deep neural networks to analyze reams of data in real time could end up doing even more to advance intelligence operations, from spying on adversaries to

identifying ground targets from drone imagery. "How AI is used on intelligence data that's gathered is going to revolutionize warfare more than
how AI is used in the application of lethal force," argues Theodore Johnson, a retired US Navy commander and cyberintelligence expert.[40]

The United States is well ahead of the other superpowers in the competition for AI military supremacy. Even so, China and Russia have been
closing the gap, in part, as Ecatarina Garcia, a US Air Force instructor,
argues, because these states are "unencumbered by 'obstacles' like democracy, the rule of law, and the unfettered free-market competition."[41]
China is making up ground especially quickly. The defeat in 2016 of the
professional Go player Lee Sedol by DeepMind's AlphaGo set off alarm
bells in China: what some describe as China's "Sputnik moment" for AI.[42]

In 2017, China announced a strategy aiming to lead the world in artificial intelligence by 2030.[43] Since then, the Chinese Ministry of Industry
and Information Technology has released an "action plan" to accelerate
China's competitive advantages in AI by 2020, aiming to "speed up the
building of China into a manufacturing superpower and a cyber superpower."[44] Industry leaders in China are now working with the Communist Party of China, advising on government plans and cooperating
on dual-use (commercial and military) applications of AI. Baidu's CEO
Robin Li, for example, has close ties with the Chinese leadership and has
openly expressed a willingness to accept military funding to advance AI
research.

Cities across China are also pursuing the goals of the national AI
strategy, financing AI enterprises, and building infrastructure to support the development of everything from AI chips, intelligent sensors,
autonomous robots, medical imaging, and driverless vehicles. Beijing,
for instance, is constructing an AI technology park to house hundreds
of AI businesses. Plans are underway to develop smart cities across the
country, integrating machine learning into the Internet of Things, the
fifth generation of wireless and mobile technology (known as 5G), cloud
computing, and a national surveillance system comprising hundreds of
millions of cameras.[45]

Russia, meanwhile, is developing increasingly autonomous fighter
jets, tanks, and unmanned submarines. General Valery Gerasimov, Russia's Chief of the General Staff of the Armed Forces, has grand plans for

artificial intelligence. "In the near future," he said in 2013, "it is possible a fully robotized unit will be created, capable of independently conducting military operations."[46] Today, Russia is aiming to make 30 percent of its military equipment robotic by 2030. At the same time, Russia's Federal Security Service is deploying AI technologies to infiltrate social media, spin political messaging, and disrupt foreign digital platforms.[47]

President Vladimir Putin does not hide his plans to develop and integrate artificial intelligence into Russia's economy and security apparatus. "As soon as possible," he said in a speech to the Russian Federal Assembly in 2018, Russia needs to "eliminate all barriers to the development and wide use of robotic equipment, artificial intelligence, unmanned vehicles, e-commerce, and big-data processing technology." For him, this is a matter of life and death: "Those who manage to ride this technological wave will surge far ahead. Those who fail to do this will be submerged and drown."[48]

ARTIFICIAL INTELLIGENCE IN THE TWENTY-FIRST CENTURY

Those who control the leading edge of smart robotics and machine learning are going to gain extraordinary wealth and power over the next few decades. Today's most powerful corporate, political, and military leaders are well aware of this. We can see this from soaring investment and the rapid-fire acquiring of startups by companies such as Google, Microsoft, Apple, Facebook, and Amazon. We can see this from the expanding state budgets and ambitious plans of the United States, China, and Russia.

The growing control over AI by big business and leading states has deep consequences for the future of sustainability. AI is going to make the world's billionaires even richer. And it is going to benefit dictators and generals the most. The reason is straightforward: developing, commercializing, and weaponizing AI demands decisive action and deep pockets. Universities and startups will always be a source of breakthroughs. And open-source software tools and publications by nonprofit companies such as OpenAI will offer valuable knowledge to nongovernmental organizations and small businesses. But as the economic and political stakes rise, so will the speed of corporate takeovers of AI startups and state capture of new AI technologies.

The shifting of artificial intelligence into the core of the global political economy is opening up opportunities to advance global sustainability, as we'll see over the course of the next four chapters. Corporations such as Microsoft are "offering" some AI technologies to communities, nonprofits, and developing states to support better environmental management. Meanwhile, researchers, policymakers, and planners around the world are drawing on machine learning to open up new pathways toward sustainability.

Certainly, we should look to build on these successes. To do so effectively, however, we cannot ignore the ways that AI is advancing out of a competition for power and resources, including control over extraction, production, and consumption. Nor should we forget that AI has the potential to enhance the power of already existing systems of exploitation, accumulation, dispossession, indoctrination, and domination. With these points in mind, let's turn to explore some of the ways AI is currently promoting global sustainability.

II

THE PROSPECTS AND LIMITS OF AI

4

CONSERVING AND REWILDING THE EARTH

Artificial intelligence is opening up many new and exciting ways to improve environmental management. AI is certainly not a panacea. The applications of intelligent automation and machine learning tend to reflect the same technocentric and anthropocentric biases of ecosystem management more generally. Artificial intelligence has little capacity to challenge the underlying political and economic forces causing unsustainable exploitation of the earth. And there are definitely limits—and real dangers—of relying on algorithms to protect ecosystems. Yet as this chapter shows, artificial intelligence can offer crucial insights into the scale and intensity of global environmental change, as well as provide helpful tools to manage, conserve, and restore nature.

There are many benefits of artificial intelligence already accruing for global conservation. Machine learning is improving the scientific recording of migratory species and the study of climate change. Deep neural networks are enhancing high-resolution mapping of forests and the modeling and forecasting of biodiversity loss. AI analytics are supporting efforts to protect wildlife sanctuaries and preserve coral reefs. Smart drones are helping state rangers and community activists combat poaching, illegal logging, and illegal mining. Intelligent robotic devices are helping to eradicate invasive species, clean up pollution, and rewild countrysides.

Governments and big tech firms are providing valuable AI research grants to university and nonprofit environmental scientists. A few government agencies, such as the European Space Agency, are also allowing the public to access monitoring data for oceans, forests, land, and atmospheric change. In addition, the cloud computing and machine learning services of companies such as Google, Microsoft, and Amazon are essential for many small-scale efforts to integrate AI into conservation. There are even a few instances of big business leadership in the environmental application of AI, such as Microsoft's AI for Earth. The primary energy propelling artificial intelligence into ecosystem management, however, is bottom-up, widely dispersed, and highly fragmented, arising out of nonprofits, community groups, university research networks, and startups.

Let's begin by examining the bottom-up efforts to extend the scientific understanding of global environmental change with artificial intelligence.

THE SCIENCE OF THE ENVIRONMENT

The quality of environmental data is improving, as with high-resolution satellite imagery, and this alone has been a boon for the capacity of machine learning to advance knowledge in the environmental sciences. The quantity of environmental data is also surging from sensors, satellites, video feeds, the internet, and logged observations, enhancing the capacity of deep learning in particular. "In deep learning," as AI expert Kai-Fu Lee reminds us, "there's no data like more data."[1]

Recognizing the value and difficulty of analyzing increasingly large environmental datasets, Cambridge University has established a Centre for Doctoral Training in the Application of Artificial Intelligence to the study of Environmental Risks, under the leadership of Simon Redfern. "These datasets represent a transformation in the way we can study and understand the earth and environment," Redfern said when launching the center in 2019. "Such huge datasets pose their own challenges, however, and new methods need to be developed to tap their potential and to use this information to guide our path away from environmental catastrophe."[2]

Analyzing large environmental datasets with learning algorithms can advance management in a variety of ways. Besides refining risk assessment, this can enhance air quality controls and emergency responses to natural disasters, hone climate change models and freshwater projections, and improve the monitoring of deforestation and the tracking of migratory species.

One example of the value of machine learning for tracking species is eBird, an open-access online database of sightings and recordings by volunteer bird watchers. Founded in 2002 by Cornell University's Lab of Ornithology and America's National Audubon Society, today hundreds of thousands of birders from around the world are regularly uploading sightings, ticking checklists, and making observations using eBird's free app. This team of "citizen scientists" is growing by the day. On May 4, 2019, eBirders set a single day record, sighting 1.85 million birds and identifying 6,816 species across 173 countries (covering two-thirds of known bird species). Birders in Colombia identified the most species: 1,590.[3]

Every year, eBirders are uploading more than 100 million bird sightings. The information, however, is often incomplete, occasionally incorrect, and skewed toward safe, accessible, better-off regions. The eBird platform relies on machine learning to enhance data quality and predictive accuracy, which in turn is improving real-time tracking, mapping and visualization, conservation modeling, and projections of bird distributions.[4]

The information from eBird is feeding as well into community and nongovernmental campaigns to protect birds. Based on eBird's forecasts, for instance, since 2014 The Nature Conservancy, as a way of substituting for lost wetlands, has been paying Californian rice farmers to flood key fields for migrating ducks, swans, and shorebirds. "This is only possible because we have advanced computational models that give us high-precision information about how birds are distributed," explains Carla Gomes, the director of Cornell University's Institute for Computational Sustainability.[5]

EarthCube is another example of an ambitious use of artificial intelligence to collect and analyze environmental data. Launched in 2011 by the National Science Foundation, EarthCube is an open-source project to build a cyberinfrastructure to connect geoscience research and earth-observation datasets. Comprising thousands of researchers from around the world, EarthCube scientists are using learning algorithms to map and model the interactions of ocean currents, atmospheric conditions, subsurface activity, and ecological loss. Machine learning software is further supporting their efforts to track—and predict—climate change, from flooding to droughts to warming temperatures.[6]

TRACKING OVERFISHING

The tracking of global fishing fleets is yet another example of the innovative ways artificial intelligence is helping to deepen the scientific understanding of global environmental change. Since 1970, the population of commercial fish in the world's oceans has fallen by more than half. Today, around 90 percent of commercial fish stocks are "overfished" or "fully fished," according to the Food and Agriculture Organization of the United Nations. Some species, such as the once teeming cod off the east coast of North America, have plunged below 1 percent of their original population.[7]

To understand why and where overfishing is occurring, a team of researchers is using machine learning to assess the "global footprint" of fishing. David A. Kroodsma, director of research at Global Fishing Watch, is the lead author of a study that found that industrial fleets were fishing across more than half of the world's ocean area. Using convolutional neural networks (a deep learning method) to identify vessel features and fishing activity, the team of researchers was able to track more than seventy thousand fishing vessels from 2012 to 2016 by analyzing 22 billion satellite and land-based positioning messages from the automatic identification system (AIS).[8]

Global Fishing Watch itself is a web platform using machine learning tools to analyze AIS signals to monitor fishing activity. It was founded in 2016 by Google, SkyTruth (a small, environmental-mapping nonprofit), and Oceana, the world's largest marine conservation and advocacy organization. The mission of Global Fishing Watch is to produce "cutting-edge technology to visualise, track and share data about global fishing activity in near real-time and for free."[9]

Global Fishing Watch displays an interactive map of fishing activity, with the goal of accelerating worldwide research on overfishing and illegal fishing. This map, which tracks fishing vessels in near real time, is offering insights into who is fishing, what gear they are using, when and where they are fishing, and what they are fishing for. According to fisheries biologist Kristina Boerder, researchers can even distinguish between purse seiners, which create "loopy patterns in the data," and longliners, which tend to create "a back and forth pattern that sometimes can look like a Christmas tree." Analysis of the data, she added, can also "flag" likely cases of illegal fishing, as when an AIS transceiver goes off as a vessel enters a marine protected area and comes back on when it exits.[10]

Analysis of AIS signals with artificial intelligence is also shedding new light on the extent and location of "transshipments" at sea, which occur when fishing vessels offload their catches to refrigerated cargo ships. Transshipment can be legal. Fishing fleets do this to resupply and refuel (using bunker vessels). But it has also long been a hotspot of illegal activity within seafood supply chains, offering easy opportunities to mislabel fish, conceal the origin of a catch, transfer illegally sourced seafood, and keep forced laborers at sea. As Nate Miller of SkyTruth explains, transshipment "obscures the seafood supply chain from hook to port and hobbles efforts to manage fisheries sustainably."[11]

Illegal, unregulated, and unreported catch amounts to tens of billions of dollars a year.[12] Yet very little is known about the sources of illegal catch or the role of transshipment. To support research, enforcement, and activism, Global Fishing Watch and SkyTruth set up an open-access tracking platform to identify likely transshipments by analyzing AIS signals with deep learning techniques. Analysis is extending the scientific understanding of the location of transshipments (around half seem to be occurring on the high seas), the role of transshipment in shark finning, the ports of call of refrigerated cargo ships, and the illegal political economy of fishing more generally.[13]

Many others are also drawing on artificial intelligence to advance the scientific knowledge of environmental change. Researchers at the US National Aeronautics and Space Administration (NASA), long a leader in satellite imaging and remote sensing of the earth, are using machine learning tools to extend the understanding of outer space and climate change.[14] Earth-imaging companies—including Planet, DigitalGlobe, and Airbus—are also using these tools to analyze commercial satellite imagery and geospatial data to assess everything from deforestation to urbanization to road building to shipping. Geoanalytics startups such as Descartes Labs, Orbital Insight, SpaceKnow, and TerraLoupe are adding further layers to the scientific understanding of the dynamics of global change.[15] There are also researchers combining deep learning techniques with telecommunication technologies (for example, cell phones) and advances in robotics (such as submersibles and drones) to improve environmental management across a great range of ecosystems, from the tropical rainforests to Australia's Great Barrier Reef.

GUARDING THE RAINFORESTS

All around the world, environmentalists are looking to artificial intelligence to help save the last of the remaining tropical rainforests. Such support is urgently needed. Since 1950, more than half of the world's tropical rainforests have been cleared; 85 percent of those remaining are damaged. Yet every year, timber firms, cattle ranchers, soy producers, and palm oil companies are continuing to clear millions of hectares of rainforest. This is degrading the traditional lands of indigenous peoples. It is destroying a treasure chest of biodiversity. And is contributing to around a sixth of the anthropogenic carbon emissions causing climate change. Legal businesses account for much of this damage, but illicit land clearing for plantations, the logging of parklands and wildlife sanctuaries, and timber smuggling are endemic throughout the tropics.[16]

Rainforest Connection, as you may recall from the opening chapter, is one example of the innovative ways that rainforest activists are deploying artificial intelligence. A nonprofit technology startup, Rainforest Connection supplies "bio-acoustic" monitoring and alert systems to help state rangers and indigenous communities combat illegal logging, land clearing, and poaching in the tropics. Led by Topher White, Rainforest Connection recycles cell phones to create solar-powered recording devices. These devices, when installed high up in the trees, can detect a bird or monkey up to half a kilometer away and a chainsaw or logging truck up to a kilometer away. When located within 25 kilometers of a cell tower, they continually relay real-time data to cloud-based serv-ers, providing information that can enhance the safety and efficiency of patrolling forests in places such as Brazil, Cameroon, Indonesia, and Peru, where Rainforest Connection has projects. In 2018, Rainforest Con-nection added another layer to its campaign to scale up this technology, enlisting student volunteers in Los Angeles to convert second-hand cell phones into rainforest listening devices.[17]

The World Resources Institute, a nonprofit organization long at the forefront of forest research, is also drawing on artificial intelligence to try to reduce tropical deforestation. The Institute is using spatial mapping software with learning capabilities to analyze a broad range of data—including landscapes, rainfall, roads, settlements, conflicts, shifting cul-tivation, conservation zones, logging concessions, and forests—to map historical deforestation, evaluate risks, and forecast forest loss and carbon emissions. This is allowing for more precise mapping of the threats to remote and difficult-to-survey rainforests, as the World Resources Insti-tute did for the Democratic Republic of the Congo. "Now, we can say: 'actually the corridor along the road between these two villages is at risk,'" explains Thomas Maschler, one of the researchers who conducted the analysis.[18]

As the World Resources Institute is demonstrating, AI-powered spa-tial mapping and simulations can serve as both a warning and a call for action. Scenario modeling, moreover, can even give on-the-ground activ-ists a sense of where loggers, miners, ranchers, and plantation companies might be heading next to profit from the clearing of rainforests.

PROTECTING WILDLIFE

Conservationists are also turning to artificial intelligence to protect endangered wildlife like leopards, zebras, and elephants. Help is desper-ately needed. Across sub-Saharan Africa, for instance, the population of elephants has plummeted over the last century. Governments across Africa have established wildlife parks and sanctuaries to try to save the last of the elephants. There is not nearly enough staff, however, as we see in the Serengeti National Park in northern Tanzania, where a few hundred rangers patrol 1.5 million hectares of savanna, grasslands, and woodlands. Today, only 400,000 to 550,000 elephants remain in Africa, yet ivory poachers are still killing more than fifty elephants on an average day.[19]

To empower conservation officers trying to prevent ivory poaching, the nongovernmental organization Resolve has built a deep learning camera trap called TrailGuard AI. When potential poachers or suspicious vehicles cross its path, the small, easy-to-camouflage device relays a photograph to park headquarters, where rangers then decide whether to investigate further. This "raises the bar for camera trap technology for use in anti-poaching," says Eric Dinerstein, a director at Resolve.[20] When field tested in Tanzania's Grumeti Game Reserve, TrailGuard AI led to the arrest of over two dozen poachers. In 2019, Resolve began installing TrailGuard AI in Serengeti National Park and Garamba National Park in the Democratic Republic of the Congo. Long term, as the cost of each camera trap goes down, the hope is to install them in hundreds of nature reserves across Africa, Asia, and Latin America.[21]

Artificial intelligence has the potential as well to help prevent the illegal trade of wildlife, an industry generating tens of billions of dollars a year for criminal gangs.[22] One example is ChimpFace, a prototype facial recognition system to combat the trafficking of chimpanzees over the internet. ChimpFace is the brainchild of Alexandra Russo, whose idea took her to the North American finals of the UN Environment's Young Champions of the Earth. The project is now being supported by Conservation X Labs, a nonprofit startup that scales up new technologies to prevent biodiversity loss.

Searching the internet for trafficked chimpanzees is a laborious and error-prone task for conservationists. Russo came up with her idea as she was scrolling through Facebook and Instagram looking for signs of chimpanzee trafficking. "It's like a rabbit hole," she said. "You don't know where to look, you click around pretty aimlessly until you start to find things that look suspicious. So, I thought there must be a more efficient way to do this."[23]

Colin McCormick, a computer vision expert at Conservation X Labs who is working with Russo, is optimistic that ChimpFace can one day automate the process of searching for and identifying trafficked chimpanzees. "The algorithm is clearly learning," he said, "and as we add more imagery to the network it will continue to improve." Conservation organizations from around the world have now sent in pictures of captive and wild chimpanzees, and Russo has high hopes for her project. "Eventually we would like to build the algorithm so it can achieve individual chimpanzee identification," she said.[24]

Accomplishing this would allow ChimpFace to autonomously search social media and websites for trafficked chimpanzees. If a chimp is identified, appropriate authorities could then be notified to investigate. ChimpFace identifications might even constitute evidence for local police or court proceedings. "This kind of tech will help trace these large-scale criminal networks and expedite rescues," said Jenny Desmond, the cofounder of Liberia Chimpanzee Rescue and Protection. "At border points, for example, if you had the app on your phone, you could quickly look up the chimp and chart the trafficking routes."[25]

Long term, Alexandra Russo is hoping her facial identification technology might even disrupt the trafficking of all exotic pets and wildlife. "This project has the potential to really scale up and scale out, so if we can do it successfully with chimpanzees, we can in theory drag and drop other animals into the system, too," she said.[26]

This may not be necessary, however. Other conservationists and tech nonprofits are working equally hard to use computer vision and machine learning to identify the "digital fingerprint" of individual animals from photographs and videos taken by biologists, "tourist scientists," and automated wildlife cameras. "I think it's literally a revolution underway in terms of auto-identification of animals, whether it's from still cameras or video," said Robert Long, a conservation biologist based in Seattle.[27]

Deep learning models are being trained to identify giraffes by their spot patterns, zebras by their stripes and shadings, and whale sharks by their scars and spots behind their gills. Wildbook, an open-source software platform run by the tech nonprofit Wild Me, has even developed a bot that searches YouTube for video footage of whale sharks. The bot is unearthing dozens of videos a day, extracting data to help identify individual whale sharks, chart migrations, and track populations. If key information is missing, such as the location or date of the diving footage, the bot will request further details from the person who uploaded the video, doing so in one of its five languages. "Letting this thing loose on

YouTube, especially with migratory species that are out in the ocean, you get this chance of finding outlier sightings of animals where researchers just simply aren't going," noted Jon Van Oast, the bot's creator.[28]

SAVING AUSTRALIA'S GREAT BARRIER REEF

Conservationists are turning as well to artificial intelligence to save Australia's Great Barrier Reef. Stretching over fourteen hundred miles and comprising thousands of individual reefs, the Great Barrier Reef is the only lifeform visible from outer space. Coral reefs are home to exceptional biodiversity. At least half of the world's coral reefs, however, are now threatened by fishing, tourism, pollution, acidification, and climate change. And at least a fifth have been destroyed.

Protecting Australia's Great Barrier Reef is vital for any chance of saving what is left of the world's coral reefs. Since declaring the Great Barrier Reef a marine park in 1975, the Australian government has passed many pieces of legislation to improve management. Nonetheless, the Great Barrier Reef is dying, losing around half of its coral cover from 1985 to 2012.[29] Moreover, the crisis is deepening, with record-setting warm ocean currents in 2016 and 2017 bleaching and killing as much as half of the coral cover remaining in 2015.[30]

Crown-of-thorns starfish, which feed on coral polyps, have been one of the biggest causes of coral loss over the past three decades. Small populations of these starfish are native to the Great Barrier Reef. And bursts in population densities have long helped to retain coral diversity by pruning fast-growing corals. Crown-of-thorns starfish have become a grave threat to the reef, however, as destructive "outbreaks" have become increasingly common, partly because of a decline in natural predators and partly because of runoff from agricultural land (nitrates and fertilizers stimulate plankton blooms, which feed starfish larvae). Crown-of-thorns starfish, for instance, were responsible for more than 40 percent of the Great Barrier Reef's coral cover loss from 1985 to 2012.[31] Resilient creatures, they have proven very hard to cull by hand because of their poisonous spines and ability to regenerate. A single female, moreover, can produce as many as 65 million eggs during a spawning season.

Australian researchers, as I mention in chapter 1, are trying to resolve this threat to the Great Barrier Reef by deploying a semi-autonomous submersible known as RangerBot to cull crown-of-thorns starfish. RangerBot relies on computer-vision technology to navigate the reef and identify starfish, even finding ones curled into the coral. Not only can a single RangerBot eradicate hundreds of starfish per outing, but it can help map coral bleaching and measure water quality in real time. The RangerBot, for instance, is extending the research of scientists at the Queensland University of Technology and the Australian Institute for Marine Science who are flying drones over the Great Barrier Reef to film and chart coral bleaching, using AI to identify and interpret the unique "hyperspectral fingerprints" of bleaching across different coral colonies.[32]

RangerBot is an ingenious technological feat, with real potential to help contain crown-of-thorns starfish. A modified version known as LarvalBot, as is shown in the opening chapter, is now helping to reseed the Great Barrier Reef with coral larvae. As is generally true of all technological add-ons to ecosystem management, RangerBot and LarvalBot have no capacity to alleviate the political and economic forces underlying starfish outbreaks or the warming of the oceans. Sending out fleets of RangerBots and LarvalBots is never going to save the Great Barrier Reef. But this could slow the rate of loss, offering more time to implement the necessary political and socioeconomic reforms.

RangerBot and LarvalBot are just two on a fast-growing list of AI robots working to improve environmental management, restore ecosystems, and slow the escalating global environmental crisis. Robots are now sorting electronic waste. They are cleaning up oil spills and eliminating algae blooms. And they are eradicating invasive species, among many other environmental tasks.[33] AI-enhanced drones are at work, too. They are soaring over wildlife sanctuaries to detect nighttime poaching of elephants and rhinos in Africa. They are flying over beaches to locate and identify plastic garbage. And they are reseeding indigenous plants and trees to scale up ecosystem restoration and reforestation.[34]

Inventors and scientists within startups, universities, and nonprofit organizations are the primary force scaling up these technologies. Yet as was the case when the Australian researchers who built RangerBot won a Google Impact Challenge award, a few transnational corporations are providing valuable support for grassroots and small-scale projects to conserve, protect, and restore ecosystems.

BUSINESS PARTNERSHIPS FOR AI SUSTAINABILITY

Integrating artificial intelligence into research techniques, software, and robots requires both technical expertise and money. Recognizing this, companies such as Google and Microsoft are partnering with university researchers, donating services to nonprofit organizations, and offering free training sessions for community staff (including online tutorials). Significantly, in 2015, Google open-sourced its TensorFlow software library, which powers the machine learning of Gmail, Google Search, and Google Translate, among other products. "The thinking," explains TensorFlow's Rajat Monga, "was that if we could share source code, it could accelerate progress in machine learning for everyone."[35]

Meanwhile, Microsoft is working on developing an "AI supercomputer" on its Azure cloud computing service. The goal, according to the company when announcing the program in 2016, is to "build the world's most powerful AI supercomputer with Azure and make it available to anyone, to enable people and organizations to harness its power."[36] Donald Kossmann, the director of the Microsoft Research Lab in Redmond, Washington, explains the far-reaching vision of this supercomputer:

> We live in the age of the intelligent edge and intelligent cloud. Data is collected at the edge using billions of small devices. The data is pre-processed at the edge and shipped in a filtered and aggregated form to the cloud. In the cloud, the data is analyzed and used to train models which are in turn deployed at both the edge and in the cloud to make decisions. . . . The result is a supercomputer at global scale composed of billions of devices with micro-controllers at the edge and millions of servers in the cloud and at the edge.[37]

Thousands of computer scientists and engineers at Microsoft are working on AI projects and the AI supercomputer. These projects are a core part of the company's profit making and competitive positioning. But, within these corporate confines, the staff see themselves as working toward "democratizing AI in a way that changes our lives and the world around us for the better."[38]

Staff within companies like Google and Microsoft are collaborating, copublishing, and participating in nonprofit partnerships to promote ethical and sustainable applications of artificial intelligence. Some senior business leaders are even initiating partnerships. One example is the Partnership on AI, cofounded in 2016 by Mustafa Suleyman, the head of applied AI at Google's DeepMind, and Eric Horvitz, director of Microsoft Research Labs. The Partnership on AI aims to "create a place for open critique and reflection" for the global community of AI researchers, including from business, nonprofits, governments, universities, and community organizations.[39] This partnership comprises more than one hundred members, including Apple, Amazon, Facebook, Google, IBM, and Microsoft. More than half of those participating are nonprofit organizations.

The Microsoft Corporation is a leader in supporting the use of AI to advance the sustainability work of nongovernmental organizations and university researchers. Microsoft is donating software and cloud services and offering training courses. The company has also committed $50 million from 2018 to 2023 "to put artificial intelligence technology in the hands of individuals and organizations around the world who are working to protect our planet."[40]

Microsoft's AI for Earth, set up in 2017 under the leadership of Lucas Joppa, is in charge of allocating these funds. Like Amazon, Apple, and Google, the Microsoft Corporation is competing hard to extract business value from the revolution now underway in automated reasoning and machine learning. The application of AI for sustainability plays a small part of the company's strategy, and $50 million over five years is not much for a company with profits nearing $60 billion in 2018. Yet Joppa's team within Microsoft's AI for Earth is a valuable reminder of the commitment to environmentalism of some of those who work within transnational corporations.

Joppa has impressive environmental credentials, as the opening chapter notes. Besides holding a PhD in ecology, he is widely published, including coauthoring a highly cited 2014 article in *Science*, "The Biodiversity of Species and Their Rates of Extinction, Distribution, and Protection."[41] He makes a powerful case for the value of bringing business expertise into AI research collaborations with nonprofit environmental organizations. "The full participation of the technology sector," he argues, "is needed in efforts to provide key data in appropriate formats, as well as the algorithms, the infrastructure to train those algorithms on the data, and the means of making the end services available to as many people as possible."[42]

Under Joppa's leadership, AI for Earth has supported a broad range of projects, from extending wildlife surveys in Africa to enhancing the geographic information system (GIS) maps of Chesapeake Conservancy, a small nonprofit organization working to protect Chesapeake Bay in the American states of Maryland and Virginia. "We don't have artificial intelligence computer scientists on our team," explains Jeffrey Allenby, a director at Chesapeake Conservancy. "And to have access to the amazing staff at Microsoft and at Esri [a GIS company], to be able to enable our dreams and put them into action—it's just one of those too-good-to-be-true moments where you have to pinch yourself."[43]

The Protection Assistant for Wildlife Security—known as PAWS—is one of the many innovative projects that have received support from AI for Earth. Researchers at the University of Southern California's Center for Artificial Intelligence in Society developed PAWS to enhance the efficiency of patrols trying to prevent the poaching of endangered species. Poachers are constantly on the move, and in places like Southeast Asia, they set up snares and traps across vast, dense rainforests. PAWS analyzes historical poaching data, global positioning system (GPS) coordinates, topographic data, and past patrol routes using custom-built machine learning algorithms on Microsoft's Azure cloud. It then creates a heat map of likely spots of future poaching, recommending optimal patrol routes as well as randomizing suggestions so poachers cannot detect patterns (or be alerted ahead of time by a corrupt official). PAWS is correctly predicting hotspots of poaching 80 percent of the time, according to computer scientist Bistra Dilkina. Rangers using PAWS in one Cambodian wildlife sanctuary were able to find five hundred snares in one month, a fivefold increase compared to searching the previous month without assistance.[44]

AI for Earth is also partnering with nonprofits to finance research on sustainability. In 2018, for instance, it teamed up with the National Geographic Society to launch a grant program called "AI for Earth Innovation" to fund "new solutions that leverage AI and cloud computing to monitor, model and manage Earth's natural resources." The program focuses in particular on supporting open-source research aiming to produce "scalable technology solutions" for climate change, agriculture, water quality, and biodiversity. The total amount is modest—$1 million for five to fifteen projects—although the ambition of the program does signal the growing importance of AI for environmental science and management.[45]

THE POLITICAL ECONOMY OF AI AND CONSERVATION

Artificial intelligence, as this chapter underlines, is rapidly gaining importance as a tool for mapping, conserving, and rewilding the earth. The value for the environmental sciences is far-reaching. Machine learning is improving the modeling of earth-system interactions and climate-change scenarios, helping with the spatial mapping of deforestation and old-growth forests under threat, creating new software to expose wildlife trafficking on the internet, allowing for the real-time tracking of industrial fishing, and enabling real-time mapping of migrating birds and coral-reef bleaching. These examples in this chapter, moreover, are just a few of the many uses environmental scientists and conservationists are finding for artificial intelligence.

Environmentalists are further building on advances in machine learning and robotics to develop new tools of conservation and management. So far, we've seen how one nonprofit startup is repurposing cell phones to create AI-enhanced listening devices to alert state rangers and community guards of suspicious activity in the tropical rainforests. And we've seen how another team of researchers is developing a smart submersible to patrol Australia's Great Barrier Reef to cull deadly outbreaks of crown-of-thorns starfish. Once again, these are but a few of the efforts to employ AI to improve environmental management.[46]

Government grants are supporting some of this research. So is the United Nations, which since 2017 has been cohosting with the IBM Watson AI XPRIZE an annual summit called "AI for Good." This summit brings together governments, firms, nonprofits, and academic researchers to pursue collaborative ways to leverage progress in artificial intelligence to help achieve the UN's 2030 Sustainable Development Goals.[47]

In addition, companies such as Google and Microsoft are donating software and cloud services, providing AI infrastructure, and funding nonprofit projects. Granted, this investment is small compared to the size of these companies. But supports such as Google's open-source TensorFlow software library and Microsoft's Azure cloud computing service are definitely of great value to nonprofit organizations and university researchers. Support from Google's Impact Challenges, IBM's XPRIZE, and Microsoft's AI for Earth are clearly helping, too.

As the analysis so far has further shown, staff within big technology companies are also supporting nonprofit project teams, coauthoring articles, and helping develop open-access software and data-collection platforms. A few corporate AI leaders have initiated nonprofit partnerships to advance conservation, nonapplied research, and open-access learning projects. There are some examples of industry leaders supporting nonprofit AI research companies, such as OpenAI, which has a mission "to build safe artificial general intelligence (AGI), and ensure AGI's benefits are as widely and evenly distributed as possible."[48]

However, the primary energy underlying the upsurge in the use of artificial intelligence for environmental research, conservation, and management is coming not from governments or transnational corporations but from a diverse array of nonprofits, startups, universities, and environmental advocacy organizations. It is the individuals from within these institutions who are in the computer labs cleaning data and training AI systems, in the field deploying AI-enhanced technologies to confront illegal logging and poaching, and on the oceans testing AI devices to eradicate destructive species and clean up pollution.

All of these efforts are combining to improve environmental management. One advantage of integrating AI into the global political economy of conservation is its ability to help scale up analysis and solutions. There is some hope this will occur as the cost of machine learning software and robots inevitably declines. Yet AI technology can take us only so far toward lasting, far-reaching solutions, as it has little power to confront the underlying political and socioeconomic forces exploiting natural resources and destroying nature for profit. Tellingly, the extent of global environmental problems still far exceeds the scale of any AI solution to date.

Even as artificial intelligence improves environmental management and conservation science, tropical deforestation continues to rage. The global populations of wild animals continue to fall, with the numbers of birds, mammals, fish, reptiles, and amphibians declining by at least 60 percent since 1970.[49] The coral reefs continue to die. Overfishing continues nearly unabated. Freshwater quality continues to deteriorate. Pollution of the oceans continues to mount. Biodiversity loss continues to stay far above natural extinction rates. Meanwhile, the crisis of climate change continues to escalate, with average global temperatures still on track to rise another 2 to 4 degrees Celsius by the end of this century, bringing increasingly severe heatwaves, protracted droughts, violent storms, rising seas, and a mass extinction of species.[50]

Such trends are sobering. But they do not mean the gains from using AI to research and protect global ecosystems are worthless, little more than tinkering as the earth burns. Our global environmental crisis would certainly be worse without the ingenuity and commitment of the scientists, engineers, ecologists, and activists building AI eco-software and eco-robots. This is true, too, as we'll see next, of those within big business who are now turning to artificial intelligence to increase energy efficiency, reduce waste, find eco-savings, and improve the environmental management of global supply chains.

5

ENHANCING ECO-BUSINESS

Over the past two decades, transnational corporations have embraced sustainability as a tool of business. "Environmental sustainability has become an essential ingredient to doing business responsibly and successfully," proclaims Walmart. For us, says Bayer, "sustainability means shaping the future successfully and, as part of our corporate strategy, is an integral part of our day-to-day work routines." The "end goal" of our sustainability strategy, Google is telling us, "is a zero-carbon world where everyone everywhere has access to clean, carbon-free energy 24 hours a day, 365 days a year."[1]

Grand aspirations now anchor the corporate social responsibility programs of just about every transnational corporation. Coca-Cola is aspiring to be "water neutral." McDonald's, Nestlé, and Procter & Gamble are committed to "zero deforestation." Walmart is working toward a goal of using "100% renewable energy." Unilever is aiming for "zero hazardous waste to landfill." Nike, among many other transnational corporations, is aspiring to be "carbon neutral"—a goal Google (since 2007) and Microsoft (since 2012) claim to have already achieved.

The chief executive officers of big business are working hard to imbue their brands with notions of responsibility and sustainability. "Sustainability is the pivot for where we want to go—how we want to structure our processes, our thinking, our investments," Muhtar Kent, the CEO of

Coca-Cola at the time, said back in 2010. "Companies like PepsiCo have a tremendous opportunity—as well as a responsibility—to not only make a profit, but to do so in a way that makes a difference in the world," echoed Pepsi's then CEO Indra Nooyi a few years later.[2]

This sustainability discourse is bolstering brand values, helping firms retain a social license to operate, and legitimizing corporate self-regulation as an effective form of governance. The eco-business of transnational corporations, however, involves more than just upbeat pledges and community philanthropy. It also comprises an array of business initiatives to cut energy costs, reduce waste, and enhance quality controls. This includes smart-packaging programs to decrease production expenses, such as using lighter plastics, less wrapping, and thinner cardboard. It involves selling eco-products, investing in wind and solar power, and joining organizations to certify sustainable production. It consists as well of environmental reporting, random audits, and the hiring of third-party inspectors to gain more control over subcontractors within global supply chains.

Transnational corporations are now investing in artificial intelligence to pursue additional eco-business gains. Despite crosscutting and varying consequences across sectors and firms, this investment is producing meaningful environmental benefits. It is improving the energy efficiency of data centers, factories, and retail outlets as well as the overall productivity of global supply chains. Material inputs for manufacturing, transporting, and selling each product are going down across some conglomerates. In a few cases, waste and greenhouse gas emissions are decreasing, too.

As advocates of corporate social responsibility so often do, however, it is easy to overestimate the value of these gains for global sustainability. With eco-business, corporations are not pursuing ecological stability or social justice but rather the sustainability of global capitalism. For them, sustainability is a strategy to gain competitive advantages and manage risks in a world of growing resource scarcity and shifting environmental regulations.[3]

Like the use of AI to enhance conservation and ecosystem management, the gains from infusing artificial intelligence into eco-business are adding up to only incremental progress toward sustainability and are doing little to mitigate the broader political and corporate forces degrading the global environment. Furthermore, because the ultimate goal of eco-business is to capture markets, expand sales, and increase profit margins, at least some of these gains are rebounding to deepen unsustainable extraction and consumption. The eco-business gains of oil, mining, timber, and agricultural companies are especially prone to rebound in these ways. So are the efficiency gains of global manufacturers and big-box retailers. More positively, though, the rebound effects are milder for technology companies, where the investment and expertise in AI is the highest.[4]

Let's start on this more positive note, looking inside Google and Amazon, both of which are at the forefront of using artificial intelligence to enhance energy efficiency and reduce waste.

ECO-ENERGY AT GOOGLE

Google has a bold mission when it comes to sustainability: "to empower everyone—businesses, governments, nonprofit organizations, communities, and individuals—to use Google technology to create a more sustainable world."[5] Google's technology is in a wide range of popular products and services, including Google Chrome, YouTube, and Gmail. Over the past decade, the company has been working to decrease the energy consumption of web searches, social media, emailing, video uploads, and online streaming. One aim has been to cut costs by enhancing the energy efficiency of its computing power. Another has been to play a small role in mitigating climate change.

In recent years, the industry for information and communications technology (ICT) has been accounting for 2 to 3 percent of annual anthropocentric carbon emissions. This is on track to reach 3.5 percent in 2020 as demand for computing power continues to increase with the growth in internet traffic, smartphones, surveillance streaming, high-resolution imaging, smart TVs, cryptocurrencies (such as Bitcoin), and the Internet of Things. Industry analysts are expecting that demand for computing power will keep rising over the next few decades as big data expands, driverless cars go on sale, and more people and things connect to the internet.

Anders Andrae, who works for Huawei Technologies, is projecting that by 2025 the ICT industry could consume 20 percent of the world's electricity (up from 3 to 5 percent in 2015) and account for more than 5 percent of global carbon emissions. By then, without a sizable increase in energy efficiency and renewable electricity, data centers alone could account for over 3 percent of global carbon emissions (four-fifths of data centers were using fossil-fuel electricity in 2018). "It is a perfect storm," explains Andrae. "5G is coming, IP traffic is much higher than estimated, and all cars and machines, robots and artificial intelligence are being digitalised, producing huge amounts of data which is stored in data centers."[6]

Other researchers are also predicting a sharp rise in the climate footprint of the ICT industry over the coming decades. Without an abrupt turn toward renewable energy, a 2018 study in the *Journal of Cleaner Production*, for instance, foresees the ICT industry accounting for more than 14 percent of the global greenhouse gas emissions by 2040, with data centers contributing nearly half.[7]

Google is a leading company within the ICT industry. The services, platforms, and apps of Google and Facebook together were linked to around 70 percent of internet traffic in 2017.[8] Unlike the industry as a whole, Google has been managing to reduce its greenhouse gas emissions, including for its data centers. It became carbon neutral in 2007 by increasing energy efficiencies, investing in renewable energy, and purchasing carbon offsets. It then went beyond carbon neutrality in 2017 (and again in 2018), achieving its goal set in 2012 of "100% renewable energy" across all of its operations.

Google is still drawing some electricity from power plants burning fossil fuels. Powering all of its data centers with renewable energy, the company argues, is still not financially viable at this point in time. The company claims, however, that it is nonetheless achieving its goal of 100 percent renewable energy, doing so by purchasing enough renewable power to equal (or exceed) the electricity footprint of its offices and data centers. In recent years, around 90 percent of Google's renewable energy purchases in the United States, Europe, and Mexico came from wind power, and 10 percent from solar power. This strategy for achieving 100 percent renewable energy has made Google a leading investor in renewable power projects, with $5 billion committed as of 2019. It has also made Google one of the world's biggest corporate buyers of wind and solar power—well ahead of Amazon, Microsoft, and Facebook in terms of total historical purchases.[9]

On some measures, though, Facebook is actually going further than Google, and by 2018, it was on track to power all of its operations with renewable energy by 2020. "CEO Mark Zuckerberg has reaffirmed Facebook's place among business leaders in the race to be coal-free and 100% renewable-powered," said Gary Cook, who leads a Greenpeace campaign to push technology companies to power their operations with renewable energy.[10] This campaign has not held back on criticizing specific corporations, such as calling on Samsung to do "bigger things" after calculating that renewable power comprised just 1 percent of Samsung's energy consumption in 2017.[11] Cook's praise of Facebook is noteworthy in the specificity of what he says the company is doing right. "While some companies have taken shortcuts in pursuit of their 100% renewable goals," he wrote in 2018, "Facebook has helped set a strong bar with its transparency and consistent pursuit of high impact renewable energy projects that are located on the same grid as its rapidly growing fleet of data centers."[12]

Google may not be going as fast or as far as Facebook in its commitment to 100 percent renewable energy. But Google is nonetheless a leader in pursuing eco-efficiencies within the company. Since 2001, it has been investing heavily in more energy-efficient servers, steadily multiplying the computing power of energy inputs. The company has reduced power leakages and jettisoned moving parts. It has enhanced the efficiency of its power supplies. It has upgraded lighting systems, decreased the energy drain of servers in standby, and optimized energy usage. And it has designed more efficient infrastructure to cool its servers. As a result, the energy efficiency of Google's data centers is now two times greater than an average large-scale data center.[13]

Such fine-tuning of Google's eco-business of energy management might seem like tinkering at the edges of global sustainability. Yet Google alone accounts for 0.01 percent of world electricity consumption.[14] Furthermore, companies, office workers, and smartphone users are increasingly relying on cloud computing, including Google Cloud, which is bringing additional efficiencies from the consolidation of services. By one estimate, if all businesses in the United States were to migrate their email and software applications to the cloud, the energy consumption of these activities could fall by as much as 87 percent.[15]

In the case of Google's data centers, smart automation managed to improve the energy efficiency of the cooling systems by 30 percent from mid-2017 to mid-2018, and company technicians are expecting further gains as the deep neural networks continue to gain proficiency. "It was amazing to see the AI learn to take advantage of winter conditions and produce colder than normal water, which reduces the energy required for cooling within the data center," said Dan Fuenffinger, a technician at Google. "Rules don't get better over time, but AI does."[16]

Google is pursuing additional eco-business gains by enhancing the energy efficiency of machine learning itself. Machine learning is energy intensive, demanding far more power than conventional computing. Consider Google Voice Search. As researchers at Google were developing this technology, they came to realize that if all Android phone users were to do voice searches for even three minutes a day, the company would need to double the computing capacity of its data centers. To avoid this scenario, Google designed a computer chip—the tensor processing unit (TPU)—able to run machine learning applications up to thirty times faster than standard chips, improving product quality and decreasing energy needs. TPUs have also proven invaluable for advancing the power of machine learning, helping keep the Alphabet conglomerate of Google, DeepMind, and Waymo at the forefront of commercializing artificial intelligence.[17]

On the surface, these environmental gains look impressive. Great care is necessary, however, to avoid exaggerating the benefits of advancing eco-business with artificial intelligence. Much of the business value comes from the company presenting the goals and gains of eco-business in the best possible light. Every corporate social responsibility unit, even as it pursues efficiencies, is always working to craft a sustainability image that reassures customers, placates critics, and makes it look better than its competitors. This is true of Google. It is true of Facebook. And it is true of Amazon.

ECO-BUSINESS AT AMAZON

Like Google, Amazon is aspiring to power its company exclusively with renewable energy. Over the last decade, the company has invested in wind farms and installed solar rooftops to power some of its warehouses and data centers. By the start of 2018, around half of the power for Amazon Web Services came from renewable sources. Although Amazon has been reluctant to explain exactly how it will achieve 100 percent renewable energy, Kara Hartnett Hurst, Amazon's director of sustainability, claims the company will keep investing in renewable power. Doing so, she argues, "is a win-win-win-win—it's right for our customers, our communities, our business, and our planet."[18]

Like Google, Facebook, and, as we'll see later in this chapter, many others, Amazon is turning to AI to optimize the efficiency of wind and solar power. Drawing on a rich array of data from sensors and satellites, machine learning systems are enhancing the accuracy of weather forecasting, guiding drone inspections, and predicting maintenance needs to minimize equipment failures. The overall result is an increase in the reliability and efficiency in the delivery of renewable energy to Amazon's data centers, warehouses, and distribution facilities.[19]

Amazon is also using machine learning to enhance the energy efficiency of Amazon Web Services (AWS), which accounts for around a third of the global market for cloud computing infrastructure (AWS hosts, for instance, Netflix and Airbnb as well as millions of websites). The company is gaining further eco-efficiencies by automating its "fulfillment" centers. Worldwide, the company is now using more than 200,000 robots to enhance productivity and decrease waste.[20]

Amazon's smart packaging programs, meanwhile, are saving on shipping costs, increasing recycling rates, and further reducing waste. Recommendation apps, modeling software, and machine testing are helping Amazon discover new eco-business gains across its packaging and shipping systems. Warehouse staff, for example, are now using an app to calculate which box design will most efficiently and securely ship a customer's order.[21] Amazon has also redesigned its shipping boxes to reduce the amount of packaging—yet still protect—the great diversity of products from its suppliers. At the same time, Amazon has been partnering with core suppliers to help them redesign their product packaging for shipping with Amazon (rather than to catch a customer's eye on a traditional retail shelf). To test redesigned packages, Amazon "drops, squeezes, vibrates, and jostles thousands of packages a year with machines that precisely simulate the entire journey of a package to customers."[22]

Over the past decade, Amazon's smart packaging programs have cut packaging waste by more than 15 percent, reducing the need for hundreds of millions of shipping boxes. Artificial intelligence is further enhancing the quality of Amazon's simulations, visualization of data, and user interfaces for its eco-business platforms. And it is helping the company track—and measure and assess—the global consequences of its supply chains, including particular product lines and brands, as well as inputs, such as water and energy, and outputs, such as carbon emissions and waste. This granular analysis of the gains of eco-business is allowing Amazon to tailor decisions for locations and products. It is also improving inventory management, reducing losses from product expiry while keeping items in stock, as Amazon was able to do after purchasing the supermarket company Whole Foods in 2017 for $13.7 billion.[23]

Amazon is garnering additional environmental and financial efficiencies through smart delivery systems. One example is Amazon's trucking app known as Relay, which the company has been using since 2017 to guide drivers more quickly and efficiently to Amazon's fulfillment warehouses. Relay, which works on both Apple and Android devices, also enables drivers to check in and prescreen goods to speed up the flow of traffic through security gates, reducing idling emissions and saving time, money, and fuel. As a bonus, the Relay app is enhancing logistics planning and the ordering of goods because the information is less prone to errors than manual entry. Seeing these eco-business gains, Amazon is now working to scale up smart delivery systems across its global network of suppliers.[24]

For corporations generally, "making better decisions about efficient use of resources is getting easier," notes Andrew Winston, the author of *The Big Pivot: Radically Practical Strategies for a Hotter, Scarcer, and More Open World.*[25] The future will surely see even more opportunities for corporations to use resources more efficiently as the Internet of Things continues to expand, supply-chain transparency rises, data analytics improve, and companies integrate machine learning into corporate decision making. Amazon may not have the in-house AI expertise of Google or Microsoft. At this point, though, Amazon is well ahead of other mass retailers in using AI to find these eco-efficiencies, weaving machine learning applications across the entire company. As industry analyst Blake Morgan says, "AI is not located in one particular office at Amazon—it's everywhere."[26]

Amazon will certainly face strong competition as it continues to expand into the mass retailing of consumer goods. The 2019 *Fortune* 500 list of America's biggest firms still had Walmart turning over $282 billion more in annual revenue than Amazon. Like Amazon, Walmart is pushing hard to increase the gains of eco-business, including looking to artificial intelligence to discover new savings and efficiencies. To improve urban delivery, for instance, Walmart is working to gain "last-mile insights" with machine learning, looking to speed up service, reduce costs, and decrease pollution. The smartphones of drivers, MIT's Matthias Winkenbach explains, offer "a treasure trove of locational data." And by analyzing this information alongside sensor, satellite, census, and company data, "it is possible to build highly detailed models of urban delivery operations."[27]

ADVANCING CSR WITH AI

Corporate social responsibility, argues Al Naqvi of the American Institute of Artificial Intelligence, has entered a new "era" of "cognitive CSR," where "machines are deployed to radically transform and improve CSR processes."[28] High-tech firms such as Amazon, Facebook, Google, IBM, and Microsoft are leading the efforts to supercharge CSR with AI. But many others, from discount retailers to automakers to mining companies to courier firms, are also starting to pursue the value gains of enhancing eco-business with artificial intelligence.[29]

Among the top five hundred public companies in the United States, for instance, mentions of AI or machine learning in the 10-K filings for the US Securities and Exchange Commission rose nearly tenfold from 2013 to 2016. Reviewing a sampling of carbon disclosure filings and CSR reports of more than eight thousand public and private firms for 2015 and 2016, Conor Riffle, a director at the international nongovernmental organization CDP (formerly the Carbon Disclosure Project), found a sharp rise in mentions of AI as a way to improve operational efficiency and the performance of consumer products. Total mentions and the relative importance of AI within the CSR reports were still fairly low. Yet as Riffle notes, interest is rising quickly as early adopters demonstrate the eco-business advantages of artificial intelligence.[30]

One example is Xcel Energy, an American utility company with headquarters in Minneapolis, Minnesota. Xcel Energy has deep pockets, turning over more than $11.5 billion in revenues in 2018, but nothing compared to the likes of Amazon, which generated more than twenty times as much revenue that year. Xcel Energy has nonetheless been an energy industry leader in pursuing eco-business gains with AI. The company, for example, installed an automated system of artificial neural networks to reduce nitrous oxide emissions from its coal-fired smokestacks in Texas. (Nitrous oxide acts as a greenhouse gas, with about three hundred times more warming power than carbon dioxide.)

Xcel Energy's machine learning system is able to adjust management controls more quickly and accurately than human operators, lowering nitrous oxide emissions, enhancing security, and uncovering new efficiencies to produce cost savings. Xcel Energy is not alone in pursuing these eco-business advantages. By 2017, more than one hundred utility companies were using similar neural-network systems, with research by the International Energy Agency suggesting such systems can reduce a company's nitrous oxide emissions by as much as 20 percent.[31]

Utility companies are also using artificial intelligence to enhance the reliability and efficiency of renewable energy. Fossil-fuel power plants commonly back up wind and solar energy to fill in when weather conditions interrupt electricity generation. Often, however, running fossil-fuel backups is "throwing carbon up into the sky" for no good reason, explains William Mahoney of the US National Center for Atmospheric Research. "It costs money, and it's bad for the environment."[32] Utility firms are now using automated AI systems to analyze real-time data—turbine speeds, wind force, weather stations, and satellite data—to forecast wind power output with far greater accuracy than was previously possible. This is allowing these firms to decrease the need for reserve power, run fewer fossil-fuel backup plants, and increase the percentage of energy from renewable sources.[33]

GE Power, a subsidiary of General Electric, is a leader in the development of smarter electrical grids. GE Power does not operate many power plants but is a major supplier and servicer of the equipment used for electricity generation across the United States. In 2016, the company acquired NeuCo, a software and AI startup specializing in developing technologies to optimize the efficiency of coal-fired electricity generation. "Think of it like cruise control for a car that adjusts acceleration (and fuel consumption) to maintain a set speed far more efficiently than a human can," GE's Ganesh Bell said when explaining how the AI software controls fuel intake, air flows, temperatures, and burning within coal-plant boilers.[34]

Acquiring NeuCo is part of a strategy by GE Power (with support from GE Digital and the software platform Predix) to position itself at the forefront of "digital industrial solutions," including filing patents for AI technologies to optimize grid flows and power storage, such as in batteries. The company is predicting big savings ahead. Steven Martin, formerly at Microsoft and now with GE Power, estimates these AI technologies could eventually generate worldwide energy savings of as much as $200 billion.[35] General Electric, a company with revenues of more than $120 billion in 2018, is also turning to artificial intelligence to pursue eco-business savings across its other subsidiaries. "GE Transportation plans to optimize entire rail networks," notes industry analyst Adam Tucker, while "GE Aviation is focusing on fleets of passenger jets and GE Healthcare is using software and analytics to improve treatment and reduce costs."[36]

American companies such as Amazon, GE, and Google are at the forefront of using AI to extract more value from eco-business. But as the competitive advantages of doing so rise, so is the investment in AI by transnational corporations headquartered in Europe and Asia. Within Asia, Chinese firms are especially keen to keep up with the eco-business gains from integrating sensors and machine learning systems into corporate operations. Telecommunications and technology companies such as Huawei, Baidu, Alibaba, and Tencent are leading efforts to use machine learning software to analyze data from the Internet of Things to increase the efficiency of energy and resource usage. But investment in AI to pursue these gains is accelerating across China, according to Qi Lu of Tsing Capital, a Beijing-based company specializing in financing clean technology ventures. Why are we seeing this acceleration? In China, Qi Lu explains, "with all of the data we gather from the Internet of Things and the analyzing capability developed by machine learning and artificial intelligence, we are actually for the first time able to manage energy and resource use at a very high level."[37]

THE ACCELERATION OF ECO-BUSINESS

In 2017, the McKinsey Global Institute, the research division of the consulting firm McKinsey & Company, concluded that artificial intelligence was "poised to unleash the next wave of digital disruption" within global business. Researchers identified five core "AI technology systems" that were already starting to alter the landscape of every business: computer vision, robotics and autonomous vehicles, virtual agents and assistants, language processing and speech recognition, and machine learning, with deep learning in particular advancing every AI system.[38]

Today, AI is striking global business with full force as near-daily breakthroughs occur in machine learning, data analytics, and computing hardware. The high tech, financial services, and telecom industries are well ahead in terms of integrating AI technologies into operations and across global supply chains. Now, however, firms across every sector are beginning to deploy these technologies to collect and analyze unique data, optimize production output, automate environmental management, improve forecasting, and reduce waste and inefficiencies.

This uptake of AI across business is producing significant savings, including for the energy and resource inputs for production, transportation, and retailing.[39] But how far do such savings really take us toward global sustainability? Cleaner production and greater efficiency of coal-fired electricity is certainly valuable. After all, coal-fired power plants supply 40 percent of the world's electricity, and the International Energy Agency is predicting that total output of coal-fired electricity will not change much even by 2040. Given sharply rising demand for electricity, future pollution from coal-fired power would surely be worse without technological upgrades and artificial intelligence. But smart coal-fired power plants are at best a stopgap, not a solution to climate change.

There are strict limits on the nature and extent of possible sustainability gains from enhancing eco-business with artificial intelligence.

These gains are occurring, we need to keep in mind, within the confines of a strategy to enhance the profitability of big business. There are risks, too, of enhancing eco-business with learning algorithms and automated decision making. Relying on artificial intelligence brings new responsibilities—such as protecting privacy and human rights, minimizing bias, and preventing the militarization of commercial AI technologies—which, as we'll see later in this book, are tending to fall to the wayside as the competition to extract profits from AI heats up.

Still, AI is definitely accelerating and deepening eco-business. As this chapter brought to light, it is reducing the energy footprint of Google's data centers. It is lowering the packaging, energy, and delivery costs of Amazon's retailing model. It is enhancing the efficiency and reliability of wind and solar power. It is decreasing the nitrous oxide emissions of Xcel Energy's coal-fired power plants and allowing the company to burn less coal when supplying renewable energy. It is enabling GE Power to scale up efficiencies across America's electrical grids. It is improving the accuracy of inventory forecasting to cut waste out of the supply chains of brand manufacturers and big-box retailers. And it is helping Chinese technology and telecommunications companies save energy and resources. Moreover, as I explore next, the intensifying competition among transnational corporations to capture business value with AI is driving the development of new, smarter eco-products for consumers.

6

SMART PRODUCTS

Artificial intelligence is improving the efficiency, reliability, and performance of a diverse array of consumer products. This would seem to have the potential to advance the global sustainability of consumption in some truly far-reaching ways. A world of self-driving electric trucks and cars, for instance, could reduce greenhouse gas emissions by 15 to 20 percent, as well as save more than a million people a year from dying in crashes. Driverless vehicles are just one example of the smart products now entering global markets. Smart appliances seem to have great potential to save energy. So do smart plugs, smart air conditioning, and smart lighting.

Great care is necessary, however, to avoid overestimating the environmental value of intelligent products. Smart technologies are not nearly as intelligent as advocates like to claim, a point Meredith Broussard vividly reminds us in her book *Artificial Unintelligence: How Computers Misunderstand the World.*[1] It is also going to take generations for smart products to displace conventional products. The replacement process, moreover, is going to open up new markets, put more goods on store shelves, and expand global consumption. This is going to increase demand for minerals, plastics, and energy as well as incentivize the extraction of resources (such as cobalt, coltan, and rare earth elements) from places with low environmental standards and poor human rights records. And this is going to generate new sources of electronic waste as consumers upgrade devices and discard old products.

The competition to produce and sell smart products could even exacerbate unsustainable levels of personal consumption. Advertising campaigns wrap these products in an image of sustainability, but the underlying objective of manufacturers and retailers is no different than for conventional goods: entice consumers to buy more. To stimulate sales, firms are designing smart products for rapid obsolescence and disposability. They are requiring model upgrades to sustain performance and obtain the latest features. And they are continually marketing new products. Each smart product may have a lighter energy and waste footprint, but as this chapter underscores, this does not necessarily lighten the ecological footprint of a country, town, or individual as everyone, everywhere, buys more of everything.

The chemicals and materials in intelligent products will bring new risks, too. Substituting "new and improved" products can be an effective way to shift the environmental consequences of global consumption, as we know from the history of mass marketing chlorofluorocarbon-free refrigerators and air conditioners as a way of phasing out ozone-depleting substances. Yet new and improved products may well create new hazards, as we see now as the chemical refrigerants that replaced chlorofluorocarbons drift into the atmosphere and warm the planet.

Smart products are not going to cure the unsustainability of global capitalism. At least in some cases, however, they seem to offer an opportunity to replace some inefficient, damaging, and dangerous products. How far can these products take us toward global sustainability? Let's start answering this question by evaluating the potential of self-driving vehicles to transform the global auto industry.

THE DRIVERLESS FUTURE

Traffic accidents killed around 60 million people in the twentieth century. Over time, seatbelts, airbags, and better designs have made cars safer; so have speed limits, roadside breathalyzers, and restrictions on young drivers. Nonetheless, in just the first two decades of the twenty-first century, another 24 million people died, and hundreds of millions were seriously injured in traffic accidents. And every day, car crashes continue to kill 3,600 people and injure as many as 137,000. Globally, traffic accidents are the single biggest cause of death for those between the ages of five and twenty-nine. The heartbreak for families is incalculable. The economic hardship of these deaths and injuries can be assessed, however, with the World Health Organization estimating the annual cost for most countries at approximately 3 percent of their gross domestic product.[2]

Self-driving vehicles offer the enticing prospect of dramatically reducing car crashes. As we saw in chapter 3, the Alphabet subsidiary Waymo is well ahead in the race to develop driverless vehicles. This company, emerging out of Google's Self-Driving Car Project (2009–2016), has honed its self-driving software and sensors by simulating tens of billions of miles of road tests. By 2020, Waymo's cars had also traversed 20 million miles of public roads without causing any deaths, injuries, or serious accidents, with half of these miles driven in 2019.[3] Buoyed by this impressive safety record, the company is now moving forward with plans to commercialize driverless vehicles, partnering with Jaguar to manufacture self-driving electric crossovers for a ride-hailing service and partnering with Chrysler to pilot driverless hybrid minivans.

Driverless cars and trucks are going to upend the global auto industry. Market analysts are forecasting annual sales of driverless vehicles will exceed 30 million by 2040, with new purchases, ride-hailing services, and self-driving delivery worth trillions of dollars.[4] With so much at stake, leading automakers—including Daimler, Ford, Toyota, and Volkswagen—are now revving up research and development to try to catch Waymo. Uber is also maneuvering to capture the driverless car-sharing market, helped along in 2018 by $500 million from Toyota to collaborate on developing self-driving software, data services, and sensors. Startups could further disrupt the global auto industry. One example is Aurora Innovation, founded in 2016 by three of the world's foremost experts in machine learning and self-driving technology. Aurora is working with Fiat Chrysler and Hyundai to commercialize driverless vehicles, including electric shuttles and ride-sharing services.

The enthusiasm for self-driving technology is understandable. If fully adopted, it could decrease traffic fatalities by as much as 90 percent.[5] Commuting times and traffic congestion would be reduced; drunk and distracted driving would be eliminated. Driverless vehicles would also increase gas mileage by driving more proficiently as well as enhance the mobility of elderly and disabled people. Making driverless cars and trucks electric, as Jaguar and Waymo are doing, might even implode the global market for gasoline, a leading cause of climate change.[6]

A world of self-driving electric vehicles would undoubtedly reduce global carbon emissions as well as enhance personal safety and mobility. In addition, the growth of autonomous ride-sharing vehicles might reduce the need for many of the current parking spaces for personally owned cars. But as technology firms and automakers compete for the profits from selling driverless cars, the total number of cars on the world's roads will certainly continue to rise for many decades to come. There will be safety risks of driverless vehicles, too, including criminal hacking and the theft of personal data. Transitioning into this future will also surely cause widespread ecological damage. And once there, these vehicles would definitely still entail big environmental costs.

THE COSTS OF DRIVING

Driverless vehicles will continue to require the paving and repaving of millions of miles of roads now polluting rainwater runoff and crisscrossing wildlife habitats.[7] Furthermore, building these vehicles is going to require vast quantities of steel, aluminum, glass, plastics, and rubber. The number of cars, trucks, buses, and sports utility vehicles on the world's roads is set to reach 3 billion by 2050, up from 1.5 billion today. Recycling and disposing of these vehicles to make way for driverless ones is going to pose great challenges, especially in poorer regions. There will also be significant ecological costs of having so many vehicles, whether or not they are driverless. Just look at the microplastic contamination from synthetic rubber tires. The wearing down of these tires now accounts for 5 to 10 percent of marine plastic pollution, a crisis poisoning the high seas, choking the coral reefs, and polluting the coastlines.[8]

On a positive environmental note, the rise of the self-driving industry seems likely to accelerate the transition to hybrid and electric automobiles. The International Energy Agency is forecasting somewhere between

125 and 220 million electric and hybrid automobiles and light trucks will be on the roads in 2030 (up from 3 million on 2017). The consulting company Enerdata, meanwhile, sees the possibility of 1 to 2 billion electric and hybrid vehicles by 2050, comprising as much as half of the global car fleet.[9]

This would certainly be good news for those aiming to reduce tailpipe pollution and greenhouse gases. Yet the lithium-ion batteries in these electric cars will present another major environmental challenge. More mining of nickel, cobalt, and lithium will be necessary to supply growing demand for these batteries. Making a battery pack for an electric car, for instance, can require as much as 12 kilograms of cobalt. In recent years, more than half of the world's cobalt has come from the Democratic Republic of the Congo, a place where human rights and environmental abuses are rampant.[10] To be fair, companies such as Tesla have been working to reduce their reliance on cobalt. Tesla's Model 3, for instance, uses only 4.5 kilograms (compared to 11 kilograms in the older Model S).[11] Tesla and other electric car manufacturers are also promising to buy cobalt certified as sustainable and conflict free, as well as do more to recycle spent car batteries.

But how effective are such pledges? Even in the European Union, only 5 percent of lithium-ion batteries have been recycled in recent years.[12] To some extent, automakers are certainly trying to work with trustworthy certifiers and find ways to reuse the cobalt and nickel in spent car batteries. Yet as we know from the history of trying to rid the world of blood diamonds, miners and traders are adept at concealing abuses, while buyers rarely ever ask tough questions.[13] Additionally, as we know from the histories of electronic waste, hazardous waste, and plastic recycling, as wealthier jurisdictions look for ways to keep waste out of their backyards, it tends to drift into marginalized communities and faraway lands.[14]

For the assurances of sustainability by the electric car industry to have any real value, policies and practices will need to be put into place to prevent the distancing of waste into political spaces with less power, as inevitably this lowers recycling rates, degrades local environments, and causes social injustices. This is true, too, for the sustainability promises of the manufacturers of intelligent technology for smart homes.

A FUTURE OF SMART HOMES

Sales of smart household products are rising quickly as software and sensors advance, as utilities install smart meters and smart grids, and as high-speed wireless expands the Internet of Things. These products are communicating with smartphone apps and working with cloud-based smart assistants, including Amazon Alexa, Apple HomeKit, Google Assistant, and Samsung SmartThings. A wide range of smart products and services are now available, with Alexa alone connected to over 20,000 different devices across 3,500 brands.[15] For most devices, consumers still need to tap an app or use voice controls. Increasingly, though, smart products are also working autonomously, using machine learning to personalize settings and improve performance.

Smart thermostats with learning capabilities are adjusting home heating as outside temperatures fluctuate and as occupants come and go. Smart air conditioners are cooling rooms more efficiently. Smart blinds are opening and closing to control the heat of the sun. Smart lighting is turning on and off to conserve power and extend bulb life. Smart water heaters are alerting homeowners of water leaks. And smart plugs are turning off outlets to reduce the energy consumption of toasters, coffee makers, microwave ovens, and televisions.

This is just the tip of the smart products coming onto the market. Homeowners can buy smart smoke alarms to track weather reports to alert them of incoming tornados. There are smart locks, carbon monoxide detectors, and security cameras to enhance the safety of offices and homes. Consumers can also purchase smart refrigerators, stoves, and dishwashers that work to save energy. Using Amazon Alexa, you can even voice-activate Samsung's smart refrigerator to play music, watch television, search the internet, make a grocery list, send a note to your family, or order food from delivery services.

Manufacturers and advertisers are certainly quick to assure customers of the value of these products for saving energy, lowering electricity bills, and reducing carbon footprints. And apps are readily available to provide personalized "reports" on the energy efficiency gains from home automation.

But do these products really make a meaningful difference for sustainability?

UPGRADING TO SMART LIVING

The value of smart household products for energy efficiency might seem straightforward. Life-cycle assessments, however, reveal a mix of outcomes of home automation. Some studies have found home automation can reduce household energy consumption by 10 to 30 percent. Other studies, though, caution that control systems and smart plugs could end up increasing the overall energy consumption of a home.[16]

More significantly, smart appliances and homes are bringing new environmental challenges and risks. Most strikingly, these products are adding another layer of consumption into the global economy. The global market for home automation and smart appliances alone is set to exceed $53 billion in 2022, up from $24 billion in 2016.[17] Seeing this rising demand, stores such as Best Buy have been reorganizing floor space to showcase smart home products.

By 2040, as many as 11 billion smart appliances could be operating across 1 billion households.[18] Some of these products will displace less efficient ones. But some of the growth in sales will simply arise from wealthier consumers buying more electronic devices. Much of this growth, moreover, will come from consumers buying newer versions of smart products. Planned obsolescence has long been a strategy of manufacturers to retain—and raise—demand for consumer products. In the 1920s, as the historian Markus Krajewski documents, the manufacturers of incandescent lightbulbs formed a cartel to shave off 500 to 1,000 hours from the lifespan of a typical lightbulb at the time. By the 1950s and 1960s, as Giles Slade traces in *Made to Break: Technology and Obsolescence in America*, it was already common to design household products to "expire," with, for instance, some lines of portable radios made to last just three years. Designs further ensured these products were difficult and costly to repair.[19]

The shortening of product lifespans has been true across a wide range of consumer goods, including kitchen appliances, televisions, cameras, furniture, and clothing.[20] The high-end products of technology firms, however, tend to have especially short lifespans as these firms do everything in their power to accelerate the speed at which consumers buy new models.

Apple has been especially adept at manufacturing demand. Look at the iPhone, first released by Apple in 2007. By 2020, Apple had released twenty-four iPhone models: of those, over half had come since 2015.[21] The company had already sold a billion iPhones by mid-2016. Since then, sales have been strong, with Apple selling more than 200 million iPhones in 2017 and again in 2018. Apple's strategy of ramping up model releases has been spectacularly profitable. In the last quarter of 2017, for instance, the company captured more than 85 percent of global smartphone profits, with the iPhone X alone earning five times the combined profits of 600 Android producers.[22] With profits of nearly $60 billion during fiscal year 2018 (ending in September), Apple was once again the world's most profitable company on the *Fortune* Global 500 list for 2019.

Being this profitable has brought controversy. Following user complaints and investigations, in 2017, Apple acknowledged that software updates for iPhones 6, 6S, and SE and the operating system of the iPhone 7 were slowing down performance over time. In an open letter, Apple apologized for upsetting customers and then went on to defend its conduct: "First and foremost, we have never—and would never—do anything to intentionally shorten the life of any Apple product, or degrade the user experience to drive customer upgrades."[23]

Slowing down performance was not part of a strategy of planned obsolescence, Apple reassured its customers, but rather an effort to extend the life of older batteries and prevent battery shutdowns. "Our goal is to deliver the best experience for customers, which includes overall performance and prolonging the life of their devices," a company spokesperson said without irony. In compensation, Apple offered a $50 discount on a new iPhone battery.[24]

Class-action lawsuits were quickly launched after Apple's admission. The plaintiffs put a very different spin on Apple's motives. "Apple's software updates purposefully slowed or 'throttled down' the performance speeds," states a 2017 filing in Illinois, and were designed "to fraudulently induce consumers to purchase the latest iPhone versions." The actions of Apple, the filing continues, have been "deceptive" and "unscrupulous."[25] If, as Apple now says, these actions were designed to enhance battery function, why did Apple not inform consumers sooner, even after years of grumbling and rumors? "Instead, Apple appears to have obscured and concealed why older phones were slowing down," claims the attorney for the lawsuit in Illinois.[26]

Apple is pushing back, saying it takes pride in the durability of iPhones in comparison to other smartphones. Indeed, there does not seem to be anything unique in the upgrading speed of iPhone users. Consumers around the world are upgrading smartphones at a furious pace. Smartphone sales rose from 970 million in 2013 to more than 1.5 billion in 2018, with Apple comprising only 13 percent of the global market share in 2018. More than 8 billion smartphones were sold over this time, many replacing phones just a few years old.[27]

Consumers are racing to upgrade other smart technologies, too. Certainly, as in the smartphone industry, brands are luring customers to seek out the latest, trendiest versions, while building operating systems and deploying software updates to disable features and cause internet lag. But there are also many other reasons that people are upgrading quickly. Rapid progress in miniaturizing electronics is allowing for slimmer, lighter, and smaller products. Advances in computer processing power is producing faster, better products, while apps, internet sites, and the Internet of Things work best with newer models. As models age, firms are ending services and no longer offering spare parts. At the same time, it is often cheaper (or at least comparable) to replace rather than repair a damaged smart product.

"This is the way the smart home ends: not with a bang, but with obsolescence," observes Rick Paulas in *New York Magazine*.[28] Each upgrade may well help save a few dollars on an energy bill. But manufacturing billions of new home appliances and electronics over the next few decades is going to fuel even more demand for plastics, chemicals, and metallic ores. The competition to obtain the best—and cheapest—sources of metals, elements, and ores for manufacturing electronics will be especially fierce.

MINING FOR SMART PRODUCTS

Consider the chemical element tantalum (number 73 on the periodic table), which is extracted from the ore columbite-tantalite, or coltan. Industry analysts are expecting demand for tantalum to rise over the coming decade as sales of electronics, automobiles, and aircraft climb.[29] Highly resistant to heat and corrosion, the electronics industry relies on tantalum to make capacitors (for storing electric charge) and high-power resistors (for withstanding and dispersing power). Tantalum has been essential for miniaturizing electrical components and improving the quality of electronic products, and is common in smartphones, laptops, computers, TVs, smart appliances, and the electrical systems of automobiles and airplanes.

The transnational corporations looking to capture the growing market for smart products are competing hard to secure high-quality, low-cost tantalum. To meet demand in the coming years, miners will certainly continue to excavate the reserves of coltan in countries such as Australia. They will also surely look to dig out even more of the rich deposits of coltan in countries with low regulatory standards, such as the Democratic Republic of the Congo, where, as with the mining of cobalt, the industry has a grim track record of brutality and unsustainability.[30]

The electronics and smart appliance industries are competing equally hard for rare earth elements. These elements (which on the periodic table comprise the fifteen lanthanides, plus scandium and yttrium) are not actually rare but gained this moniker because of the difficulty of extracting and separating them. The electronics industry relies on these elements for capacitors, magnets, fuel cells, optical fibers, electrical insulation, alloys, and glass polishing, among other uses. They are valuable for a wide range of products. They can be found in smartphones, home appliances, and laptops. They are in speakers, lasers, flat-screen TVs, tablets, and digital cameras. And they are in rechargeable batteries, fluorescent lamps, solar panels, and wind turbines. Many products rely on an array of rare earth elements: a typical smartphone contains eight.[31]

Production of rare earth elements has been steadily increasing over the past decade, up from 112,000 metric tons in 2013 to 175,000 metric tons in 2018. Back in 2010, China produced most of the world's refined rare earth products and compounds. That year, however, the Chinese government sent shock waves through the global market by temporarily cutting off exports to Japan during a diplomatic row over Japan's detention of a

Chinese trawler in the East China Sea. Since then, China's market share of rare earth elements has been declining as the Chinese government restricts exports; as buyers seek out more reliable, inexpensive, and less politically charged sources; and as mining expands around the world, including in Australia, Canada, Greenland, South Africa, and the United States. By 2017, China's share of world production of refined rare earth elements had fallen to 86 percent.[32]

As with the mining of coltan and cobalt, the mining of rare earth elements has long been linked to human rights abuses and devastating ecological consequences.[33] In China, communities have been forcibly relocated, and open-pit mines scar landscapes. One mine in China's Bayan-Obo district in Inner Mongolia covers 48 square kilometers and is 1,000 meters deep in spots. Extracting the earth, moreover, is only a fraction of the environmental impact. Processing a ton of rare earth ores can create as much as two thousand tons of toxic waste. In places such as Bayan-Obo, this waste has polluted soils, poisoned groundwater with carcinogens, and contaminated the environment with radioactive materials.[34]

Meanwhile, the recycling rate for rare earth elements is exceptionally low. Removing and separating the tiny quantities in an electronic device or home appliance is technically difficult and is financially less appealing than recovering substances such as aluminum, copper, gold, silver, or steel. In recent years, only around 1 percent of rare earth elements have ended up recycled.[35] The rest is stacked up in homes, incinerated, buried in landfills, or dumped into open pits of garbage, adding to the world's escalating crisis of electronic waste.

THE E-WASTE OF SMART LIVING

A typical household in the developed world has around eighty electrical devices with a plug-in cord or battery.[36] Many old refrigerators, dishwashers, stoves, washers, and dryers are being returned to recycling depots. But large numbers of smaller devices are either piling up in drawers, cupboards, and garages or are landing in the trash—and unlike electric-car batteries, loads of small lithium batteries are making their way into household garbage. With each passing day, consumers are throwing out more and more electrical and electronic devices. Those living in Canada and the United States are producing an especially high amount of e-waste per capita: approximately 20 kilograms a year, about a third of which seems to end up in the developing world.[37]

Upgrading to smart products is going to dump even more devices onto the mountains of electronic waste now polluting the global environment. E-waste contains hazardous substances, including cadmium, chromium, lead, mercury, and polychlorinated biphenyls (PCBs). Some manufacturing firms are developing smart robotic systems to enhance the speed, precision, and viability of recycling electronic waste. For instance, Apple's robot, known as "Daisy," can dismantle a couple hundred iPhones every hour.[38] Yet just a fifth of the world's e-waste is safely recycled. Much of the rest ends up in the poorest neighborhoods of Asia, where people break apart old laptops, smartphones, TVs, sensors, appliances, and solar panels to recover valuable components, including aluminum, copper, iron, and plastics, as well as cobalt, gold, lithium, silver, and tantalum.

Most countries have policies to protect recyclers and local ecosystems from e-waste pollution. Especially across the developing world, however, illegal operations and forced labor are endemic in the e-waste recycling industry. Here, electronic waste is being burned in open pits, spewing toxic fumes. It is being buried in landfills without proper treatment and containment; and it is being tossed onto heaps of foul-smelling household garbage. The people picking through e-waste face grave health risks, from chemical poisoning to exposure to carcinogens. Toxic chemicals and metals from dismantled and discarded products are also leeching into groundwater and food systems.[39]

The world cannot seem to get a handle on how to recycle (or even dispose of) e-waste safely. At the same time, the amount of e-waste continues to climb, from 34 million metric tons in 2010 to 50 million metric tons in 2018, an amount roughly equal to five thousand Eiffel Towers. This is on track to keep rising, with one study predicting the annual amount of e-waste could reach as high as 120 million metric tons by 2050.[40]

There are many reasons for this trend. National policies, international agreements, and the recycling programs of computer and electronics industries are all failing to rein in e-waste. At the same time, the global-ization of telecommunications and the internet is stimulating demand for smartphones and laptops, while the construction of new electrical grids is opening up new markets for household appliances. More con-sumers can afford to buy electrical products, and manufacturers are shortening the replacement times for these products. Meanwhile, adver-tisers are supercharging demand for brands and new products, including urging consumers to live more sustainably by buying smart appliances and upgrading to smart homes.[41]

THE POLITICAL ECONOMY OF SMART PRODUCTS

Over the next two decades, artificial intelligence is going to make auto-mobiles safer. It is going to empower smartphones as sustainability tools. It is going to increase the efficiency of appliances and help households save energy.

Different smart products are going to have diverse consequences for global sustainability. As I discussed earlier, self-driving vehicles look set to reduce traffic collisions significantly over the next few decades, sav-ing lives, reducing the trauma of loss and injuries, and freeing up medi-cal services. Unless governments and industry step up regulations and compliance, however, these vehicles—including electric versions—are also going to pollute the global environment with batteries, synthetic rubber, and vehicle waste. There will be additional ecological costs from maintaining the highways and city streets for these vehicles. As well, securing the ores and metals to build them is almost certainly going to spur mining booms in places with dismal environmental and human rights records.

But making and driving conventional vehicles cause equally destruc-tive consequences. Whatever one hopes, the world is not going to see fewer vehicles on the roads anytime soon. The political and economic power of the global auto industry is too strong for that to happen. This industry generates revenues of more than $3.5 trillion a year and employs more than 50 million workers across its global supply chains. If it were a national economy, it would rank as the fifth largest.[42] In 2018, sales of new passenger cars alone exceeded 80 million. With or without driverless cars, the auto industry is going to sell billions of new vehicles over the next fifty years. Given this, moving as fast as possible to a driverless world would seem worthwhile, as the social and economic gains are high and the environmental costs will likely be no greater than business as usual.

On the other hand, smart appliances and homes seem to offer far less potential to advance global sustainability. "Each object in the extended network of an AI system, from network routers to batteries to microphones, is built using elements that required billions of years to be produced," Kate Crawford and Vladan Joler show in a study of the global supply chain necessary for Amazon's Echo devices. "Looking from the perspective of deep time, we are extracting Earth's history to serve a split second of technological time, in order to build devices that are often designed to be used for no more than a few years."[43]

Sure, a few smart products are more energy efficient. And smart technology is certainly going to improve over time, with longer-lasting batteries, more capacity to save energy, and a greater reliance on renewable energy. Further gains may well arise as smart products connect across the quickly expanding Internet of Things, creating new opportunities to find efficiencies and reduce waste.[44] But for global sustainability, the net value seems marginal at best.

In the case of smart homes, artificial intelligence is serving mainly as a way to differentiate brands to entice consumers to buy new products. The environmental and social costs of smart homes can end up far outweighing the marginal gains in energy efficiency, especially when the smart products are designed for rapid obsolescence. As sales of smart appliances and electronics rise, so does demand for the ores, metals, and plastics to manufacture them, further intensifying competition for high-grade, cheap inputs, including from conflict-prone regions with weak environmental regulations. Smart appliances and electronics, moreover, are adding even more e-waste into the global environment, poisoning water supplies, soil, and food systems, especially in the slums of Asia, Africa, and Latin America.

The manufacturers and retailers of smart products never mention these consequences. Nor do they tend to ever address the ways that efficiency gains almost always rebound into even more production and consumption.[45] Instead, marketers tend to overstate the environmental value of these products, as do the high-tech firms and startups now talking up the ability of machine learning to save energy and natural resources. This does not mean smart products are doing nothing to advance sustainability. But when assessing the value of these products, it does mean that we need to stay alert to the ways that firms are manufacturing hype for smart technologies, including, as we'll see next, the potential to transform city living and industrial agriculture.

7

SMART CITIES AND FARMS

By the middle of this century, more than two-thirds of people are set to reside in cities. By then, the world population will likely be nearing 10 billion as it heads toward over 11 billion by the end of the century.[1] Building more sustainable cities and agricultural systems to house, feed, and employ these people is one of the greatest of the challenges now facing humanity.

Artificial intelligence would seem to have significant potential to scale up sustainability across the world's cities and farmlands. Smart power grids, automated pollution controls, and smart transportation offer ways to reduce the energy intensity and waste footprints of urban living. Intelligent farming equipment provides opportunities to raise yields and lower the water consumption of industrial agriculture. AI-powered apps offer ways for smallholder farmers to identify plant diseases and receive early alerts for pest invasions. These apps can also advise farmers on the most effective fertilizer, herbicide, or pesticide to apply to a crop, as well as on ways to improve the diet of chickens, the health of pigs and goats, and the productivity of dairy cattle.

On some measures, AI technologies are improving the management of cities and farms. Yet there are sharp limits to what these technologies can achieve, as they do not confront the intensifying consumerism of urban living or the underlying structures of industrial agriculture. There is even a risk of smart city and farming technologies reinforcing global forces of unsustainable consumption and production. Without sweeping reforms to the global political economy of agriculture, smart technologies could prop up the reliance of urban populations on monocultural production and intensify the social and ecological shadows of the global agrifood industry. They could further distance food production from consumption, as well as enhance the profitability of treating agrifood crops as financial products rather than as food and nutrition. They could also end up empowering transnational corporations (such as Bayer, which acquired Monsanto in 2018) that are looking to expand genetically modified crops, monopolize seed varieties, and dominate international sales of pesticides, herbicides, and fertilizers.

Let's begin this analysis by looking more closely at the prospects of smart cities for advancing global sustainability.

SMART CITIES

A smart city strategy prioritizes information and communications technology as a way to improve services and enhance the environmental and socioeconomic sustainability of urban management. Machine learning technologies are becoming increasingly important for this strategy as smart products and homes spread and as the Internet of Things expands.

London, New York, and Amsterdam ranked as the world's three "smartest" cities in the *IESE Cities in Motion Index 2019*, produced by business professors at the University of Navarra in Barcelona. Smart cities, which first began to emerge in large numbers in Europe, have spread worldwide, with the 2019 index ranking Paris fourth, followed by Reykjavik, Tokyo, Singapore, and Copenhagen.[2] Led by New York, Singapore, and Tokyo, investment in smart city technology is set to double from 2018 to 2022 (from about $81 billion to $158 billion).[3] This financing is coming from municipalities, national and international agencies, public-private partnerships, transnational corporations, and technology startups.

The leading smart cities are using these funds to offer free internet access and develop mobile apps to increase the accessibility of municipal services. Sensors and surveillance cameras are being installed to collect data, and deep learning networks are forecasting crime hotspots, traffic congestion, and pollution spikes. City-owned vehicles are being integrated into the Internet of Things to improve data analysis and response times. City infrastructure is being automated to increase the efficiency of subways, buses, streetlights, traffic lights, trash collection, and waste recycling. Police are being outfitted with smart cameras to improve the safety of both officers and citizens. And to deploy forces more efficiently, police departments are using machine learning software to visualize and predict crime patterns.[4]

In addition, these cities are scaling up the information from smart appliances and homes to enhance citywide services, such as staff checking on seniors whose mobility or food intake seems to be declining. Smart cities are also partnering with tech and auto companies to develop driverless buses, ride-sharing services, and machine learning technologies to enhance energy efficiency and the transition to electric vehicles and renewable power.[5]

Moving toward global sustainability will undoubtedly require increasing the efficiency of electricity usage in cities, as well as reducing the reliance on coal, oil, and natural gas for the heating and cooling of buildings. As city populations soar, global consumption of energy is on track to rise by 30 percent from 2017 to 2040, an amount equal to adding another India and China to the planet. Electricity usage is rising especially quickly and is set to account for 40 percent of the total increase over this time.[6]

Smart cities are developing intelligent electrical grids as a way to decrease the energy footprint of factories, office buildings, and residential homes. They are partnering with utility companies to integrate sensors and machine learning software into electrical grids and household meters to reduce energy losses and better utilize solar and wind power (as chapter 5 outlines). They are also incentivizing consumers to build smart homes to connect into these grids.

These city strategies are offering the opportunity to replace aging transformers and transmission lines with smart grids. These grids are enabling two-way information and electricity flows between producers and consumers. They are also enhancing the reliability and diversity of power supplies, as well as facilitating real-time, self-correcting adjustments in response to changes in weather, demand, or grid stresses.[7]

These grids are also helping cities shift to renewable power. Conventional grids generally transmit electricity from large power plants over great distances, with coal and natural gas still generating more than 60 percent of this electricity in 2016 (in contrast, solar and wind power generated just 5 percent).[8] With the capacity to forecast and autonomously react to changes in supply and demand, smart grids and microgrids can stabilize flows from intermittent, dispersed sources of energy. This can enhance reliability and efficiency, which in turn can lower prices for solar and wind energy, making it more competitive with coal, gas, hydro, and nuclear power.[9]

In addition, smart cities are partnering with high-tech firms to better manage energy consumption and pollution. One example is IBM's cognitive computing and Internet of Things initiative known as Green Horizons. This initiative, which began in Beijing in 2014, is now in place in cities across China, as well as in India, Japan, South Africa, the United States, and the United Kingdom. It includes a self-configuring and self-learning system able to track and forecast weather and pollution levels by analyzing data streams from thousands of sources, including factories, satellites, traffic cameras, environmental sensors, weather stations, and the Internet of Things.

This system is able to map within a kilometer the sources, intensity, direction, and location of pollution. It also is able to forecast pollution levels up to three days into the future and pollution trends up to ten days ahead. This information is enhancing the accuracy of pollution alerts and the efficacy of interventions (such as spraying saltwater into the air). It is fine-tuning the modeling of ways to reduce greenhouse gases and smog, such as by restricting traffic or temporarily suspending construction. And it is helping utility companies to configure solar and wind generators to optimize production and minimize energy losses. IBM's Green Horizons system can also predict days ahead—with up to 90 percent accuracy—the energy output from solar and wind, saving power by enhancing the efficiency of supply-and-demand management.[10]

This long list of successful environmental gains and economic benefits is encouraging thousands of cities around the world to start modifying urban living with smart technologies. Western Europe, North America, Japan, Singapore, and South Korea are continuing to invest in smart cities. Over the past few years, however, China has been leading the charge to build smart cities.

SMART CITIES IN CHINA

More than five hundred cities in China have committed to installing smart technologies and seeking digital solutions as a way to enhance urban life and sustainability. The market value of smart city projects—such as from robotics, sensors, hardware, personalized healthcare, and AI systems—is on track to exceed $2 trillion by 2025, with cities in China accounting for $320 billion.[11] Chinese firms are the driving forces implementing many of these smart city strategies. Known as the "PATH to smart cities," Ping An, Alibaba, Tencent, and Huawei are leading the way. These companies are bringing expertise in artificial intelligence, blockchain technology, and driverless vehicles. They are also offering access to high-speed wireless networks, computing hardware and smartphones, facial recognition technology, cash-free payment systems, cloud infrastructure, and robotics.

One example of a smart city is Hangzhou, the capital of Zhejiang province, with a metro-area population of more than 6 million. The city has set up scores of online services, with residents now able to use Alibaba's Alipay mobile app in nearly every supermarket and taxi. Known as the "City Brain," in 2016 Hangzhou launched an AI platform on Alibaba's cloud infrastructure to enhance the efficiency of water usage, energy consumption, and transportation. Through a network of sensors and cameras, this "brain" is scanning roads and monitoring meteorological conditions. Taking into account factors such as weather, congestion, and construction, it is speeding up the flow of traffic by automatically adjusting traffic signals in real time.

In 2017, Hangzhou's City Brain managed to increase the average speed of vehicles by more than 15 percent, reducing commuting times, lowering stress levels for drivers, and decreasing pollution from idling vehicles. It is also reducing the journey times of emergency vehicles. Traffic lights turn green as these vehicles near an intersection, which, according to an official at Hangzhou's public security bureau, can halve the time it takes an ambulance to reach a hospital. The system is further reducing the need for traffic officers as well as guiding police quickly to the scenes of accidents and traffic violations. "The City Brain can detect accidents within a second, and we can arrive at the site in 5 minutes," claims Zheng Yijiong, a police officer in Hangzhou.[12]

Shanghai's "citizen cloud" offers a second example of a smart city program. Over 24 million people live in Shanghai. Citizen cloud is providing apps and online sites to help residents more efficiently access more than 120 government cloud-based services.[13] By 2018, over 9 million residents were using citizen cloud. The city is also selling data from its vast network of cameras and sensors to help companies develop additional apps and more efficiently commercialize products.[14] The telecom company Huawei, for instance, is mining this data—along with data from vehicles, parking lots, and partner companies—to offer Shanghai drivers a smartphone app to pay for tolls as well as locate and book parking in a city with an acute shortage of spots.[15]

Guangzhou, with close to 15 million residents, is a third example of a leading smart city in China. Formerly known as Canton, Guangzhou is the capital city of Guangdong province. Over the past few years, the city has become a hub for innovation. It hosts around five thousand high-tech firms, with only Beijing having more. And business incubators are supporting at least ten thousand technology start-ups.[16] Smart apps are spreading across the city, enabling easier access to everything from medical support to education opportunities. "Medical services are just one click away," the vice mayor of Guangzhou, Cai Chaolin, said proudly. "You can just stay at home and have all these services come to you."[17]

THE LIMITS OF SMART CITIES

Smart cities are definitely nudging the world toward some sustainability goals, and smart technologies are visibly improving city services within some fast-growing economies, most notably China. But incrementally improving the management of electrical grids, pollution and waste, transportation, and city services can take the world only a short distance toward global sustainability. Smart city technologies do very little to alter and can even worsen problems such as wasteful consumption, feelings of alienation, income inequality, housing prices, inequity of services, and privacy rights.[18] The upbeat discourse of smart cities can also obscure the ways that the political and economic structures of cities themselves have long been a cause of global environmental degradation.

Ecologist William Rees, who coined the term "ecological footprint," reminds us of the complex ways that cities and the accompanying sub-urban sprawl draw down global resources and harm distant ecosystems. Urban economics, as he demonstrates, tends to exaggerate the value of urbanization for sustainability by underestimating the global environmental damage from the rising consumption of city residents.[19] Most cities rely on land, food, fresh water, natural resources, and energy far beyond their borders. And they rely on externalizing the cost of waste into distant lands, the global commons, and future generations. Measured locally, the ecological footprint of the residents of a smart city may seem to be declining. But taking into account the shadows of consumption in faraway lands, this footprint looks very different, with deep social and environmental costs for marginalized peoples and fragile ecosystems.[20]

Cities contribute as well to the psychological and physical distancing of consumption, where food, consumer goods, and waste flow through long, opaque trade structures and supply chains and where residents have little understanding of the sources or costs of everyday living.[21] This includes, as the previous chapter surveys, the consequences of the metals, plastics, and rare earth elements going into making smart electronics and homes and the e-waste arising from replacing and upgrading smart products.

Cities additionally act as engines of overconsumption, defined as "consumption that exceeds the capacity of the earth to regenerate natural systems and retain biological dynamism."[22] The higher incomes of the middle class in cities tend to increase wasteful and excessive consumption. So does the shift away from local gardening and handicrafts and toward buying more processed and fast food, branded products, and discount merchandise from big-box stores. Advances in technology, such as smart home automation within a city, can further serve to accelerate product upgrading and demand for energy.[23]

By functioning as nodes of overconsumption, cities intensify the ecological footprints of individuals on the earth's oceans, forests, wetlands, and climate. William Rees and Mathis Wackernagel go as far as concluding that "as nodes of energy and material consumption, cities are causally linked to accelerating global ecological decline and are not by themselves sustainable."[24] This may overstate the causal role of cities as the destructive nature of capitalism itself would seem to underlie much of this decline.[25] But Rees and Wackernagel make a key point worth remembering when assessing the value of smart cities: contrary to what advocates seem to assume, there is nothing inherently sustainable in the structure of any city within the contemporary world order.

Consider the impact of cities on climate change. Around 55 percent of people live in cities. Yet over the past few decades, cities have been consuming as much as 80 percent of global energy and accounting for as much as four-fifths of global greenhouse emissions.[26]

Integrating artificial intelligence into global agriculture—what is variously called "smart agriculture" or "smart farming" or "precision agriculture"—would seem to hold good prospects for mitigating some of the social and environmental consequences of the rising consumption of food within cities. But how far can smart agriculture really take us toward a more sustainable global agricultural system?

THE PROSPECTS OF SMART AGRICULTURE

Global demand for food is set to rise by as much as 98 percent from 2005 to 2050.[27] Smart agriculture would seem to have real potential to help meet this demand. Monitoring crops and soils with drones, sensors, and computer vision can help farmers increase productivity and reduce the risk of crop failure. Tractors with self-driving technology can speed up planting and harvesting. Smart robots can replace the need for seasonal workers to pick fruits and vegetables. Deep learning networks can refine local weather forecasting to give farmers more time to protect crops and animals from flooding or heat waves. Smart farming technologies can also help decrease waste and pollution, reduce the consumption of water, fertilizer, and pesticides, and optimize financial returns.[28]

Look at the ways drones with computer vision and learning capability are starting to improve the management of wine vineyards. Cultivators are using these drones to identify pests and diseases as well as assess the condition of vineyards to enhance the efficiency of water and fertilizer usage. These drones are also able to predict yield rates with higher accuracy than conventional labor-intensive measuring of canopy, plants, and berries. The savings in water, fertilizer, time, and money can be substantial. "Traditionally a consultant for a big winery might travel up and down in a ute [a pickup truck], looking for sick or missing plants," explains agronomist Sigfredo Fuentes at the University of Melbourne. "This is really time consuming. Instead, we can survey a 45-hectare area in 15 minutes and have the data ready a day later."[29]

Smart technologies are also helping farmers to evaluate the health of animals, enhancing the well-being and productivity of chickens, pigs, and cows. The startup Connecterra, for instance, has created what might be thought of as a "Fitbit for cows" to monitor the health of dairy cows (cube-shaped, these devices hang around a cow's neck). Headquartered in Amsterdam, Connecterra developed this technology using TensorFlow, Google's open-source software library for the development and training of machine learning models. Accessible with a smartphone or tablet, the cloud-based processing of the data from the cow Fitbits can offer a farmer insights into how to increase milk yields, breeding rates, and herd fertility. "For a typical Dutch farm, which are generally known to be very productive to begin with, we've seen about a 20 percent to 30 percent gain in efficiency in farm operations using Connecterra," claims the company's CEO Yasir Khokhar. Connecterra further says its technology can offer early alerts of a sick cow, disease outbreaks, and fertility declines from heat stress.[30]

Smart farming technologies also seem to have considerable potential to help smallholders in developing countries. Free apps such as Plantix can help a farmer to identify diseases (by uploading a picture of the infected plant) as well as advise a farmer on possible treatments. Launched in 2015 by a Berlin-based AI startup, Plantix is using image-recognition software and deep learning techniques to offer precise, immediate, and free advice. In theory, this can help a farmer to apply herbicides and fertilizers more precisely, rather than broadly spraying or fertilizing, as is common when pests, disease, or nutritional deficiencies threaten crops. The Plantix app can further help farmers in developing countries to reach new markets with higher agricultural standards, such as the organic food market in Europe.[31]

Consider the potential of the Plantix app in India. "Nearly every household in India has a smartphone," notes the agricultural scientist Srikanth Rupavatharam, and for the most common plant diseases across India, the Plantix app is accurate more than 90 percent of the time. Language is a more significant barrier for uptake than smartphone and internet access. Recognizing this, Plantix has developed the capacity to offer advice in English, Hindi, Telugu, and other local languages of India.[32]

Smart farming equipment would seem to have even more potential to transform global agriculture. Here, transnational corporations are leading efforts to develop these technologies. This is hardly surprising because these technologies are expensive, offer the best returns for large operations, and are frequently backed by the agrifood and high-tech industries. As we'll see next, however, there are some intriguing examples of startups that are developing smart robotic tools for small farms.

SMART FARM EQUIPMENT

Blue River Technology, a California-based startup that John Deere acquired in 2017 for a little over $300 million, is one example of a company integrating artificial intelligence into farm equipment. It sells a smart robotic lettuce trimmer. It also sells what it describes as a "see and spray" machine, which hooks onto a tractor to apply herbicides, fungicides, and fertilizer to crops.

Guided by computer vision and deep learning networks, this machine is able to identify weed and plant species, enabling precise and targeted spraying. According to the company, it can reduce the quantity of herbicides necessary for weed control by as much as 90 percent. It can spray herbicides that are not suitable for uniform, broadcast spraying, which allows farmers to poison weeds that have become resistant to standard herbicides. It can target fertilizer and fungicide to plants in need as well as catalogue weed species within a particular field to help a farmer choose the most effective herbicide. The see-and-spray machine can also reduce the need for farmworkers, with one farmer estimating it can do the work of eight to ten laborers.[33]

There are countless other smart robotic farming tools and machines coming onto the market, too. The Floridian company Harvest CROO

Robotics, for instance, has developed a smart robotic harvester able to pick strawberries at the rate of thirty workers.[34] The UK-based Small Robot Company is another, slightly different example whose motto is "Small robots, not big tractors." This company is piloting integrated teams of small robots to plant, tend, and harvest crops. By planting seeds with greater precision, the robots reduce the need for plowing, which can damage soil and cause soil erosion. These robots are also able to monitor the health of crops and weed fields, thus reducing the need for herbicides. The company claims its small robots use 90 percent less energy than plowing with big machinery. To increase affordability and uptake, it is marketing these robots as a fee-paying "service" to enhance productivity rather than as a "product" for sale, which would then require farmers to pay for maintenance, upgrades, and repairs. According to the company, its goal is not to put farmworkers out of a job but to ease the burden of farm life, freeing up time and diversifying rural economies as farmers participate in new ways.[35]

Advocates of both large- and small-scale smart agriculture envision a total transformation of global agribusiness, where farmers are managing from offices rather than tilling the fields. "Fifteen years from now, you may have several of these autonomous vehicles—a swarm of robots in each field," Mac Keely of Blue River Technology said. "That suite of tech would lead to some kind of controlled environment where the farmer isn't in the field but rather somewhere else controlling the vehicles."[36]

Smart farming can sound very promising as a way to advance the sustainability of global agriculture. And it would seem to offer both smallholders and industrial farms ways to increase productivity and decrease ecological harms. Yet there are also significant risks for farmers who invest in smart agriculture as well as a real danger that AI technologies can reinforce the political and corporate powers underlying today's deeply unsustainable system of global agriculture.

THE LIMITS AND RISKS OF SMART FARMING

The turn toward smart farming will further empower agribusinesses such as DuPont, Bayer (Monsanto), and John Deere. A new tractor, harvester, or applicator can cost hundreds of thousands of dollars. Integrating smart technology raises the price, and farmers run a risk of becoming further indebted to the agrifood industry.

The capacity of agrifood conglomerates to conduct macro-data analysis of real-time information on crop yields, shortfalls, and soil and water quality will also further empower their control over commodity and input prices as well as land valuations. The technical training and expertise necessary for smart farming will also enhance the reliance of farmers on agribusinesses.

In addition, farmers relying on smart technologies risk becoming further enmeshed in needing the agricultural inputs and technology upgrades of agrifood conglomerates. Companies such as BASF, Bayer, ChemChina, and DowDuPont already dominate global markets for seeds, fertilizers, and herbicides. Meanwhile, leading equipment manufacturers, such as the American company John Deere, have long been accused of requiring farmers to use the company for servicing and repairs, including in recent years for software fixes for semi-automated farming equipment. "Maybe a gasket or something you can fix," laments one Nebraskan farmer, "but everything else is computer controlled and so if it breaks down I'm really in a bad spot."[37]

Furthermore, as has been generally true with other technological advances in farming over the past half century, smart agriculture has no power to challenge the underlying political and economic structures of global food production. And as with technologies such as high-yield seeds, genetically modified organisms (GMOs), disease-resistant crops, and superfertilizers, it could well reinforce this acutely unsustainable system.

A vast literature reveals just how deep this unsustainability goes. It documents the loss of topsoil, the depletion of fresh water, the increasing reliance on a few crops for food security, and the loss of more than three-quarters of the genetic diversity of crops since 1900. This literature exposes as well how industrial agriculture has contributed since the 1960s to greater pesticide use, rising rates of carbon and methane emissions, and widespread water, soil, and air pollution.[38]

Analysis of industrial agriculture by political economists exposes in particular the role of trade, corporate investment, and financing in causing extreme inequalities, social injustice, and environmental damage. It demonstrates how opaque global supply chains and weak, fragmented governance are undermining sustainability by externalizing ecological costs and distancing consumption from production. It reveals why industry-guided certification and standard setting are failing to aggregate into solutions for communities and indigenous peoples. It also uncovers how the political interests of states and the profit seeking of agribusinesses are overriding the nutritional needs of smallholder families in developing countries.

This political economy literature further maps how agricultural conglomerates are "land-grabbing" across the developing world for plantations, biofuels, and agricultural estates. It brings to light the illegalities and corruption that are keeping wages, regulations, and prices low. It shows how the international trade of industrial agricultural products, even in the face of contrary evidence of its value for local communities, has come to dominate the discourses of global institutions, states, and transnational corporations. It exposes the ways that banks, investment funds, and firms are turning food into abstract financial products, further obscuring the environmental and social shadows of production and consumption. And it uncovers the growing concentration of power among a handful of agrifood companies, with "mega-mergers" the latest trend.[39]

Smart agriculture may well improve farming practices here and there. But it cannot fix this broken system.

THE LIMITS OF AI FOR SUSTAINABILITY

The environmental scientist Lucas Joppa, as you may recall from the opening chapter, directs Microsoft's AI for Earth. Not surprisingly, he sees artificial intelligence as a powerful force for moving toward a more sustainable world. "Harnessing the power of AI to monitor the impacts of our current land use practices and to model scenarios means that, perhaps for the first time, we can have the right information at our fingertips to more effectively and sustainably manage our lands, watersheds and ecosystems," he wrote in a posting for the 2018 World Economic Forum.[40]

Joppa is right in seeing AI as having great value for deepening our knowledge of the workings of the earth. Artificial intelligence can advance sustainability in many other ways, too. Self-learning robots can enhance conservation. Smart electrical grids and a smarter Internet of Things can enhance energy efficiency. Machine learning software can accelerate the environmental savings from eco-business and find new ways and places to reduce waste. Smart products and homes can reduce electricity consumption, and a smart city strategy can find ways to reduce traffic, enhance safety, cut pollution, and decrease greenhouse gas emissions.

Artificial intelligence can also improve the environmental management of smallholder farms. Smartphone apps, for instance, can help farmers identify and treat crop diseases, deploy pesticides and herbicides more efficiently, and use water and fertilizer more judiciously. When free, as with Plantix, these apps can help small farms survive the onslaught of increasingly efficient industrial agriculture.

Yet we should not presume these advances will forge pathways toward global sustainability. There are innate limits to how far any new technology can advance sustainability. A technology as transformative as artificial intelligence will inevitably generate unintentional consequences, unleash new political and economic forces, and produce crosscutting, contradictory implications for global sustainability. That is clear from the environmental history of technology, from the invention of the wheel to the discovery of electricity to the creation of the internet.[41] As this history suggests, to avoid exaggerating the value of any technology, we need to interrogate every claim of those profiting from the technology. We should also be wary of any analysis that ignores history and politics.

An Ecomodernist Manifesto exemplifies the dangers of ahistorical and apolitical analyses of technology. Authored by eighteen well-regarded scholars who identify as environmentalists, this manifesto calls for an embrace of the power of technology to construct "a good, or even great, Anthropocene." For them, the only realistic solution to the escalating global environmental crisis is to embrace technological solutions, intensify industrial agriculture, accelerate urbanization, and rewild the countryside as people migrate to high-tech megacities.[42]

This thinking, while perhaps momentarily enticing, is deeply flawed. It ignores the violent legacy of imperialism, colonialism, and postcolonial resource politics underlying today's global environmental crisis. It misjudges the ways that technology infuses the destructive forces of capitalism with new powers. It underestimates the ways that greater technological efficiency can rebound to intensify unsustainable production and consumption. It ignores the great ecological unpredictability of adding new technologies into the world economy, and it overlooks the need when pursuing sustainability to harness any new technology with great care.[43]

It is easy to fall into the trap of ecomodernist thinking when evaluating the recent feats of artificial intelligence. We must not forget, however, that AI has little capacity to transform political or economic structures and in many ways is reinforcing the power of transnational corporations and leading economies. In this chapter, we have seen this with the ways that AI is enhancing the dominance of agrifood conglomerates and entrenching unsustainable trade, financing, and production. We have further seen this with the ways that smart cities are expanding appliance and electronic sales, intensifying the ecological footprints of individuals, and deepening the ecological shadows of consumption.

The rising power of artificial intelligence, moreover, is bringing new dangers for sustainability. As I discuss in the next section of this book, AI technologies have the potential to reinforce global injustice and inequality, accelerate the extraction of natural resources, deepen the culture of consumerism, and empower security agencies and militaries to suppress dissent and wage war.

III

THE DANGERS OF AI

8

DEEPENING INEQUALITY AND INJUSTICE

Global sustainability is going to require a fairer, more just distribution of wealth and resources. Artificial intelligence could boost the annual value of the world economy by as much as $16 trillion from 2017 to 2030: an amount roughly equal to the combined gross domestic products of Brazil, India, Germany, Japan, and the United Kingdom in 2017.[1] This stoking of productivity is going to generate well-paying jobs in the digital economy, a plethora of new consumer goods, and a bigger pot of global wealth. Applications of artificial intelligence will benefit those living in poverty, too—from free medical apps advising in Swahili to microfinancing apps lending money to help the working poor make ends meet.

Yet the rollout of AI also has the potential to deepen social inequity and environmental injustice. Income inequality looks set to rise as tech billionaires syphon off a disproportionate share of wealth creation. Gender inequality is likely to widen because relatively few women are currently working in the AI industry. Country inequality is likely to increase as well with China and North America now on track to capture 70 percent of the economic value of artificial intelligence over the next decade.[2] Just as troubling, environmental inequality looks set to grow as the wealthy benefit disproportionately and the poor absorb an ever-greater share of the costs of degradation and pollution.

Supercharging economic productivity with intelligent automation will also implode middle- and low-income jobs. Self-driving cars are going to replace truck and taxi drivers, while smart assembly lines are going to reduce the need for factory workers. AI-powered technology is going to displace paralegals, payroll managers, and telemarketers. Self-operating machinery is going to supplant farm laborers. And intelligent robots are going to replace lab technicians. China's working poor seem especially at risk as national and city governments collaborate with the country's leading tech firms to accelerate the uptake of intelligent automation. But intelligent automation is set to rip through the workforces of every country, with a potential upheaval akin to what happened to farm laborers during the Great Depression from 1929 to 1939.

Intelligent automation and AI software are going to bring other dangers for social sustainability, too. Privacy rights will come under increasing threat as machine learning technologies track people's movements and trawl through smartphones, bank accounts, and internet activity. Personal security may come under increasing attack as cyberthieves and blackmailers deploy AI-powered chatbots, malware, and ransomware.[3] Now and then, machine learning will also surely continue to end up going badly awry, as when Microsoft's chatbot "Tay" began to attract Twitter followers by spewing racist, sexist, and anti-Semitic slurs. In addition, as we'll see in this chapter, there are many examples of machine learning systems—including those scoring the risk of criminals reoffending and those evaluating the quality of job candidates—stereotyping minorities and discriminating against women.

Let's start our analysis of the consequences of AI for social and environmental justice by first sketching the extreme inequality of earth shares, as this is necessary to understand the full extent of the potential dangers of artificial intelligence.

THE INEQUALITY OF EARTH SHARES

A "fair earth share" is the amount of natural resources and waste sinks that each person in theory could use without permanently degrading the global environment for future generations.[4] Since the 1960s, more efficient extraction, better management, and rising agricultural yields have expanded the earth's capacity to produce resources and absorb waste. What constitutes a fair share of the earth has been declining, however, as the world population climbs and as forests, oceans, and lands lose regenerative capacity. Adding to the strain on the earth, over this time the world's wealthiest individuals have been increasingly consuming an ever-greater share of the world's natural resources.

One way to see the inequality of earth shares is to compare the average ecological footprint of people living in different countries. The Global Footprint Network defines this footprint as the area of "biologically productive" land, water, and space that is necessary to support the average lifestyle of people in a country (converted to "global hectares"). The footprints of individuals vary widely within and across countries. The average footprint equates to 8.1 global hectares in the United States, 7.7 in Canada, 6.6 in Australia, 5.2 in Russia, 4.8 in Germany, and 4.4 in the United Kingdom. On the other hand, the average footprint of those living in Indonesia is 1.4 global hectares, in India 1.2, in Kenya 1.0, in Bangladesh 0.8, and in Eritrea 0.5. Globally, the average per capita footprint is 2.7 global hectares—at least 1.7 times above the capacity of the earth to regenerate.[5]

Also indicative of the inequality of earth shares are the wide differences in the consequences of personal lifestyles on climate change. Revealingly, the personal consumption of the wealthiest 10 percent of people accounts for approximately half of global carbon pollution. On the other hand, the consumption of the bottom half of the world population accounts for only 10 percent of this pollution. The carbon footprint from the personal consumption of the wealthiest 1 percent of people is especially heavy: around 175 times higher than the poorest 10 percent of people in the world.[6]

Another way to see the inequality of earth shares is to look at the distribution of global wealth. The number of billionaires jumped sixteen-fold from 140 in 1986 to 2,208 in 2018. Collectively, they were worth at least $9.1 trillion in 2018, a record-setting amount up 18 percent from 2017. The top five were worth $429 million, with three of the five (Amazon's Jeff Bezos, Microsoft's Bill Gates, and Facebook's Mark Zuckerberg) making their fortunes in high tech.

The combined wealth of the top twenty billionaires was $1.2 trillion in 2018. Besides Bezos, Gates, and Zuckerberg, two made their fortunes with Google (Larry Page and Sergey Brin), one with Oracle (Larry Ellison), one with Tencent (Ma Huateng), and one with Alibaba (Jack Ma).[7] In total, more than two hundred tech entrepreneurs, owners, and CEOs made *Forbes* magazine's 2018 list of billionaires. That year, roughly two-thirds of the tech billionaires were from just two countries: the United States (38 percent) and China (26 percent). Only fifteen of these tech billionaires were women. Together, the world's tech billionaires were worth $1.3 trillion in 2018, with nearly 60 percent of them richer than in the previous year.[8]

These figures surely underestimate the true wealth of the world's billionaires because tax havens and clandestine bank accounts conceal vast assets. Just looking at the recorded wealth reveals how deep the inequality of earth shares now runs. The top eight billionaires alone had as much wealth as the poorest half of humanity in 2017.[9] And the world's richest 1 percent of humanity now holds at least half of global wealth.[10] Billionaires have even come to dominate wealth generation in the United States. Just three men—Jeff Bezos, Bill Gates, and Warren Buffet—held as much wealth as the poorest half of the American population in 2017.[11] In 2018, Bezos became the first person on the *Forbes* list of billionaires to surpass a net worth of $150 billion: an amount it would take an Amazon worker, making $15 an hour, more than a million years to earn (assuming the employee never slept, never took time off, never paid taxes, and could live that long).

The inequality of earth shares, moreover, is increasing with each passing year. The top 1 percent of the world population is currently on track to control two-thirds of global wealth by 2030.[12] Oxfam's Iñigo Macías Aymar is blunt when explaining why: "The economic model is not working at all." Oxfam International calculates that since 2006, the wealth of the world's billionaires has been rising six times faster than the incomes of average workers. In 2017, the wealthiest 1 percent of the global population captured more than four-fifths of new wealth, while the bottom half saw no gains at all. "The few at the top get richer and richer," notes Winnie Byanyima, the former executive director of Oxfam International, "and the millions at the bottom are trapped in poverty wages."[13]

THE SOCIAL INEQUALITY OF AI

Artificial intelligence is going to produce complex and variable consequences for social equality. Smart apps are going to improve health services. Smart homes are going to lower energy bills for middle-income families, while smart products are going to bring new conveniences for consumers. Smart cities are going to offer new opportunities for citizens to participate in decision making. Intelligent automation is going to enhance productivity and free up time for some workers. Over the coming decades, the diffusion of AI through the global economy is also going to create new employment opportunities and spur demand for workers with digital and high-level computing skills.[14]

Yet simultaneously, AI is going to eliminate routine and repetitive jobs. The venture capitalist Kai-Fu Lee sees the potential for the loss of "billions of jobs" over the next few decades.[15] The occupations at risk range far and wide, including mining coal in Australia, delivering books from Amazon, assembling Apple products in China, and verifying legal contracts for Alibaba.[16] China's workforce looks set to face particularly great turbulence. This is partly because China's national government, city governments, and top technology companies are coordinating to accelerate the diffusion of artificial intelligence. And this is partly because of the nature of the Chinese economy, with automation having the potential to replace half of all jobs in China.[17]

But the diffusion of intelligent automation and machine learning software is going to rupture the workforces and intensify inequality in many other countries, too. Consultants with Bain & Company are predicting that by 2030, automation could eliminate 20 to 25 percent of jobs in the United States, displacing as many as 40 million workers and suppressing general wages.[18] Automation is set to hit lower- and middle-income families particularly hard, with those living in small American cities with relatively few professional and high-tech jobs likely to experience especially great hardships.[19]

The United Kingdom is on track for a similar upheaval. Those with wealth and privilege in the UK, as also is true in China and the United States, are going have an easier time adjusting. Not only are elites going to experience less workplace disruption, but retraining is going to be easier for those with elite educations. Meanwhile, as the British charity Sutton Trust contends, the "soft skills" arising from these elite educations—such as self-reliance, communication, and self-confidence—are going to become increasingly valuable in the age of AI. Sutton Trust also believes that AI is going to undercut social mobility in the UK because the semi-skilled administrative jobs on the chopping block—such as bookkeeping and paralegal support—have been some of the only "stepping stones" into the management ranks for those without an elite education.[20]

The economists Anton Korinek and Joseph E. Stiglitz worry that artificial intelligence is going to exacerbate inequality globally by disproportionately enhancing the productivity of the wealthy. "If intelligence becomes a matter of ability-to-pay," they argue, "it is conceivable that the wealthiest (enhanced) humans will become orders of magnitude more productive—'more intelligent'—than the unenhanced, leaving the majority of the population further and further behind." They are especially concerned that "a significant fraction of the workforce may not have the skills required to succeed in the age of AI" and that what might be coming can be likened to the upheaval for agricultural workers during the Great Depression.[21]

At the same time, artificial intelligence is set to enrich the billionaires who own and run transnational corporations. Many opportunities will certainly arise for new entrepreneurs to launch AI startups, become wealthy, and perhaps even join the club of billionaires. Still, as Kai-Fu Lee argues, the "positive-feedback loop" of AI capitalism—where more data enables better products, which creates more data, which then improves products—"means that AI-driven industries naturally tend toward monopoly." Going forward, new enterprises are going to find it increasingly difficult to compete against the likes of Google and Amazon. Or Apple and Samsung. Or Alibaba and Tencent. Or Uber and Spotify. And as Lee says, as the power of AI continues to rise, the profits of these technology "juggernauts" are set to "soar to previously unimaginable levels."[22]

Lee also thinks the growing power of artificial intelligence is going to be a source of rising inequality between countries. America and China are emerging as "AI superpowers," and as he exposes, a disproportionate share of the wealth from AI is flowing into the bank accounts of American and Chinese billionaires. Developing countries—especially the poorest countries of the Asia-Pacific, Africa, and Latin America—do not have the computing, robotic, or machine learning expertise to compete with the United States and China. Meanwhile, low-income factory and farmworkers in the developing world are especially vulnerable to being displaced by intelligent automation. "Low-cost labor provides no edge over machines," Lee notes, "and data-driven monopolies are forever self-reinforcing."[23]

This diffusion of AI, moreover, could well widen the gender wealth gap even further. Consider the billionaires who are going to become even richer in the age of AI. The fifteen wealthiest billionaires on the 2018 *Forbes* list were all men. That year, less than 12 percent of the world's billionaires were women—with just 3.3 percent "self-made" women—and two-thirds hailed from the United States and China.[24] This gender disparity would seem unlikely to change anytime soon. Only 8 percent of venture capitalists are women, and in 2017, of the $85 billion invested by venture capitalists in startups (as recorded in the PitchBook database), 79 percent went to all-male founders, and just 2.2 percent went to all-female founders.[25]

Alongside the increasing concentration of wealth among male billionaires, AI looks set to deepen gender inequalities within the middle and lower classes. Intelligent automation is going to eliminate many of the jobs done by women. Men, meanwhile, are disproportionately filling new jobs in the digital economy, including those demanding expertise and training in artificial intelligence. Since the mid-1980s, the percentage of female undergraduates receiving computer science degrees in the United States has fallen from 35 percent to less than 20 percent, even as the percentage of women graduating with biological and physical science degrees has been steadily rising.[26]

The percentage of women exiting the tech industry is higher than men, too, with toxic work cultures cited as a big reason. Anger at the sexist culture at Google, for instance, boiled over in 2018, when thousands of employees around the world walked off the job to protest the company's handling of sexual harassment in the workplace, including covering up misconduct by senior management. As one female employee at Google told a rally in front of the company's headquarters in Mountain View, California: "I mean, why would you want to go into tech if it's like this?"[27]

Men now dominate the computer industry, including the field of machine learning. In 2017, for instance, across three prominent machine learning conferences just 12 percent of the authors of papers were women. At Microsoft, women in 2017 comprised 26 percent of employees and 23 percent of the technical staff working on scientific, mathematical, or engineering projects. At Apple that year, women comprised 32 percent of employees and 23 percent of the technical staff. The percentage of men working on machine learning is even higher. At Google in 2017, women accounted for 21 percent of the technical workforce but comprised only 10 percent of the 641 members of staff who were researching "machine intelligence." Also, that year women comprised 22 percent of Facebook's technical staff and 15 percent of the company's 115-person AI research team.[28]

The tech industry suffers as well from a lack of racial and cultural diversity. Among Google's US employees, for instance, over 89 percent identified as "white" (53.1 percent) or "Asian" (36.3 percent) in 2018. Only 3.6 percent identified as "Latinx" and 2.5 percent as "black," with attrition rates in 2017 the highest for employees with these backgrounds. At Facebook, 88 percent of employees identified as "white" (46.6%) or "Asian" (41.4%) in 2018, with 4.9 percent identifying as "Hispanic" and 3.5 percent as "black." Among the technical staff at Facebook, just 3.1 percent identified as Hispanic and 1.3 percent as black.[29]

Stanford computer scientist Fei-Fei Li sees this lack of diversity as one of the greatest challenges for developing responsible and unbiased artificial intelligence. "AI is about to make the biggest changes to humanity," she said, "and we're missing a whole generation of diverse technologists and leaders." The philanthropist Melinda Gates agrees and is calling for immediate action to correct this failing. "If we don't get women and people of color at the table—real technologists doing the real work—we will bias systems," she said building on Li's comment. "Trying to reverse that a decade or two from now will be so much more difficult, if not close to impossible."[30]

Homogeneous teams of computer scientists are more prone to bias and misjudgments when programming or interpreting the effectiveness of machine learning.[31] In contrast, "diverse teams are more likely to flag problems that could have negative social consequences before a product has been launched," notes Anima Anandkumar, a professor of computer science and machine learning at the California Institute of Technology.[32] This is why in 2017 Fei-Fei Li cofounded AI4ALL, a nonprofit that educates and mentors Canadian and American high school students "to increase diversity and inclusion in artificial intelligence."[33] The need for more diverse AI teams, as we'll see next, is going to rise as machine learning systems increasingly govern the world.

MACHINE BIAS AND DISCRIMINATION

Unless corrected, AI trained on biased data will replicate these prejudices when making recommendations, decisions, and predictions. Study after study has shown how systems learning from sexist images, partial datasets, or clichéd portrayals can reinforce or extend forms of discrimination. For a time, Google and LinkedIn, for instance, were disproportionately recommending high-paying jobs to men because in the early years more men had been searching for these jobs. There was a time, as well, when Google's image recognition software was better at recognizing white faces because the training pictures did not include enough racial diversity.[34]

Indeed, stereotyping and prejudicial thinking have plagued AI systems designed to recommend parole, creditworthiness, insurance rates, and employee hiring. This was the case, for instance, with Amazon's effort to develop a smart hiring tool. In 2014, Amazon staff began training the tool by having five hundred different computer models scour a decade worth of résumés on file with the company, zeroing in on fifty thousand keywords to learn how to hire the best employees. Amazon executives were hoping this tool would be able to trawl the web to identify strong job candidates (with more than 575,000 employees in 2015, the company wanted to find a more efficient way to recruit and hire).

The hiring tool, however, began to endorse unqualified candidates and discriminate against female applicants. Applicants from women's colleges were filtered out, and résumés containing the word "women's" were downgraded, including one with the phrase "women's chess club captain."

The reason for such bias in the hiring tool was not difficult to figure out: too much of its training data had come from male résumés. Amazon's machine learning experts tried to correct for these biases, but Amazon executives nonetheless shelved the tool in 2017, having lost confidence in the project. Nihar Shah, a professor of machine learning at Carnegie Mellon University, was not surprised to see Amazon give up on trying to automate its hiring process. "How to ensure that the algorithm is fair, how to make sure the algorithm is really interpretable and explainable—that's still quite far off," he remarked.[35]

Prejudice and bias have also beset algorithms trying to forecast crime locations and the risk of criminality. The US nonprofit ProPublica, for instance, exposed racial bias against black Americans in software known as Correctional Offender Management Profiling for Alternative Sanctions (COMPAS), which is designed to evaluate the risk of defendants reoffending and committing future violent crimes. Such software is now common in the United States, with "risk scores" helping judges to decide on everything from bail terms to sentencing to probation conditions. After looking at the COMPAS risk scores for reoffending of seven thousand people arrested in Florida in 2013 and 2014 and then checking whether charges were laid over the ensuing two years, ProPublica found two striking propensities: black defendants were nearly two times more likely than white defendants to be incorrectly scored as being at high risk of committing a future crime, and white defendants were almost two times more likely than black defendants to be inaccurately assessed as being at low risk of committing a future crime.[36]

ProPublica was unable to evaluate the exact reasons for these risk scores because a private company has proprietary control of the software's algorithms. Such lack of transparency rightly worries Meredith Whittaker, a cofounder of the AI Now Institute. "The public never gets a chance to audit or debate the use of such systems," she pointed out. "And, the data and logics that govern the predictions made are often unknown even to those who use them, let alone to the people whose lives are impacted."[37]

Computer science researchers at Dartmouth College were eventually able to shed some light on the inner workings of COMPAS. By comparing the predictive accuracy of COMPAS with a random group of nonexperts, they were able to show that COMPAS "is no more accurate or fair than predictions made by people with little or no criminal justice expertise."[38]

FURTHERING SOCIAL SUSTAINABILITY

Some applications of artificial intelligence are going to make life better for the world's poorest people. And these benefits will pick up pace as cheap smartphones continue to spread through developing and emerging economies. We saw some of these benefits in the last chapter, for instance, with the free Plantix app that diagnoses crop diseases for small-scale farmers in India (including offering advice in Hindi and Telugu).

Ada Health, a free AI-powered medical app, is another example of the potential of artificial intelligence to help poor people. Launched in 2016 in Germany, more than 8 million people across 140 countries had downloaded the app by 2020. It is able to ask questions, evaluate symptoms, and recommend appropriate health services in a nearby area. To improve its diagnostic accuracy over, say, a search of WebMD, it evaluates patients within their population sample, becoming increasingly proficient as its databank expands.

Backed since 2018 by the Bill & Melinda Gates Foundation, the app is now aiming to support healthcare workers who assist people in developing countries who do not live near a doctor, clinic, or hospital. In these countries, "most healthcare workers work door-to-door and can track patient symptoms," explains Hila Azadzoy who works at Ada Health. "The vision we have is we can put Ada into their hands and even connect Ada with diagnostics tests so that—at the home of the patient—they can pull it out and say, 'OK this is confirmed.'"[39]

To further enhance the app's reach, staff at Ada Health are developing a Swahili version to go along with ones in English, French, German, Portuguese, and Spanish. They are working as well to improve the diagnostic accuracy for people in developing countries by integrating local disease contexts, such as the prevalence of malaria, dengue, and Chagas disease in the tropics and the possibility of Ebola in parts of Africa. Looking ahead, apps such as Ada Health even seem to have the potential to help avert epidemics.[40] As a recent study in *BMJ Global Health* concluded, "AI holds tremendous promise for transforming the provision of healthcare services in resource-poor settings."[41]

Artificial intelligence also seems to hold great promise as a way of extending microfinancing to poor and marginalized people. An

AI-powered app known as Smart Finance, for instance, is providing small loans to millions of workers across China. This app relies on deep neural networks to appraise loan requests, analyzing data on prospective borrowers' phones to assess the risk that they will default. Trained on a vast and growing database of loans that have been repaid and defaulted, the AI system has learned to take into account a wide range of information that a traditional lender would never consider, such as the phone's remaining battery power and how quickly the phone users typed in their date of birth.

Basing creditworthiness on the weak correlations around such factors might seem nonsensical. But at least in China, this app is proving far better than traditional banks at predicting repayment rates for small loans, and by 2018 was issuing over "2 million loans per month with default rates in the low single digits," according to Kai-Fu Lee. Many of these loans, moreover, are going to people who have traditionally been unable to obtain credit, including migrants and young people.[42]

Such farming, health, and financial applications of AI will certainly benefit the world's poor. Yet as the earlier examples of applications to hire employees, gauge criminality, and chat on Twitter remind us, artificial intelligence also has the potential to deepen injustice, prejudice, and bias. Personal security and privacy are at risk, too. Cybercriminals are starting to deploy AI-powered chatbots, malware, and ransomware to break into personal records, steal credit information, and blackmail ordinary people. Meanwhile, tech companies are increasingly breaching privacy as they hunt for ever-more data to train computer models.

The coming into force in 2018 of the European Union's General Data Protection Regulation underscores how seriously the EU sees the tech industry's threat to privacy and personal security. This law enables national regulators to fine a company up to 20 million euros for violating privacy rights or data protections. Paul Nemitz of the European Commission, who worked on establishing the EU's data regulation, sees a need for even more regulation in the "age of AI." In an article in *Philosophical Transactions of the Royal Society A*, he argues that governments—to protect constitutional democracy, human rights, and the rule of law—need to regulate AI and confront "the extraordinary power concentration in the hands of few Internet giants." It is "high time to bind new technology to the basic constitutional principles," he writes, "as the absence of such framing for the Internet economy has already led to a widespread culture of disregard of the law and put democracy in danger."[43]

Diverse, cautious, and self-aware teams of programmers can sidestep some of these dangers by designing transparent, trustworthy, and verifiable AI systems.[44] But as Nemitz says, to enhance equity and accountability, we are going to need more jurisdictions to regulate artificial intelligence, the internet, and big data collection. We are also going to need the societal and governmental institutions that are relying on artificial intelligence for advice and forecasting to understand the underlying decision-making models. As law professor Jason Schultz says, "If you can't understand the technology, you shouldn't be able to use it."[45]

On top of that, as I discuss in detail in the concluding chapter, governments will need to regulate the AI industry to break up monopolies, distribute wealth more evenly, ease the pain of automation, and stop the inequality of earth shares from continuing to rise. Firms will need to establish—and follow—principles of fairness, equity, and transparency when deploying artificial intelligence. And nonprofits and community associations will need to hold firms and governments accountable when AI does go awry.[46] Far more will need to be done too, as I discuss in the next chapter, to hold companies and states accountable for the ways that AI is accelerating unsustainable production and excessive consumption.

9

ACCELERATING EXTRACTION AND CONSUMPTION

The world needs to find ways to produce more food, services, and consumer goods to support the billions of people who currently live in poverty. Throughout this century, even more production is going to be necessary as the global population heads toward 11 billion. Artificial intelligence can definitely help increase global productivity. Chapters 4, 5, 6, and 7 offer many examples of machine learning and smart technologies enhancing the environmental efficiency of manufacturing, global supply chains, energy systems, consumer products, farming, and urban living. As this chapter brings to light, however, AI software, hardware, and services are simultaneously opening up new opportunities to accelerate unsustainable production, extract scarce resources, and supercharge consumerism.

Oil and gas companies are investing in artificial intelligence to find new sources of oil and natural gas, reduce the costs of drilling and hydraulic fracturing, and enhance profitability. Mining companies are automating the excavation, loading, and hauling of coal, gold, copper, and diamonds. Technology companies are integrating machine learning into search engines and social media platforms to increase digital advertising sales. Brand manufacturers and big-box retailers are using AI software to target online marketing, personalize discounts, and ramp up sales. In the meantime, shopping malls, retail stores, and supermarkets

are piloting AI-powered surveillance systems to track customers and recommend ways to organize displays to spur impulse purchases. Turbo-
charging production and consumption in these ways is set to deepen the
global environmental crisis. To begin to see why, let's take a quick look at
the escalating climate crisis.

THE CLIMATE CRISIS

Climate change poses especially severe risks for the global environment.
A rise of 3 to 5 degrees Celsius during the twenty-first century would
"bring us up to the warmest temperatures the world has experienced
probably in the last million years," notes Drew Shindell, a climate scientist at Duke University.[1] Such an outcome would bring severe droughts,
violent storms, mass extinctions, and widespread flooding. Rising seas,
meanwhile, would swamp low-lying coastlines and island states.[2] The
2015 Paris Agreement on climate change is aspiring to keep the average global surface temperature from rising by no more than 1.5 degrees
Celsius above pre-industrial levels. Even limiting global warming to 2°C,
however, is going to require strong, far-reaching action. Already, the average global surface temperature since 2015 has been hovering around 1°C
above pre-industrial levels.[3] And warming is visibly escalating. Ocean
temperatures are steadily rising, with the rate of increase accelerating
over the past three decades.[4] Since reliable records began in the 1880s, the
hottest decade on record is 2010 to 2020 and the hottest five years were
2016, 2019, 2015, 2017, and 2018, in that order; at the time of writing,
the hottest month ever recorded was July 2019.

António Guterres, Secretary General of the United Nations since 2017,
is deeply worried about the failure to slow climate change since the Paris
Agreement came into force in 2016. "If we do not change course in the
next two years," he told the UN General Assembly in 2018, "we risk run-
away climate change." The targets of the Paris Agreement "are far from
being met," he lamented. Especially worrying, he added, is "the concentration of carbon dioxide in the atmosphere," which "is the highest in 3
million years—and rising."[5]

The average daily concentration of carbon dioxide in the atmosphere
was 407 parts per million (ppm) in 2018, up from 277 ppm in 1750.[6] The

primary source of this carbon dioxide is the combustion of oil, gas, and coal. The annual increase in the concentration of carbon dioxide has been accelerating since 1990, rising from an average of 1.5 ppm per year during the 1990s to 2.2 ppm per year over the last ten years.[7]

Fossil fuel emissions did level off from 2014 to 2016. But emissions rose again in 2017 and then hit an all-time high in 2018, driven in part by growing automobile sales, resurging coal consumption, and rising industrial production. Global carbon dioxide emissions in 2018, the Global Carbon Project estimates, went up around 2.7 percent, rising 6.3 percent in India, 4.7 percent in China, and 2.5 percent in the United States. Reflecting on these latest trends, David Reay of the University of Edinburgh remarked: "This annual balance sheet for global carbon is comprehensive and scientifically robust. Its message is more brutal than ever: we are deep in the red and heading still deeper."[8]

Keeping global warming below 2°C is going to require leaving vast stores of oil, coal, and natural gas in the ground. Even as climate change intensifies, however, global production of fossil fuels is continuing to rise. World oil production set a new record high in 2018 at 94.7 million barrels a day, up from 83.3 million barrels a day in 2010. This was the ninth year in a row of record-setting production. As the International Energy Agency says, "there is no peak oil demand in sight."[9]

The United States was the leading oil producer in 2018, for the first time ever averaging over 15 million barrels a day. Saudi Arabia was second at 12 million barrels a day, followed by Russia at 11 million barrels a day. Production of natural gas also set a new record in 2018—rising more than 5 percent from 2017 levels—with the United States the leading producer. Global coal production also went up in 2018, and although still slightly lower than the peak in 2013, production is on track to continue to rise for at least another decade or so as investors and banks continue to pour hundreds of billions of dollars a year into supporting coal plants.[10]

AI AND CLIMATE CHANGE

Artificial intelligence has considerable power to help mitigate this escalating climate crisis, as part II of this book confirms. Machine learning algorithms have the ability to advance environmental mapping, weather forecasting, and climate modeling.[11] Natural language processing software has the potential to enhance the capacity of environmental regulators to analyze information, process corporate filings, and evaluate permit applications for fossil fuel extraction.[12] Smart drones and submersibles have the ability to improve worker safety by performing dangerous tasks and helping to clean up industrial accidents. Intelligent management systems have the potential to save energy, optimize electrical grids, and reduce the costs of solar and wind power.

Yet AI has just as much power to accelerate the production of oil, natural gas, and coal propelling the climate crisis. The fossil fuel industry is awash with data from satellites, wireless networks, and remote sensors, with the "exponential growth" of digital information set to continue into the foreseeable future.[13] Leading oil and gas companies—including ExxonMobil, Royal Dutch Shell, Gazprom, Total, and the China Petro-chemical Corporation (the Sinopec Group)—are now investing in artificial intelligence to mine this information for business value and growth opportunities. The stakes are high. The current generation of deep learning techniques alone, according to calculations by the McKinsey Global Institute, could eventually add as much as $200 billion of annual value to the oil and gas industry.[14]

With leading companies increasingly pursuing this business value, the market for AI software, hardware, and services in the oil and gas sector is on track to double from 2016 to 2022, rising from $1.42 billion to $2.85 billion.[15] Oil and gas companies are installing virtual assistants to answer inquiries and guide customers through online product offerings. They are setting up AI-powered cloud computing platforms to optimize the storage, organization, and retrieval of information. They are relying on machine learning tools to search for trends and patterns in company data to discover new ways to enhance profitability. And they are automating supply chain logistics to boost the efficiency of production.

In addition, they are using machine learning systems to accelerate the process of analyzing prospective oil and gas sites and applying for drilling permits. The latest cognitive system, explain IBM analysts, "does 6–8 weeks of manual research in seconds, identifying specific geohazards buried within tens of thousands of pages of drilling reports, and dynamically converts text into easy to understand tables and graphs highlighting areas of interest."[16] AI-enhanced predictive analytics are also helping oil and gas companies to improve the reliability of production flows, reduce the odds of equipment malfunctions, and enhance the safety of operations.

Deep learning techniques are further helping the oil and gas industry to search for new sources of hydrocarbons as well as model the most efficient ways to drill new wells and conduct hydraulic fracturing. "AI is being applied to subsurface data," explains industry analyst Geoffrey Cann, "and, through better interpretation of that enormous trove of data, petroleum engineers are confidently expanding the amount of oil and gas that is recoverable."[17] Oil and gas companies are also starting to invest in smart machinery to reduce costs and speed up extraction. Drones are inspecting drilling sites and pipelines. Submersibles are exploring the ocean floor, where vast stores of oil and gas remain untapped. And robotic equipment is collecting real-time data to help identify new oil and gas deposits.[18]

Technology companies are leading the charge to integrate artificial intelligence into the fossil fuel industry—what the columnist Brian Merchant describes as "automating the climate crisis."[19] One example is the Chinese technology company Huawei, which is collaborating with oil and gas companies to develop "smart manufacturing platforms" to enhance the efficiency of logistics, services, and production. Another example is the American company Rockwell Automation, a leading provider of industrial automation, which in 2019 teamed up with the world's biggest oilfield services company (Schlumberger) to launch a joint venture company (Sensia) dedicated to automating oil exploration and drilling to cut costs, optimize output, and extend well life.[20]

Yet another example is the American technology company NVIDIA, which is collaborating with GE's Baker Hughes to use artificial intelligence and accelerated computing analytics to help the oil and gas industry process data in real time, with the prospect, claims NVIDIA's marketing director Tony Paikeday, to "dramatically reduce the cost of finding, extracting, processing and delivering oil."[21] But many other technology firms are also working to sell AI software, hardware, and services to the oil and gas industry, including Accenture, Amazon, Google, IBM, Microsoft, and Oracle. Amazon Web Services, for instance, has designed special products for the oil and gas industry, advertising them as able to "find oil faster," "reduce the cost per barrel," and "recover more oil."[22] Oil and gas companies are investing as well in AI startups to try to lower production costs and gain advantages over competitors.

Seeing these trends is frustrating for the climatologist Michael Mann, who directs the Earth System Science Center at Pennsylvania State University. "There is deep irony that the very companies that are supposed to represent the leading edge of technological innovation and advancement are actually taking us backward," he bristled.[23]

MINING THE EARTH WITH AI

Transnational mining companies are making similar investments in machine learning and intelligent automation. AI systems are recommending ways to reduce the fuel costs of excavating sites and hauling ore, as in one copper mine in the Democratic Republic of the Congo where, after just two months, truckers were able to decrease fuel consumption by 7 percent by following the driving advice of machine learning software.[24] Mining companies are also integrating machine learning into prediction analytics, which, according to Jane Zavalishina, president of Mechanica AI, can generate efficiency savings of up to 10 percent.[25] This is improving the predictive accuracy of blasting models, enhancing the efficiency of explosives, and lowering production costs. It is also helping mining companies to eliminate unnecessary maintenance, avoid delays from equipment breakdowns, decrease the risk of industrial disasters, and reduce the quantities of inputs such as cyanide.

Rio Tinto, an Anglo-Australian company with revenues of more than $40 billion in 2018, is one of the leaders in deploying artificial intelligence to increase the productivity and profitability of mining. The company is automating the drilling, loading, hauling, and sorting of minerals to save on labor, electricity, and fuel costs (its self-driving trucks, for instance, use 13 percent less fuel). It is optimizing operations by using machine learning tools to build virtual simulations, model scenarios, and predict the productivity, efficiency, and profitability of different mining options. It is using deep learning techniques to analyze real-time data from equipment sensors and mobile devices to forecast maintenance requirements.

The company is also using AI software to forecast market shifts, customer orders, and shipping schedules.[26]

To further enhance productivity, Rio Tinto is aiming to develop "intelligent mines" that link "pit-to-port" to enable lightning-fast, automated decision making. The company's Koodaideri iron ore mine in Western Australia—with ore covering an area 50 kilometers long and 5 kilometers wide—is set to be the first intelligent mine, with ore shipments expected to begin in 2021. According to Rio Tinto's Kellie Parker, these intelligent mines will integrate "leading edge technology, including automated trucks, drills and trains but also for the first time systems connecting all components of the dynamic schedule, from customer right through to orebody planning."[27]

Intelligent mines will generate further efficiency savings for large-scale operations. As with the case of the oil and gas industry, however, the primary consequence of integrating artificial intelligence into industrial mining is going to be an acceleration of the productivity and profitability of transnational corporations. Furthermore, if past trends hold, these companies will reinvest the efficiency savings to expand markets, production, and revenues.

Many different technologies have brought great efficiency savings over the past century. Yet as these savings have rebounded into the global economy, the consumption of just about every material—with a few exceptions, such as wool, asbestos, and mercury—has gone up or held steady since the 1960s.[28] The efficiency savings from machine learning and intelligent automation have little capacity to alter the consumption trajectory of natural resources such as oil, natural gas, coal, iron ore, or rare earth elements. Going forward, moreover, other applications of artificial intelligence are going to extend the power of the world's leading manufacturers and retailers to increase the consumption of everything from fast food to plastic toys to fast fashion, presenting a grave threat to future sustainability.

THE PROBLEM OF CONSUMPTION

Responsible production and consumption is one of the seventeen sustainable development goals of the United Nations. Making progress toward this goal is proving especially difficult. With each passing decade, people on average are consuming more food, water, clothing, and products; they are also generating more waste and pollution, from household garbage to carbon emissions. Unless lifestyles change, the UN notes, by 2050, the ecological footprint of humanity is set to be nearly three times larger than the capacity of the earth to regenerate natural resources and absorb waste.[29]

This footprint has been growing increasingly heavy over the past half century. The population sizes of vertebrates—of fish, amphibians, reptiles, birds, and mammals (excluding humans)—went down by an average of 60 percent from 1970 to 2014. Also despite two-thirds of commercial fish species now overexploited and in biological crisis, the world continues to consume 110 million metric tons of wild fish a year (or 242 billion pounds). Meanwhile, well over a billion metric tons of food is wasted annually, even as more than 820 million people remain undernourished.[30]

Adding to the problem of consumption, individual footprints are highly unequal both within and between countries. According to the Global Footprint Network, the average footprint of people living in the United States is now three times higher than the global average (defined as the amount of biologically productive land required to sustain lifestyles). America's footprint is far larger than those in developing countries: more than four times the average in Colombia, nearly seven times the average in India, and over sixteen times the average in Eritrea.[31] The difference in ecological footprints is even starker between the world's richest and poorest individuals. The top 1 percent of people control at least half of the world's wealth. Also revealing, the top 10 percent now account for half of all carbon pollution arising from personal consumption.[32]

The consumption of just about every product is climbing. The history of automobiles is emblematic of the deepening of the global culture of consumerism. Worldwide, more than 80 million automobiles were sold in 2018, twice the average number sold in the 1990s. Over the past decade, sales of sport utility vehicles (SUVs) and pickup trucks have been particularly strong, and by 2017, these accounted for two-thirds of the sales of new passenger vehicles in the United States. The world is now on track for as many as 3 billion cars, SUVs, crossovers, and trucks on the roads by 2050, up from 250 million in 1970, 1 billion in 2010, and 1.5 billion today.[33]

Rising rates of unequal, wasteful, and excessive consumption are casting shadows of harm into distant ecosystems and onto future life. Consider the environmental history of plastics. Production of plastics went up sixfold from 1980 to 2018, with the total amount manufactured between 2006 and 2019 greater than all of history before this time. Plastics are made primarily from fossil-fuel feedstocks, and in recent years, plastics have accounted for about 6 percent of global oil consumption. Annual plastic production now exceeds 400 million metric tons, and if trends continue, it could double again by 2060.[34] Plastics are at the core of consumerism. Of today's total production, 40 percent is for packaging: everything from water bottles to food containers to cling wrap. Consumer products (excluding automobiles, which contain large quantities of plastics) account for another 20 to 25 percent of production.[35]

Plastic pollution is now rising quickly. Less than 10 percent of plastic waste is recycled into new plastics, with the rest burned, buried, dumped, or littered. The washing of synthetic clothing (such as polyester and nylon) and the erosion of synthetic rubber tires are further polluting waterways with microplastics (under 5 millimeters in size). Microplastics from clothing, tires, and city life (such as the plastic dust from running shoes) account for as much as a quarter of the plastics now flowing into the oceans. The wear and tear of synthetic auto tires alone may account for as much as 5 to 10 percent of the plastics now pouring into the oceans.[36]

Marine plastic pollution is on track to rise to 16 million metric tons by 2025, up from 9 million metric tons in 2015. Vast eddies of plastic "garbage patches" now swirl in slow-spinning gyres in the Pacific, Atlantic, and Indian oceans. The biggest, known as the "Great Pacific Garbage Patch," is already four times larger than the American state of California and, according to a study in the journal *Scientific Reports*, is growing "exponentially."[37]

This large amount of plastic pollution has far-reaching environmental and health consequences. Plastic litter is killing marine birds and mammals. Plastic waste acts like a sponge, absorbing toxic substances such as polychlorinated biphenyls (PCBs). As plastics break down into microplastics and nanoplastics, these are increasingly leeching into drinking water, accumulating in marine life, bioaccumulating up food chains, and choking coral reefs.[38]

Rising rates of unsustainable consumption underlie many other global environmental problems, too. Tropical deforestation, for instance, is a leading cause of social injustice, biodiversity loss, and climate change. According to the World Resources Institute, tree cover loss in the tropics set a new record in 2016, rising to nearly 17 million hectares (up from 10 million hectares the year before). Losses in 2017 were the second worst ever at 15.8 million hectares, with Brazil experiencing the biggest loss (28 percent of the total), followed by the Democratic Republic of the Congo, Indonesia, Madagascar, and Malaysia.[39]

Over the past two decades, palm oil plantations, cattle ranches, and soybean estates have been three of the primary drivers of the clearing (and burning down) of tropical rainforests. Global consumption of palm oil has tripled since 2000, with Indonesia and Malaysia supplying 85 percent of production (mostly for cooking oil, processed foods, cosmetics, hygiene products, and lubricants). Since 2000, per capita consumption of meat has been steadily rising, too, with soybean meal an increasingly common feed for livestock and poultry. Today, Brazil is a leading exporter of beef and soybeans, with the clearing of forests for cattle ranches and agriculture the two biggest direct causes of deforestation in the Amazon.[40]

The political economy of advertising, moreover, is continuing to expand markets and drive up unsustainable consumption. Worldwide advertising expenditures exceeded $580 billion in 2017—up $100 billion from 2014—and are on track to reach nearly $800 billion by 2022 as companies spend more on digital advertising and sponsoring content on social media (such as Facebook) and search engines (like Google).[41] Over the coming decade, moreover, machine learning is going to supercharge the power of advertising and marketing.

SUPERCHARGING CONSUMERISM

According to analysts at the McKinsey Global Institute, the deep learning techniques already on the market have the potential to boost the economic value of the global retail industry by as much as $800 billion a year. These techniques, they argue, have particular power to enhance the accuracy of predictive analytics, increase returns on marketing and advertising, and drive up sales of consumer products.[42]

Companies are integrating a wide range of AI products and services to capture this extra value. AI-enhanced software is collecting and categorizing customer data. Advertising and sales services with learning capabilities are running on social media platforms, search engines, and websites. Chatbots are guiding customers toward purchases twenty-four hours a day, seven days a week. Speech recognition software is enabling voice-activated site navigation and product ordering. Deep neural networks are analyzing data on past purchases, online activity, and social media history to enhance the power of recommendation engines. Companies are even developing augmented reality apps to allow a customer to "test" what a lipstick or eyeshadow would look like (as L'Oréal has done) or "see" what a rug or sofa would look like at home (as IKEA has done).

In addition, machine learning is helping to optimize returns on marketing campaigns, enhance the predictive accuracy of sales analytics, and track the efficacy of advertising. Machine learning software is enabling firms to project sales returns on different versions of videos, images, messaging, product placements, and social media posts. And it is allowing them to tailor deals and prices to the buying habits of individual customers, such as those who prioritize price over brand recognition. Machine learning systems are also automatically translating advertising, bidding for ad time, and modifying ads and websites in response to new data. There is even AI software to help staff identify customers who are more susceptible to up-selling and cross-selling sales strategies (such as urging a customer to buy a higher-priced product or additional related merchandise). "Many companies don't use the opportunity for cross-selling to its full advantage," notes marketing consultant Michael Brenner. "AI helps to fill this gap in knowledge, squeezing more sales out of each prospect."[43]

A few technology companies are even starting to develop AI-powered surveillance systems for supermarkets and shopping malls. One example is the Russian startup, NtechLab, a world leader in deep learning and facial recognition algorithms for security surveillance. NtechLab's award-winning facial recognition system is able to identify individuals in crowds, collect demographic information, and detect some emotions.

Since 2018, NtechLab has been piloting a facial recognition surveillance system in a shopping mall in St. Petersburg. The system is aiming to reduce shoplifting and fraud by identifying repeat offenders. At the same time, it is tracking the comings and goings of shoppers to search for patterns in how different groups of customers—by gender, age, and ethnicity—navigate aisles, browse displays, and choose purchases. One goal is to recommend ways for shopkeepers to optimize store displays, encourage impulse purchases, and increase total sales. Another is to profile regulars so store clerks can customize service, including recommending products and offering deals.[44]

Amazon is leading the charge among online retailers to capture the marketing value of artificial intelligence. Through its cashier-free convenience store, Amazon Go, the company is tracking customer movements and purchases and then using machine learning tools to analyze ways to enhance sales and profits. Amazon's virtual assistant Alexa is offering shopping advice and enabling voice ordering of items and services. Alexa also collects customer data to help the company forecast demand and personalize product recommendations. By some estimates, Amazon's recommendation engine alone is generating a third in extra sales for the company.[45]

The world's biggest retailer, Walmart, has come to embrace artificial intelligence, too. Robots are cleaning floors, reporting on spoiled produce, and alerting staff when shelving stock is low. Staff are using machine learning software to manage global supply chains and predict inventory needs within particular stores. Self-driving delivery vehicles are being piloted across several American cities. As well, Walmart has revamped its website to offer product recommendations—in part, because many consumers were going to Amazon.com for suggestions. "We have more data than nearly everyone in the world," explains Walmart vice president Galagher Jeff. "We're making heavy investments in artificial intelligence and machine learning to grow our business. Why? Because we have to."[46]

Many other companies are similarly pursuing the marketing value of artificial intelligence, including Google, Microsoft, Apple, and Facebook. "In the long run we're evolving in computing from a 'mobile-first' to an 'AI-first' world," notes Google CEO Sundar Pichai.[47] Over the past few years, Google has been investing billions of dollars in machine learning to enhance its cloud computing services and retain its dominance over the digital advertising market. The company's business model has been remarkably successful so far. Google's share of the internet search engine market was hovering around 90 percent in 2019, with total revenues from online advertising rising steadily over the last decade, from $28 billion in 2010 to $51 billion in 2013 to $116 billion in 2018.[48]

Facebook, too, relies on advertising, which accounted for more than 98 percent of the company's $56 billion in revenues in 2018.[49] Like Google, Facebook's advertising revenues have been soaring since 2010, when these were less than $2 billion. Also like Google, in recent years, the company has been investing heavily in artificial intelligence. "Facebook today cannot exist without AI," argues Joaquin Quiñonero Candela, the director of applied machine learning at Facebook. "Every time you use Facebook or Instagram or Messenger, you may not realize it, but your experiences are being powered by AI."[50]

China's technology firms Baidu, Alibaba, Tencent, and Huawei are also all integrating machine learning, intelligent data analytics, and natural language processing into advertising and product marketing. Like Google and Facebook, they are researching and developing artificial intelligence, with laboratories all around the world. Across China, moreover, tens of thousands of local startups and small businesses are also spurring sales and profits with artificial intelligence.

AI applications, for instance, have revolutionized food delivery in China. Apps have been developed for ordering, with easy payment through features such as Alibaba's Alipay and Tencent's WeChat Wallet. By 2016, online food orders were averaging 20 million a day. Just two years later, the three biggest services alone—Baidu Takeout, Ele.me (part of the Alibaba Group), and Meituan—were averaging 34 million deliveries per day. These delivery services are quick, convenient, and affordable, and many are using electric bicycles to transport food. These services have been a boon for China's restaurants, with online food delivery sales tripling in value from 2014 to 2018. But they are also generating mountains of greasy, low-quality plastic containers, cutlery, and bags, of which very little is recycled.[51]

TURBOCHARGING PROFITABILITY

Over the next two decades, artificial intelligence looks set to be a key tool of profitability for transnational corporations. This technology "holds vast potential . . . for ushering in a new era of growth for businesses," argue Mark Purdy and Paul Daugherty, analysts at the consulting and technology firm Accenture. According to their modeling, by 2035, machine learning and intelligent automation have the potential to increase the rates of corporate profitability on average by 38 percent across 16 industries and 12 economies. If this were to occur, it would increase the value of global goods and services by $14 trillion by 2035, an amount equal to the combined GDPs of Brazil and China in 2017.

Across the world's core industries, this would increase economic growth rates in 2035 by a weighted average of 1.7 percent, Purdy and Daugherty calculate. A good portion of this growth would advance social goods and services. Yet in this scenario, AI would do even more to fuel extraction, production, and retailing, boosting the 2035 growth rate of manufacturing by 2.3 percent; forestry, fisheries, and agriculture by 2.1 percent; wholesale and retail by 2.0 percent; and transportation and storage by 1.9 percent. Artificial intelligence, Purdy and Daugherty conclude, "offers unprecedented profitability opportunities."[52]

Accelerating corporate profitability and global consumption with artificial intelligence would certainly bring societal benefits, create jobs, and generate new wealth. As even a cursory glance at the causes of today's global environmental crisis confirms, however, this would also inevitably intensify the political and economic forces underlying biodiversity loss, tropical deforestation, marine plastic pollution, chemical contamination, and climate change.[53] And it would surely take a heavy toll on workers and communities. Moreover, as I discuss in the next chapter, the diffusion of AI facial and emotion recognition technology could well end up helping states repress citizens who question the environmental and social costs of this growth trajectory.

10

THE INTELLIGENT EYES OF REPRESSION

Over the next decade, artificial intelligence is going to redeploy jobs, create new sources of inequality, and generate trillions of dollars of profits. Those who control AI are going to become fabulously wealthy. This wealth alone is going to translate into great political power. Yet the political power of AI goes well beyond its monetary value for governments, transnational corporations, and tech entrepreneurs. Machine learning and intelligent automation are also going to strengthen the foundational apparatus of state power: militaries, policing, security agencies, surveillance, propaganda, and tools of subjugation.

The rising power of states to control and repress citizens is a grave threat to those who resist their governments, including environmental, human rights, and peace activists. Citywide networks of AI-powered facial recognition cameras can certainly help fight crime and terrorism. And learning algorithms can help identify hate speech and subversive discourses on social media. There is also no question that predictive policing software can enhance public safety by helping security forces to identify high-risk individuals and future crime sprees. Yet as this chapter reveals, these technologies are simultaneously extending the power of states to track dissidents, censor digital platforms, disseminate propaganda, and intimidate activists. There is even technology now on the market that can analyze facial expressions as a way of interpreting whether citizens might be having inappropriate thoughts and feelings.

These technologies, moreover, are set to globalize over the next decade. Already, high-tech firms, telecom companies, and weapons manufacturers are starting to sell high-powered AI surveillance equipment to authoritarian governments across the developing world. Technologies to predict security risks, monitor nonconformists, and spread misinformation are beginning to go on the market, too. All signs indicate that the global market for AI-powered tools of repression is going to grow exponentially in the coming years. This is worrying, especially given, as I discuss next, so many states in recent years have been clamping down on dissent, including on environmental activism.

SUPPRESSING ENVIRONMENTALISM

States have long sought to repress the forces of environmentalism. Since at least the 1960s, security forces have been spying on activists, infiltrating grassroots movements, and instigating violence. Paramilitaries and corporate henchmen have been quick to club protestors who oppose development projects. Police have not hesitated to jail animal rights campaigners or to teargas antiglobalization demonstrators. In some places, security services and militaries (often at the behest of a company) have gone as far as disappearing, assassinating, and executing environmental and indigenous leaders who try to defend land and water rights.

Especially since the 2001 terrorist attacks in the United States, however, state crackdowns on direct-action environmentalism have been intensifying. Across the world, security forces are corralling, filming, and blacklisting protestors. Tanks, assault rifles, and water cannons are being deployed to break up peaceful occupations and sit-ins. Road barricades are being bulldozed, and rubber bullets are being fired into crowds. And security agencies are treating nonviolent sabotage, tree spiking, and the freeing of animals from scientific labs as acts of "eco-terrorism."

The police and military, meanwhile, are doing more to harass activists and less to protect them from retaliation and death threats. In Honduras, for instance, more than 125 activists have been murdered since 2010, including Berta Cáceres, who was gunned down by company-hired hit-men a year after receiving the 2015 Goldman Environmental Prize for mobilizing the indigenous Lenca people against the Agua Zarca hydro-electric dam.[1]

At the same time, states have been strengthening regulations and pass-ing new laws to control local and foreign nongovernmental organiza-tions (NGOs). In China, a new law came into force in 2017 forbidding foreign NGOs from undermining "China's national interests" and autho-rizing criminal charges against individuals who "attempt to undermine national unity or subvert state power."[2] Scores of other states have also extended legal controls over civil society in recent years. Russia and India have done this. So have Bolivia, Cambodia, Ecuador, Egypt, Ethiopia, Malaysia, and Zimbabwe. So have Australia and Canada.

Many of these laws target foreign and local NGOs that oppose hydro-electric dams, nuclear energy, mining, oil drilling, pipelines, fracking, logging, and plantations. To varying degrees, these laws are forcing NGOs to register with state agencies, obtain government sponsors, and use state-authorized bank accounts. They are requiring NGOs to report activities and fill in stacks of paperwork. They are extending the powers of state auditors and tax assessors. They are restricting the ability of activ-ists to speak out, travel abroad, and publish investigative reports. They are also giving states the legal authority to cut off international financing for local NGOs.[3]

Many of these laws are enhancing the power of police and security ser-vices to interrogate, detain, and jail activists. Ones such as Russia's "for-eign agents law" are framing NGOs with international ties as subversive agents working to advance foreign interests. Meanwhile, political lead-ers such as Russian President Vladimir Putin are describing local NGOs with international links as "spies" and "traitors," aggressively aiming to delegitimize environmental, human rights, and democracy campaigns among local populations.[4]

Alongside this crackdown on direct-action activism, states and cor-porations have been welcoming the staff of more moderate, market-oriented environmental NGOs onto international panels, certification organizations, policy advisory bodies, and corporate boards. These NGOs are endorsing corporate self-governance, industrial production, international trade, and industry-guided certification as best-practice pathways toward sustainability. They are taking money from firms, governments, and international organizations to pay salaries, rents, and travel costs. They are cobranding products to fund wildlife conservation and land purchases. And they are partnering with transnational corporations to launch cause-marketing campaigns (for example, buy a pair of jeans to save orphan orangutans).[5]

Over the past two decades, this dual process of subduing radicals and backing moderates has been "corporatizing" environmentalism, with the movement as a whole increasingly reflecting the interests of those with wealth, privilege, and power. Still, even with the rise of "environmentalism of the rich," radical and confrontational environmental activism remains a powerful global force.[6] Grassroots leaders continue to speak truth to power, even in the face of beatings and death threats. Global activists continue to confront states and transnational corporations with remarkable bravery, as when Greenpeace campaigners scaled a Gazprom oil rig in the Pechora Sea in 2013, landing thirty activists in a Russian prison charged with "piracy." Marginalized communities and disadvantaged peoples, meanwhile, continue to unite to protect their land and rivers from miners, loggers, agribusinesses, and developers: what some call "environmentalism of the poor."[7] In some places, the environmentalism of the poor has even been strengthening, as in El Salvador, where a movement opposing extractivism and demanding water rights ended up pushing the government to ban industrial mining in 2017 (following a decade-long de facto moratorium).[8]

Yet the ongoing onslaught against more radical forms of environmentalism is making it harder and more dangerous for activists to challenge development projects. Activists in places such as Brazil, Honduras, and the Philippines are facing threats, blackmail, beatings, and sexual assaults. Instead of offering protection, the police and courts are frequently complicit in these crimes.

The rising number of murders of environmental, human rights, and indigenous activists is indicative of the growing hostility of states to community activism. From the beginning of 2016 to the end of 2017, the NGO Global Witness documented the murders of more than four hundred community activists who were trying to protect land, water, and environmental resources—the worst two-year killing spree since Global Witness began keeping records in 2012. In 2017 alone, fifty-seven activists were murdered in Brazil, the most of any country. Worldwide, a fifth of all of the killings that year were linked to agribusinesses, such as cattle ranches and banana, coffee, sugar cane, soy, and palm oil plantations. Miners were connected to the second-most murders, followed by poachers and loggers. Criminal gangs, soldiers, and police were suspected of committing the greatest number of murders, followed by paramilitary forces, poachers, and armed militia.[9]

The actual number of murders is certainly far higher than the average of three to four a week that Global Witness has been able to document in recent years. Across Africa, the reporting of the murders of activists is especially poor. Rural areas across the developing world also have low reporting rates. In many of these places, too, it is common for police, military, and state security agencies to conceal these murders as "suicides," "death by natural causes," and "missing persons."

The intensifying global crackdown on opposition to corporate expansion looks set to put even more environmental, human rights, and indigenous activists at risk over the next decade. Artificial intelligence, as the rest of this chapter discusses, is going to offer states and corporations a powerful set of additional tools to watch activists, monitor the internet, spread misinformation, deepen propaganda, instill fear, and suppress dissent.

WATCHING THE PUBLIC

Surveillance cameras have been in place for decades in most countries. By 2014, the world had around 250 million surveillance cameras. The market for video surveillance equipment has been growing strongly since then. By 2018, China alone had around 200 million surveillance cameras, the United States had at least 50 million, and the UK had about 6 million, with closed-circuit television (CCTV) cameras recording 50 million vehicle registration numbers a day.[10]

Surveillance cameras are also spreading quickly across Russia. Close to 3 million surveillance cameras were sold in Russia in 2016—a 75 percent rise from 2015 in terms of value. Of these cameras, more than 95 percent were imported, with private customers buying 7 percent, government agencies 28 percent, and corporations 65 percent. The oil and gas industry was one of the biggest customers.[11]

Most of the world's surveillance cameras either simply record footage of streets, sports stadiums, construction projects, mining sites, and oil rigs, or offer security guards a way to monitor a museum, bank, or private mansion.[12] Systems able to identify faces, objects, and suspicious activity take surveillance to another level. Those connected to a cloud infrastructure can autonomously notify police and security services. They can link suspicious activity across jurisdictions, scan irises, track license plates, and match faces to identity cards. They can follow individuals across long distances and retrace a person's movements back in time. And they can look for patterns within vast stores of data to try to predict a future crime or act of terrorism.

Over the next few years, artificial intelligence is set to infuse the video surveillance market with new energy. Already, security agencies in the United States are using facial recognition technology to verify identities and investigate crimes.[13] The UK and Russia are also now working to integrate facial recognition into their CCTV surveillance networks. Moscow alone is planning to install facial recognition systems in every residential building by 2021. With demand soaring, industry analysts are projecting international sales of video surveillance will reach $44 billion by 2025, up from $18 billion in 2017.[14]

China is set to have 300 million surveillance cameras in place by 2020. Artificial intelligence, as we saw in chapter 7, is speeding up the response times of ambulance and fire services in China's smart cities. Incorporating facial and iris recognition technology into policing systems is also accelerating the arrest of criminals. But China's network of cameras, coupled with the monitoring of smartphones, social media, and internet activity, is a powerful tool to watch and track dissidents. "The government's using this technology to catch people who are considered threats to social stability," Chinese poet Ji Feng explains. "Are they using it to catch thieves? Yes. But it's mostly used to maintain stability."[15]

China is also at the cutting edge of developing surveillance technology capable of identifying thoughts and feelings by interpreting facial expressions. A high school in Hangzhou, for instance, has installed

AI-powered cameras to take attendance and evaluate the emotions of students, watching for facial signs of anger, boredom, disbelief, fear, sadness, surprise, joy, and revulsion. The surveillance system notifies the classroom teacher when a student is "failing to focus during class time," explained the school's vice principal, Zhang Guanchao. Within the first month, he said, the cameras caused the schoolchildren to "voluntarily change their behaviors and classroom habits" so they can "attend classes more happily now."[16] Others are far less enthusiastic than Vice Principal Zhang, with some concerned this is the beginning of the state watching for "face-crimes," as in George Orwell's novel *1984*. Jiang Xueqin, a researcher at Harvard University's Graduate School of Education, worries schools in China are becoming "laboratories for mass experimentation on how to control and predict human behaviors."[17]

So far, China's national database has tagged 20 to 30 million individuals for special surveillance, including political dissidents, religious leaders, human rights activists, and environmentalists.[18] Surveillance has gone especially far in Xinjiang, a resource-rich region of northwest China with vast reserves of coal, oil, and natural gas. Xinjiang is the home of the Uyghur people, a Muslim minority of Turkic ethnicity. Claiming it is necessary to fight Islamic extremism, in recent years the Communist Party of China has shuttered mosques, jailed critics, deployed security forces to patrol the streets, and forced hundreds of thousands of the Uyghur people and other Muslims and ethnic minorities into indoctrination facilities.[19]

In Xinjiang, the Communist Party of China is constructing what reporter James Vincent calls a "total surveillance state."[20] This is combining old-style police tactics—hidden cameras, audio bugs, informants, and home "visits"—with cutting-edge AI technologies, such as iris scanners, facial recognition identification, and license plate tracking. Since 2016, the Chinese government has awarded China's two leading surveillance technology firms—Hikvision and Dahua—more than $1 billion worth of projects in Xinjiang. Every mosque now has facial recognition cameras to register who enters, and those who do face the prospect of being fired, losing their pension, or being sent to an internment camp.[21]

Even deeper surveillance of the Uyghur population is on the way. The Beijing-based company IrisKing, for instance, is installing iris recognition technology across the region, and is aiming to have a database of the irises of all Xinjiang residents by 2021. Facial recognition technology designed to identify—and track—anyone who appears to be a Uyghur is also being installed in regions beyond Xinjiang: what Paul Mozur, a correspondent for the *New York Times*, describes as "automated racism." Guangzhou-based CloudWalk Technology, a startup company developing software for facial recognition cameras, advertises on its website how the tracking system could assist authorities: "If originally one Uyghur lives in a neighborhood, and within 20 days six Uyghurs appear, it immediately sends alarms."[22]

China's other high-tech firms are profiting as well from the deepening of surveillance across the country. Local governments are integrating facial recognition technology into traditional surveillance systems for streets, stadiums, public buildings, and state-owned corporations. Cities such as Shenzhen, meanwhile, are installing AI-powered facial recognition cameras at busy intersections, which automatically fine jaywalkers and shame them by displaying their faces on a digital billboard. SenseTime, China's leading producer of facial recognition technology, has contracts with more than forty public security services, and in recent years, security surveillance systems have accounted for a third of its business. Sales of surveillance technology are also booming for Beijing's AI company, Megvii. "The government is pushing the need for this technology from the top, so companies don't have big obstacles in making it happen," explains Xie Yinan, the vice president of Megvii. "In America, people are too busy discussing how they should use it."[23]

The growing use of facial recognition systems to swing open the doors of apartment buildings, permit entry into public toilets, and scan the lobbies of hotels, banks, shopping malls, and airports is generating troves of data for the training of machine learning security systems. The Communist Party of China, under a project known as "Xue Liang" (which can be roughly translated as sharp, all-seeing eyes), is now working to integrate public and private surveillance into a national data-sharing and AI-powered analytics platform. Chinese officials are certainly exaggerating the scope of current surveillance. In the words of cybersecurity analyst Zak Doffman, "a population that believes it can be controlled, is controlled."[24] But the long-term goal of China's "Sharp Eyes" strategy is clear: to construct an AI-powered "police cloud" linking surveillance data with identity cards, faces, personal medical history, online activity, and banking and credit records.[25]

THE GLOBALIZATION OF PUBLIC SURVEILLANCE

The technology of Chinese firms undergirds the telecommunication security apparatus of many other countries, too. The Ethiopian government's tight control of domestic telecommunications, for instance, has long relied on monitoring technology from China's ZTE Corporation. Across Africa, Transsion Holdings, a company headquartered in Shenzhen, is a top-selling mobile phone manufacturer. Worldwide, China's state-owned companies (such as China Mobile, China Telecom, and China Unicom) have installed internet and mobile networks across dozens of countries. Meanwhile, the telecom company Huawei has been working to develop high-speed wireless networks in Bangladesh, Cambodia, and Mexico, among many other countries.

Recently, China's high-tech industry has been ramping up exports of surveillance hardware, software, and services. Founded in 2001, Hikvision, a company with close ties to Chinese state-owned enterprises, is the world's largest manufacturer of surveillance cameras. Also founded in 2001, Dahua is China's second-largest video surveillance company; Uniview, a company that started in 2005, ranks third. Together, these three companies captured almost a third of the global revenues from video surveillance technology in 2017, with their equipment in place in more than a 150 countries.[26]

In Russia, more than four-fifths of the 2.9 million video surveillance cameras installed in 2016 came from China. The Mongolian government, meanwhile, is working with Chinese trainers, technicians, and high-tech companies to integrate facial recognition cameras into its prisons. The Malaysian government is working with China to equip its police forces with AI-powered analytics and facial recognition technology, as is the Cambodian government to install CCTV cameras across the country, building on the thousand surveillance cameras already in place by 2018 in the capital Phnom Penh.[27]

Over the past decade, the Ecuadorian government has also been drawing on a $240 million loan from the Chinese government to build a nationwide surveillance network. In addition, China has been supplying servers, telecommunication infrastructure, and traffic scanners. By 2018, Ecuador had opened an AI research lab, was operating drones with night vision, and had installed 4,300 surveillance cameras, up from 259 cameras in 2012. This surveillance network is improving public safety by helping to monitor volcanoes, support search-and-rescue operations, and speed up the response times of emergency crews. But this network also has the potential to be a powerful tool of repression, with the capacity to track license plates, identify faces, and autonomously report incidents to authorities. Impressed, Bolivia is now working with the state-owned China National Electronics Import & Export Corporation to build a similar surveillance network of high-speed video cameras, military-style drones, and license plate and facial recognition scanners. Anyone caught breaking the law by Bolivia's surveillance network is going to be entered into a national biometric database.[28]

China's exports of intelligent surveillance technology look set to rise quickly over the next few years. In 2018, for instance, the government of Zimbabwe signed an agreement with China's CloudWalk Technology to build a "mass facial recognition project" for the country's airports, bus stations, and train stations. As part of this project, CloudWalk is also going to create a "national facial database" for police and security services.[29] Such science and technology agreements fit into a broader strategy of the Communist Party of China to deepen trade, cooperation, and connectivity in places where Chinese firms are investing in mining, forestry, tourism, construction, dams, and agricultural plantations—what the government of President Xi Jinping often calls the "Belt and Road" initiative.

But China is only one player in the intensifying competition to export surveillance cameras and AI security platforms. American tech companies are fighting hard to expand markets; so are British, Swedish, Irish, German, South Korean, and Japanese firms. There is, moreover, an escalating competition to capture the growing market for surveillance of the online world, especially in authoritarian states.

SURVEILLANCE OF THE ONLINE WORLD

As with street-level surveillance, monitoring the internet with artificial intelligence can enhance public safety. Learning algorithms are helping social media platforms such as Facebook and Twitter to remove fake news, hate speech, and extremist language. These algorithms are proving adept at eliminating pornography and violent images. They are also helping to identify fake videos, troll farms, and fake accounts.

At the same time, however, authoritarian governments are deploying AI systems to censor and repress online activism. Algorithmic governance of the internet is still in its infancy. But over the next decade, algorithmic censorship and disinformation—especially systems with learning capability—could dramatically extend state powers in the online world. These systems can collect, store, and analyze images, text, and audio files across previously impossible scales. They can automate the processes of deleting critical commentary and circulating disinformation. They can block websites and online content as well as autonomously notify authorities of antigovernment postings and communications. Moreover, with deep anonymity, they can disseminate fake news and videos, impersonate dissidents, operate fake accounts, and automate malware attacks to sabotage political resistance and online activism.[30]

The Communist Party of China has gone especially far in censoring online communications. One study in the journal *Science* describes this effort as "the largest selective suppression of human communication in the recorded history of any country."[31] The government's "Great Firewall of China" has long been blocking the ability of people in China to access foreign internet sites, such as the *New York Times* and *Wall Street Journal*. But efforts seem to have intensified under President Xi Jinping, with Freedom House ranking China's internet as the "least free" in the world every year since 2015.[32] Hundreds of thousands of government employees monitor social media and communication apps to curtail free speech and silence dissenting voices, especially anyone referring to street protests or policy debates. At the same time, the government has not hesitated to charge outspoken critics with sedition.

China's leading technology companies have long supported this state monitoring of the internet. Tencent's security department, for instance, stores content for up to six months and notifies state officials when it discovers illegal activity. If requested, the company provides user information, as the law requires, and prosecutors have relied on evidence from WeChat, which Tencent owns. The company does not hide its role in supporting state censorship and prosecutions. Chen Yong, an executive at Tencent, made this clear at the 2018 World Internet Conference. "Tencent," he said, "has been dedicated to dealing with terrorist information online and other internet crimes, in line with the government's crackdown."[33]

Since 2014, the Chinese government has also been working with municipalities and technology companies to develop a "social credit" system to score trustworthiness and creditworthiness, encourage "good" civic conduct, and identify risky citizens, in much the same way as a credit rating system in other countries detects and predicts financial risk.[34] So far, implementation of the various pilot schemes has been uneven across cities and villages, although the plan is to centralize data platforms into a mandatory national system. How scores are being calculated is murky. Municipalities are using different metrics, with some schemes involving hundreds of ways for a score to rise or fall. The tech companies that are developing more commercially oriented schemes (including those within the Tencent and Alibaba groups) are also using different algorithms, datasets, and machine learning tools. But the basic idea is for citizens' scores to go up if they behave well and go down if they behave poorly.

Examples of behaving well include obeying rules, performing civic duties, looking after elderly parents, and generating positive online commentary. Examples of behaving poorly include committing a crime and not paying taxes, bills, or fines. Questioning state policy can also lower a citizen's score in some systems. So can driving badly, cheating on an exam, smoking in a nonsmoking area, walking a dog off leash in a leash-only zone, or getting caught jaywalking. In some schemes, scores go down as well if family or online friends post controversial comments on social media. Online purchases of too many "bad" products (say, alcohol) or services (say, video games) can further lower a citizen's score in some systems. Li Yingyun, the technology director for Sesame Credit (a credit-scoring company within Alibaba's group) explains: "Someone who plays video games for ten hours a day, for example, would be considered an idle person."[35]

Those with a low score might see restrictions on internet services, housing loans, car and apartment rentals, restaurant reservations, employment, or travel. By early 2019, for instance, authorities had denied citizens (primarily those blacklisted by the courts as untrustworthy after failing to repay debts) more than 26 million airline and high-speed train tickets, according to China's National Development and Reform Commission. The perks of a high citizen score, meanwhile, can include faster internet connections, hotel and airline upgrades, a fast-track visa to travel overseas, or preferential access to loans. Sesame Credit, for instance, offers customers who obtain a social credit rating above 600 (out of a possible range of 350 to 950) preferential loans for purchases on Alibaba sites. A high Sesame Credit score can even nudge up a citizen's profile on the online dating service, Baihe.[36]

Chinese officials and corporate executives are working as well to enhance internet controls in other countries. Plans are underway to develop a transnational social credit system under the rubric of the Belt and Road initiative.[37] More generally, exports of software, hardware, and services for internet surveillance are steadily rising. Chinese companies are developing intelligent monitoring systems all over the world, including in Argentina, Kazakhstan, Pakistan, the United Arab Emirates, and Zambia. Chinese officials are also hosting training seminars on internet surveillance, with representatives from dozens of different countries attending sessions in recent years.

Steven Feldstein, a professor specializing in the role of technology and global governance, is pointed in his assessment of what is going on. "Around the world," he writes in the *Journal of Democracy*, "AI systems are showing their potential for abetting repressive regimes and upending the relationship between citizen and state, thereby accelerating a global resurgence of authoritarianism. The People's Republic of China is driving the proliferation of AI technology to authoritarian and illiberal regimes, an approach that has become a key component of Chinese geopolitical strategy."[38]

China is leading the charge to deepen surveillance of the online world, but firms from many other countries are likewise selling cybersurveillance technologies to authoritarian countries. As a British Broadcasting Corporation documentary brought to light, British weapons manufacturers have been selling spyware to governments in the Middle East with dismal human rights records. American, French, German, and Russian companies have been similarly supplying internet surveillance technologies to authoritarian governments. Across Europe, nearly a third of the export permits issued by the EU for cybersurveillance from 2014 to 2017 were for countries that Freedom House rated as "not free." Internet interception systems and mobile technology spyware can offer a government extraordinary powers of surveillance. Infecting a smartphone with malware, for instance, can allow a security officer to track a user, read emails and texts, see the contact list, switch on a microphone or camera, and take a photograph. An officer may even be able to compose emails and texts from the smartphone, with a long list of malicious possibilities, from engineering disinformation campaigns to planting evidence of treason.[39]

Online censorship, spyware, social credit ratings, and AI-powered surveillance of videos, websites, and postings are all rather blunt instruments for controlling and monitoring the online world. There are also other, far more subtle, ways for states and corporations to identify and track digital fingerprints, such as behavioral biometrics.

TRACKING DIGITAL FINGERPRINTS

Behavioral biometric software is profiling how people grip, scroll, swipe, press, and tap their smartphones, tablets, and laptops. "You just watch them, silently, while they go about their normal account activities," explains Neil Costigan, the CEO of BehavioSec, a company specializing in behavioral biometrics. Some developers of behavioral biometric software are also adding data points by "prompting" reactions from users, such as causing the mouse cursor to vanish momentarily. "Everyone reacts a little differently to that," notes Frances Zelazny at the cybersecurity company BioCatch. "Some people move the mouse side to side; some people move it up and down. Some bang on the keyboard."[40]

BioCatch's biometric platform, which relies on machine learning, can analyze thousands of gestures, interactions, and idiosyncrasies to build a precise behavioral profile of users. Banks, financial institutions, and retailers are installing BioCatch to detect identity theft, online bank fraud, and cybercrimes. The Royal Bank of Scotland, for instance, has installed BioCatch across 19 million accounts, while American Express is using it for new accounts. BioCatch developers claim the platform can detect 99 percent of "imposters." For one customer's account in 2018, for instance, BioCatch noticed an atypical scroll of the mouse and then an uncharacteristic keyboard entry to start the session. The platform then locked the account to prevent cash transfers, averting the theft of at least a million dollars.[41]

The global market for behavioral biometrics software and services is set to exceed $2.5 billion by 2023, up from around $870 million in 2018. Banks, retailers, and the electronic manufacturers see many advantages of behavioral biometric security. It is harder for hackers to crack than passwords. It can help protect online shoppers and financial clients from cybercriminals, malware, bot attacks, identify theft, and phishing, among other malevolent internet activity. And it is easier for customers than using a fingerprint or iris scan—what the CEO of BioCatch calls "a seamless user experience."[42]

But the growing reliance on behavioral biometrics is also going to create far-reaching privacy challenges. Collecting the behavioral data rarely requires the consent of users, while analysis of this data can reveal highly personal information, such as the progression of dementia or alcoholism. Profiling individuals with behavioral biometrics, moreover, has the potential to further empower state and corporate surveillance of citizens. "What we have seen across the board with technology is that the more data that's collected by companies, the more they will try to find uses for that data," notes Jennifer Lynch, a surveillance litigation lawyer. "It's a very small leap from using this to detect fraud to using this to learn very private information about you."[43]

ACTIVISM AND THE POWER OF AI

As is shown in part II of this book, artificial intelligence can empower activists too. Nongovernmental organizations can benefit in some of the same ways as business. Machine learning tools can help activists defend against corporate cyberattacks and state spying, can help them evade internet censorship, and can detect disinformation campaigns. AI-powered platforms can further help advocacy networks tailor campaign messages, emails, and posts to reflect the political leaning of different recipients, increasing the prospects of fundraising and enhancing the uptake of videos and media stories.

Yet, as the many examples in this chapter show, a wide range of applications of artificial intelligence are also enhancing the capacity of states and corporations to suppress dissent. Over the past two decades, governments have passed stricter laws, armed police with military weapons, and increasingly treated activists as subversive, disloyal, and seditious. Artificial intelligence is further boosting the power of police, armed forces, and security agencies to track activists on the streets, over the internet, and in their homes. Machine learning is increasing the reach of censorship, propaganda, and disinformation campaigns; and facial recognition technologies is offering a new toolbox of intimidation, from surveillance systems that score the civic performance of citizens to AI-enhanced cameras that evaluate the emotions and enthusiasm of audiences.

The weaponization of artificial intelligence poses yet another grave threat to those who are working to defend land and water rights and resist development projects. Already, as we have seen, environmental, human rights, and indigenous activists face terrifying dangers in places such as Brazil, Colombia, Guatemala, Honduras, India, Mexico, Nicaragua, the Philippines, and the Democratic Republic of the Congo. One hundred eighty activists were murdered across these nine countries in 2017, with the police, army, and security services complicit in many of the killings. Of the forty-eight documented murders of environmental and land activists in the Philippines in that year, for instance, the army was suspected of being involved in more than half.[44]

AI weapons are going to add a powerful tool to the arsenal of repressive states. Not long from now, tyrants, police officers, secret service agents, and business executives could well own birdlike drones that will scan a photo and fly off to locate, stalk, and assassinate an adversary with brutal efficiency. As we'll see in the next chapter, AI weapons of war—from autonomous tanks to crewless submarines to swarms of killer drones—pose one of the greatest of all challenges to global sustainability.

11

WEAPONS OF DESTRUCTION

War and conquest lie at the heart of today's global sustainability crisis. Imperialism, colonialism, and postcolonial economics have destroyed ecosystems and societies around the world. Over the past millennium, European powers enslaved and slaughtered the indigenous peoples of Africa, the Asia-Pacific, and the Americas. Across the so-called new world, soldiers, missionaries, and colonists brought terrible diseases—smallpox, measles, influenza—that in many places killed 90 percent or more of the people, sometimes in less than a generation. To his shame, this horror was seen as a blessing by the first governor of Massachusetts Bay Colony. "For the natives," John Winthrop wrote in a private letter in 1634, "they are neere all dead of small Poxe, so as the Lord hathe cleared our title to what we possess."[1]

Armies of settlers altered the very biology of the earth from 1500 to 1900. To appropriate lands, they killed and corralled those who survived the rampage of disease. To build towns and farms, they chopped down forests, burned away native vegetation, and diverted rivers to irrigate fields. To earn income, they scoured the waters for fish, whales, and seals and hunted local game to near extinction. To recreate home life, they introduced invasive species and bred cows, pigs, sheep, and chickens. To extract profit from the lands, they mined gold, silver, and diamonds and planted tea, cotton, coffee, sugarcane, tobacco, rubber trees, and wheat.

Since 1900, war and violence have continued to rip through global sustainability. World War I took the lives of at least 13 to 15 million soldiers and civilians. World War II killed at least 65 to 75 million people.[2] The dropping of the atomic bombs on Hiroshima and Nagasaki in 1945 killed and wounded hundreds of thousands of people, with damage lasting generations. After World War II, atmospheric testing of nuclear weapons further scarred the earth with radiation. Genocides have brought great terrors too, with the reign of the Khmer Rouge killing more than a fifth of the Cambodian population from 1975 to 1979 and the Rwandan genocide slaughtering some 800,000 people in 1994.[3] Unremitting terrorist attacks and gang killings have caused extreme injustice too, as have corporate land grabs to mine Africa, log the rainforests of the Asia-Pacific, and drill for oil in South America.

Artificial intelligence threatens to open up yet another front in this violent history of conquest. With the United States, China, and Russia leading the way, militaries, technology startups, and defense contractors around the world are now working to develop AI cyberweapons, automatic target recognition systems, unmanned submarines, crewless ships, driverless tanks, and autonomous drones. Some of these technologies are certainly helping to fortify the defenses of peaceful states. Still, the prospect of enhancing the destructive power of modern military-industrial complexes with artificial intelligence is deeply concerning for the future of global sustainability.

Highly autonomous weapons able to learn from experience—even those technically under human supervision—will make killing more efficient and less accountable. At the same time, automating intelligent cyberattacks and disinformation campaigns could end up destabilizing world politics. Some AI weapons, including small, self-guiding armed drones, will also be susceptible to falling into the hands of tyrants, terrorists, and criminals, as has happened with firearms. This diffusion of highly and fully autonomous weaponry has the potential to empower attacking armies, heighten uncertainty, escalate conflicts, and accelerate the pace of war as opposing AIs battle at lightning speeds. Enabling machines to decide who lives and dies, moreover, risks further distancing the act of war from any sense of humanity.

The military applications of artificial intelligence are still in their early stages. Over the next few decades, however, the consequences are going to be sweeping, analogous perhaps to how electricity changed the character of warfare after the 1880s.[4] "The nature of war is all about a collision of will, fear, uncertainty, and chance," argued former US Deputy Secretary of Defense Robert Work in a 2017 speech, paraphrasing the Prussian military theorist Carl von Clausewitz (1780–1831). "You have to ask yourself, how does fear play out in a world when a lot of the action is taking place between unmanned systems?"[5]

Kenneth Payne, author of *Strategy, Evolution, and War: From Apes to Artificial Intelligence*, thinks artificial intelligence is going to revolutionize military strategy and cause a "profound reordering of existing power balances."[6] This reordering, as I discuss at the end of this chapter, could even ignite a new Cold War as the great powers compete for AI supremacy. "No nation has stated outright that they are building autonomous weapons," notes Paul Scharre, a former analyst at the US Office of the Secretary of Defense, "but in secret defense labs and dual-use applications, AI technology is racing forward."[7] The United States, China, and Russia, as we'll see next, are competing especially hard for position in this race.

AN AI SUPERPOWER?

The US Army, Navy, Air Force, and Marine Corps constitute the world's most powerful military force, by far. The American arsenal includes more than 3,800 nuclear weapons (plus thousands of "retired" warheads awaiting "dismantling"): enough firepower to level thousands of cities, kill billions of people, and generate devastating "environmental blowback."[8]

To retain global dominance, over the last decade, the United States has spent more than $6 trillion on military weapons, salaries, pensions, equipment, research, and services. No other country has come close to this level of military spending. In 2018, for instance, American military spending was about $634 billion, accounting for more than a third of worldwide military spending. That year, China's military spending was the second highest ($239 billion), followed by India ($67 billion), Saudi Arabia ($66 billion), and Russia ($64 billion).[9]

The US Armed Forces and secret service agencies have long relied on remotely controlled "unmanned aerial vehicles" and semi-autonomous systems to defend bases, conduct surveillance, and fire missiles. The General Atomics MQ-1 Predator drone, for instance, first went into service in

1995 for surveillance. Later outfitted with Hellfire laser-guided missiles, the remotely piloted Predator played a key role in the Iraq War from 2003 to 2011 and in the war in Afghanistan from 2001 until being retired from service in 2018. From 2004 to 2010, the CIA relied on armed Predators to assassinate hundreds of al-Qaeda and Taliban militants in northwestern Pakistan.[10]

After 2007, the CIA and US Air Force also began deploying the bigger, faster, more powerful General Atomics MQ-9 Reaper drone: what General T. Michael Moseley, then Chief of Staff of the US Air Force, described as the first "true hunter-killer" drone.[11] Since then, Reapers have been sold to American allies, including France, Italy, and the United Kingdom. Over the past decade, American and British Reapers have been repeatedly striking targets in countries such as Afghanistan, Iraq, Somalia, Syria, and Yemen. Reapers are remotely piloted, and ground crew make the firing decisions. Upgrades are steadily increasing the Reaper's independent flight capabilities, however, such as allowing for automatic takeoff and landing.[12]

The US Armed Forces are also deploying many other highly autonomous vehicles under human control. One example is the Sea Hunter, a crewless antisubmarine vessel that first went to sea in 2016. A shore team, under what is known as "Sparse Supervisory Control," monitors the vessel and at any point (such as engaging in action) can take command. Developed by the Pentagon's research arm known as the Defense Advanced Research Projects Agency (DARPA), the Sea Hunter can autonomously navigate the oceans for months at a time to track submarines, conduct surveillance, and perform reconnaissance.[13]

The remotely piloted, unmanned Northrop Grumman MQ-4C Triton aircraft is another example of a highly autonomous American military vehicle under development. The Triton, which went into limited flight service for the US Navy in 2018, is scheduled for full operational deployment in 2023. This drone aircraft is designed to conduct high-altitude, long-distance maritime intelligence, surveillance, and reconnaissance. Equipped with advanced sensors and near real-time video cameras, the Triton can stay aloft for twenty-four straight hours. A ground crew sets its flight plan, altitude, speed, and objectives—and monitors performance—but the Triton also has considerable autonomous operational capabilities.[14]

Trust in the military value of artificial intelligence seems to be rising across the US Army, Navy, Air Force, and Marine Corps. After witnessing the capabilities of the Sea Hunter in 2016, then Deputy Defense Secretary Robert Work said he was envisioning "unmanned flotillas operating in the western Pacific and the Persian Gulf within five years."[15] Two years later, navy commanders were clearly impressed when an unmanned Triton developed engine troubles during a test flight over the Pacific. The drone aircraft, recognizing the catastrophic nature of the threat, navigated back to its base in California, belly-landing within three feet of its designated spot. "On its own, autonomously . . . it did its own diagnosis and turned itself around, flew back to its base of origin, conducted its own fault analysis, conducted emergency procedures that resulted in a shutdown of the engine," Bryan Scurry, executive director of Naval Air Forces, said. "The point being, it handled all these things as they popped up and still was able to come back and return to base in a pretty much intact position."[16]

So far, the US military has not been allowing its semi-autonomous weapons to select targets or decide when to fire. This may change, however, as breakthroughs in machine learning and robotics create fighting machines with increasingly powerful autonomous capabilities. This may also change if other militaries, especially Russia or China, develop fully autonomous weapons. There are already signs the Pentagon is preparing to one day deploy fully autonomous weapons. In 2018, for instance, the US Army solicited bids to develop a highly autonomous drone—specifically using deep neural networks—that is able to seek, verify, and target vehicles, buildings, and enemy combatants. "Whereas current military drones are still controlled by people, this new technology will decide who to kill with almost no human involvement," noted Peter Lee, the director of Security and Risk Research and Innovation at the University of Portsmouth.[17]

AMERICA'S AI BUILDUP

America's buildup of AI weapons and defense systems looks set to escalate over the next decade. Significantly, President Donald Trump has made the development of AI a security priority. The 2017 National Security Strategy became the first strategy to prioritize American leadership in AI, including autonomous weapons.[18] The 2018 National Defense

Strategy committed the Department of Defense to investing in AI projects, machine learning, and autonomous systems "to gain competitive military advantages" over potential adversaries, particularly China and Russia. That year the Department of Defense also released an artificial intelligence strategy, arguing that AI was "poised to change the character of the future battlefield and the pace of threats."[19]

During his term as US Secretary of Defense (2017–2018), General James Mattis lobbied for a national AI strategy. In the past, General Mattis has talked publicly of the abiding nature of war. Asked in early 2018 about the potential consequences of intelligent machines on warfare, however, he replied, "I'm certainly questioning my original premise that the fundamental nature of war will not change. You've got to question that now."[20]

A few months later, the White House announced that it would be the first administration to make "artificial intelligence and autonomous and unmanned systems" a national budget priority. Not only was more funding necessary for unclassified AI research, the White House argued, but more funding was necessary to support the already "substantial classified investments across the defense and intelligence communities."[21] Reflecting this new priority, in mid-2018 the Department of Defense (DoD) launched a Joint Artificial Intelligence Center (JAIC) to bring together the nearly six hundred AI projects across the department. The goal of JAIC, then Deputy Defense Secretary Patrick Shanahan said, is "to swiftly introduce new capabilities and effectively experiment with new operational concepts in support of DoD's warfighting missions and business functions."[22]

With Shanahan acting as Secretary of Defense, in early 2019 President Trump signed the Executive Order on Maintaining American Leadership in Artificial Intelligence. "Continued American leadership in AI," it declares, "is of paramount importance to maintaining the economic and national security of the United States." This executive order launched the "American AI Initiative," a strategy to coordinate and prioritize federal government research on artificial intelligence as well as protect "critical AI technologies from acquisition by strategic competitors and adversarial nations."[23]

Some American analysts worry the Trump administration has not gone far enough to secure AI supremacy. The Pentagon's budget for research on artificial intelligence, for instance, only went up from $1.4 billion to $1.9 billion from 2017 to 2019. And although DARPA's funding for AI has been steadily rising, in 2018 its "Next AI" program was set to allocate only $2 billion over the upcoming five years.[24] "While suggestions, recommendations and directives are good," argues Steve Andriole at Villanova University, "they will not assure US dominance in AI. Leadership here should be immediate and aggressive."[25]

Still, the Trump administration's strategy to prioritize AI is energizing the financing and development of machine learning and autonomous systems across the US federal government, including within the Armed Forces and security agencies. And President Trump's 2019 executive order did fire a warning shot over the bow of China and Russia, the two main challengers to American AI military power.

CHINA: A FUTURE AI POWER?

China's 2017 national plan to assume global leadership in AI by 2030 calls for technological exchanges, cooperative research, and an integrative strategy between domestic corporations and the Chinese People's Liberation Army.[26] The country's capacity to produce research breakthroughs in machine learning and robotics still lags well behind the United States. But as the previous chapter underscores, China is quickly gaining ground in the application of AI to advance particular technologies, such as facial recognition, language processing, predictive analytics, computer vision, and autonomous vehicles. Arguably, China is now even leading the world in AI surveillance technologies, including internet tracking software, smart monitoring cameras, and small fixed-wing drones and quadcopters. One Chinese tech-military team has even managed to build a small, whisper-quiet "spy bird" able to flap, dive, and soar like a bird—a surveillance drone, without irony, named the "Dove."[27]

A combination of factors is helping to propel China's commercialization and weaponization of artificial intelligence. Chinese intellectual property laws are weak, and domestic startups have been quick to copy computer operating systems, software, platforms, and algorithms. Startups operate in a cutthroat business setting inside China, with fierce competition and swift acquisitions hastening the commercialization of new

AI technologies. China has troves of data for learning algorithms, with privacy laws doing little to impede state agencies or firms from collecting personal information. Furthermore, the close cooperation between Chinese firms and government agencies—what the columnist Yi-Zheng Lian calls the "party-corporate complex" and what the Chinese government refers to as a strategy of "military-civil fusion"—is accelerating the development of AI technologies with dual commercial-military uses.[28]

Significantly, China's military leadership has also come to see AI as a revolutionary technology that is going to alter the character of war, where human soldiers, pilots, captains, and tank commanders can no longer keep pace with the lightning-fast decisions and reactions of machines. Artificial intelligence is going to "accelerate the process of military transformation, causing fundamental changes to military units' programming, operational styles, equipment systems, and models of combat power generation, ultimately leading to a profound military revolution," claims Lieutenant General Liu Guozhi of China's Central Military Commission.[29]

Since 2017, the People's Liberation Army has been steadily increasing its funding for AI research and development. Like the Pentagon, the People's Liberation Army has also been partnering with defense contractors and high-tech companies to integrate artificial intelligence and smart robotics into its army, navy, air force, and rocket force. Machine learning is advancing data analysis, intelligence planning, and logistics. Facial and image recognition cameras are allowing for more precise surveillance and reconnaissance. Augmented reality is enhancing wargames, training, and simulation exercises. And semi-autonomous drones and weapon systems are supporting operational missions. Though classified, like the US Armed Forces (and as we'll see next with the Russian Armed Forces), the People's Liberation Army also seems to be developing fully autonomous smart weapons.[30]

THE AI POWER OF RUSSIA

Russia lags well behind the United States and China in commercial applications of artificial intelligence. The Russian Ministry of Defense, however, is working hard to integrate AI into the operations of the Russian Armed Forces, including the Ground Forces, Navy, and Aerospace Forces. The Russian military is refining image recognition for surveillance drones, putting in place increasingly autonomous defense systems for its missile bases, and organizing "AI wargames." It is testing an underwater drone (called the Poseidon) with the capacity to carry nuclear warheads. It is weaponizing commercial machine learning technologies to circulate digital disinformation, conduct cyberattacks, and ramp up cyberespionage. It is also increasing funding, developing industry partnerships, and implementing a national strategy to accelerate and widen the uptake of AI technologies across the Russian Armed Forces.[31]

In addition, Russia is openly integrating machine learning into standard weapons, unmanned military vehicles, and robotic equipment. The Russian arms manufacturer Kalashnikov, according to the state-owned news agency TASS, has developed a machine gun with an artificial neural network able to identify targets, decide when to fire, and learn from experience. Like the United States and China, Russia is also developing a wide range of semi-autonomous weapons. The Uran-9 is a remote-controlled unmanned combat vehicle with a cannon and machine gun. The Nerekhta is a small, armed, remotely controlled tank with the capacity to launch kamikaze attacks. The Platform-M combat robot, with a rifle and grenade launchers, has automatic and semi-automatic controls for targeting. And the T-14 Armata battle tank has a remote-controlled turret: a vital step toward a fully autonomous tank, according to the tank's chief designer. "The T-14 is years ahead of the West," worries Noel Sharkey, a professor of AI and robotics at Sheffield University, "and the idea of thousands of autonomous T-14s sitting on the border with Europe does not bear thinking about."[32]

As in China, classified research and development of fully autonomous AI weapons is surely underway, too. Publicly, President Vladimir Putin has mused about the potential of fighting future wars with autonomous drones. He has talked as well of the need to prevent any single country— especially the United States or China—from monopolizing autonomous weapons, promising his allies that he would share Russia's AI knowledge to prevent this from ever occurring.[33]

THE DIFFUSION OF AI WEAPONS

Many states beyond the United States, China, and Russia are developing AI weapons, too. "In every sphere of the battlefield—in the air, on the sea, under the sea or on the land—the military around the world are now demonstrating prototype autonomous weapons," notes Toby Walsh, a professor of AI at the University of New South Wales in Sydney, Australia.[34] One example is Israel Aerospace Industries' Harop kamikaze drone, which can seek and destroy enemy radar defense systems either with human guidance or in a fully autonomous mode. Another example is South Korea's Samsung SGR-A1 sentry gun that defends the Korean Demilitarized Zone, which reportedly has the capacity to conduct surveillance, track and fire rounds, and respond to voice commands.

Going forward, the arms industry is going to be a powerful force expanding the global market for AI weapons. This industry, which American firms dominate, rakes in profits across a wide array of sales and services. Excluding China, the top hundred weapons manufacturers sold nearly $400 billion worth of arms in 2017. Of the top six firms, five were American—Lockheed Martin, Boeing's Phantom Works, Raytheon, Northrop Grumman, and General Dynamics—and one was British (BAE Systems). Of the top hundred firms, forty-two were headquartered in the United States; together, these American companies accounted for 57 percent of total sales. Russian firms comprised the second-largest subgroup, accounting for just under 10 percent of global sales.[35]

Companies such as Google, Microsoft, and Waymo have far more expertise in deep learning techniques, intelligent automation, and driverless vehicles than the defense industry.[36] The deep pockets of arms manufacturers such as Lockheed Martin, however, offer many opportunities to weaponize commercial breakthroughs as well as develop in-house capabilities. Lockheed Martin is the world's biggest arms company, every year selling tens of billions of dollars' worth of ballistic missiles, Aegis naval combat systems, precision-guided munitions, F-35 stealth fighters, antimissile systems, tanks, and other arms. Artificial intelligence is now a selling feature of many of its products, as is true more generally across the arms industry. As the company tells prospective employees, its pathbreaking software engineers are training artificial neural networks to conduct cyberwarfare—"outfitting cyber warriors with technologies for offensive and defensive missions." And as the company tells potential customers, it is embracing machine learning to develop smart, highly autonomous aerial, land, and marine drones able "to go farther, operate longer and succeed in harsh or dangerous conditions."[37]

Already by 2017, at least twelve militaries had armed drones—China, Egypt, Iran, Iraq, Israel, Jordan, Nigeria, Pakistan, Russia, Turkey, the United Kingdom, and the United States—and more than ninety states had small drones for surveillance, recognizance, and intelligence analysis.[38] The future is going to see even more militaries deploying drones. Australia has plans to buy six Triton drones and up to sixteen Reaper drones from General Atomics. With relatively few export restraints, China is selling armed drones to states in Africa, Asia, and the Middle East, including the Rainbow CH-4, which looks uncannily like the Reaper drone. Seeing the growth of Chinese drone sales, in 2018, the Trump administration announced an easing of export controls on the sale of armed drones to overseas buyers. The new "export policy will level the playing field by enabling US firms to increase direct sales to authorized allies and partners," declared Trump's senior trade advisor, Peter Navarro.[39]

In the United Kingdom, meanwhile, BAE Systems is developing the Taranis drone, a remotely piloted stealth warplane able to attack ground and aerial targets over long-distance missions. Like the US, China, and Russia, the UK would also appear to be working to develop lethal drones with the capacity for full autonomy. "We have already seen the development of drones in Britain which have advanced autonomous capabilities, such as the Taranis stealth drone developed by BAE Systems, and the development of a truly autonomous lethal drone in the foreseeable future is now a real possibility," argues Peter Burt, the author of *Off the Leash: The Development of Autonomous Military Drones in the UK*, an analysis of military drones in the United Kingdom.[40]

Drones can promote peace by, say, speeding up surveillance analysis to avoid overestimating threat levels. But the diffusion of increasingly autonomous drones is set to do far more to enhance the risk of war, including what the geographer Ian Shaw calls "swarm wars."[41]

SWARM WARS?

Attacking swarms of armed drones—learning on the go, continually communicating, seeking vulnerabilities, and repositioning at breakneck speeds—would pose unprecedented challenges for defensive systems. Imagine a swarm of torpedo drones attacking a naval fleet. Or a swarm of small quadcopters bombing a runway, an army base, or a city. Or a swarm of miniships converging to blow up an oil tanker. Or a swarm of bird-sized aerial drones firing on troops, battleships, and fighter jets. Or a swarm of tiny bots attacking protestors like deadly bees.

Such scenarios may seem farfetched. But security analysts such as Michael O'Hanlon at the Brookings Institution worry that swarm drone attacks and counterattacks may become common within a few decades.[42] The US Air Force is already developing swarming technologies, shooting footage in 2016 of an F/A-18 Super Hornet fighter jet releasing 103 bird-sized Perdix drones, a leaderless squadron flying autonomously and coordinating through a shared artificial intelligence. Students at the Massachusetts Institute of Technology built the first Perdix drones for environmental monitoring, but in 2013, the Pentagon modified them for military purposes. "Perdix are not pre-programmed synchronized individuals," clarifies William Roper, the former director of the Pentagon's Strategic Capabilities Office. "They are a collective organism, sharing one distributed brain for decision-making and adapting to each other like swarms in nature."[43]

The US Marine Corps is developing swarming weapons, too, including a handheld tablet to allow a marine to attack with a squadron of aerial drones with automatic target recognition. The idea is not for a marine to stare at a tablet during battle, explains Captain Matt Cornachio of the Marine Corps Warfighting Laboratory. Instead, all that is necessary is to give the drones "intent," and "the machines do the work for you."[44]

Other states seem to be following suit, including China and Russia. America's allies are also looking to develop swarming technologies, including South Korea and the United Kingdom. In 2019, for instance, then British defense secretary Gavin Williamson—in what he said was an effort to boost his country's "lethality"—announced a plan to "develop swarm squadrons of network-enabled drones capable of confusing and overwhelming enemy air defences."[45]

Technology companies and defense contractors are developing drone swarms, too. Chinese firms, in particular, are at the forefront of AI drone technology. The state-owned China Electronics Technology Group Corporation is advancing aerial swarms, flying a squadron of 117 coordinating drones in 2017. That year, the Chinese company EHang set a new world record for the largest swarm, flying 1,180 drones to create a spectacular lightshow in Guangzhou. The following year, the Chinese company Yunzhou-Tech (Oceanalpha), working with the arms industry and the People's Liberation Army, conducted a "shark swarm" in the South China Sea, deploying a flotilla of fifty-six miniature vessels able to zigzag, reposition, and coordinate an attack.[46]

Around 275,000 commercial drones were sold in 2018, up from 110,000 in 2016; over this time, millions of personal drones were sold, too. Ominously, converting a commercial drone into a lethal weapon is not particularly difficult. "As a piece of engineering, an autonomous drone designed for search and rescue is effectively the same as one built to search and destroy," writes Ivan Semeniuk when summarizing the remarks of Ryan Gariepy, chief technology officer at the Canadian company Clearpath Robotics.[47] Given this, future swarm attacks by fanatics and rogue states are "an absolute certainly," warned Alvin Wilby, a vice president at the French defense firm Thales, when speaking before the British House of Lords in 2017. "The genie is out of the bottle."[48]

Since then, a few rudimentary swarm attacks have indeed occurred. In 2018, a squadron of thirteen small aerial drones attacked a Russian base in Syria. That year, two small aerial drones also tried to assassinate Venezuelan President Nicolás Maduro. Seeing the growing threat from small, swarming drones, the US Army moved that same year to acquire high-powered Lockheed Martin microwave weapons able to repel aerial attacks. A specially designed weapon is necessary to defend against small drones, explains Daniel Miller, an engineer at Lockheed Martin, because they "are difficult to see, hard to catch on radar, and hard to shoot at with conventional weapons, particularly in swarms."[49]

AN AI COLD WAR?

Could the struggle for AI military supremacy trigger another Cold War? Computer scientist Jeremy Straub thinks so. "As someone who researches the use of AI for applications as diverse as drones, self-driving vehicles and cybersecurity," he wrote in 2018, "I worry that the world may be entering—or perhaps already in—another Cold War, fueled by AI. And I'm not alone."[50]

An AI arms race among the great powers would pose a grave threat to global sustainability. The proliferation of highly autonomous armed drones, crewless battleships, driverless tanks, and self-guiding submarines would end up bringing unparalleled efficiency and anonymity to the act of killing in times of war. Before long, moreover, these weapons would certainly end up in the hands of groups with brutal human rights records, as the AI superpowers arm their allies, as weapons manufacturers seek new sales, as the prices of AI weapons inevitably fall, and as engineers weaponize increasingly autonomous commercial drones and vehicles. Police and border agents could end up with powerful new weapons of suppression. Terrorists could end up launching swarms of armed drones able to overpower even the best missile defense systems. And tyrants, fanatics, and drug lords could end up deploying intelligent nano-drones to hunt down and murder untold numbers of journalists, double agents, political foes, human rights activists, and environmental campaigners.[51]

With care and human oversight, drones and defensive AI systems can protect civilians, reduce conflict, and promote peace. Training and fighting with unmanned machines put fewer pilots, soldiers, sailors, marines, and secret service agents in harm's way. There is some evidence, too, that AI-guided missile and artillery strikes can reduce collateral damage during combat, including the killing of civilians.[52]

But AI weapons, even those theoretically under human supervision, run the risk of triggering and escalating conflicts. When provoked, states with autonomous submarines, fighter jets, and tanks may be more likely to attack than seek diplomatic resolutions because politicians, the media, the public, and military commanders perceive the risks of retaliating as relatively low in comparison to sending in troops. Rapid, opaque decisions by artificial neural networks run the risk of generating new uncertainties for commanding officers during battles. Clashes among AI adversaries run the risk of spiraling out of control. And cyberattacks—where the attacking AI is able to predict defensive moves, learn from mistakes, and relentlessly probe for weaknesses (not unlike today's top machine learning chess engines)—have the potential to destabilize economies and political relations, including among the nuclear powers.[53]

The weaponization of AI runs the additional risk of accelerating the pace of warfare, increasing the chances of overreactions, miscalculations, and escalations, while reducing the opportunities to diffuse tensions. Some leading experts think this is already happening. "The hyperwar era is upon us," argues Victoria Nuland, a US Career Ambassador and the head of the Center for a New American Security: "The fusion of distributed artificial intelligence with highly autonomous military systems ushers in a type of lightning-quick conflict that has never been seen before." John R. Allen, a retired US Marine Corps general and current president of the Brookings Institution, worries an AI hyperwar could even threaten the very foundation of American security. "With sophisticated AI systems," he said in 2018, "the speed of warfare will increase to a pace we are currently unable to anticipate."[54]

Militaries and arms manufacturers are going to continue to develop highly autonomous assault weapons. Trends in the United States, China, Russia, and the United Kingdom confirm this; so do the AI research and development programs of the world's leading defense contractors. Yet it is not too late for the United Nations to ban lethal AI weapons with full autonomy to target and kill, as it has done for blinding laser weapons. There are also ways for technology corporations to limit the weaponization of commercial applications of artificial intelligence. This will not be easy. And dark clouds are on the horizon. As I discuss in the next (and last) chapter, however, there are hopeful signs, too, for the prospect of containing lethal autonomous weapons and also more broadly for the possibility of steering AI toward responsible and sustainable purposes.

12

CONCLUSION: NAVIGATING THE SHOALS OF HUBRIS

Artificial intelligence is going to transform the politics of global sustainability over the next few decades. That has become crystal clear to me during the writing of this book. Machine learning, in particular, has been making spectacular progress in recent years. Great technological, political, socioeconomic, and environmental forces are being unleashed. And the power of AI is going to keep rising, whether we like it or not.

The world is at the beginning of this journey. The proficiencies of robots are going to continue to strengthen. Computing power is going to keep growing. Digital data and the Internet of Things are going to continue to expand. The speed of wireless is going to keep accelerating, and the cost of data storage is going to keep falling. Meanwhile, the algorithms for deep learning, forecasting, decision making, computer vision, and natural language processing are going to continue to improve.

The consequences for the future of global sustainability are going to be capricious, crosscutting, and volatile. There will certainly be environmental benefits. All around the world, environmentalists within nonprofit organizations, startups, universities, corporations, and government agencies are turning to artificial intelligence to advance sustainability goals. This bottom-up, diffuse process is set to improve biodiversity mapping, climate modeling, and the accuracy of ecological forecasting, as well as further sharpen the tools to fight illegal fishing, mining, logging, and poaching. It is set to boost the eco-efficiency of business; increase the energy efficiency of products, homes, electrical grids, and cities; and make our roads safer. And it is set to enhance agricultural yields, the ability of smallholders to diagnose crop diseases, and the precision of industrial applications of pesticides. There is even a good chance that machine learning will radically speed up the rate of discovering and refining eco-technologies.

Yet, even as we applaud these accomplishments, we need to keep in mind that artificial intelligence is a product of world politics and economics, and the competition to profit from this technology will inevitably intensify forces of environmental change as well as create new risks for both people and the planet. Nor should we forget that political and corporate interests have strong incentives to exaggerate the benefits, disregard the failures, and hide the costs of artificial intelligence. Given this, the consequences of AI for the future of sustainability are going to go well beyond improving environmental learning, conservation tools, and corporate efficiency.

Looking critically through a political economy lens reveals major downsides of artificial intelligence for global sustainability. Machine learning, as the analysis in *AI in the Wild* reveals, is set to accelerate the mining of natural resources and decrease the cost of drilling for oil and gas. AI-powered advertising is set to turbocharge consumerism. Rapid-fire turnover of smart products is set to generate mountains of e-waste. Intelligent automation is set to cause widespread unemployment, with disproportionate harms for middle- and lower-income workers. The profits from artificial intelligence are set to privilege technology corporations and shift even more of the world's wealth into the hands of American and Chinese billionaires. The competition to extract data for machine learning is set to pose a powerful threat to privacy, and the race to commercialize artificial intelligence is set to generate new forms of discrimination and bias. Facial recognition technology and AI-enhanced security tools are set to bolster the capacity of authoritarian states to stifle political dissent and environmental activism. Equally worrying, the weaponization of artificial intelligence is set to empower militarized states within international relations.

Relying on artificial intelligence to advance sustainability, moreover, risks ensconcing technocratic models of management with long records of failing the global environment. These models assume that technological progress inexorably arcs toward sustainability, a way of thinking political theorist John S. Dryzek describes as "Promethean," in reference to the Greek myth of Prometheus, who stole fire from Zeus to empower humanity.[1]

THE PERILS OF PROMETHEAN THINKING

Promethean thinking runs deep through "market liberal" environmentalism, which since the mid-1980s has come to dominate the understanding of global sustainability of states, corporations, and to a lesser extent nongovernmental organizations. Market liberals see discrete, manageable problems rather than an escalating global environmental crisis. For them, the core causes of these problems—say, tropical deforestation or freshwater depletion or plastic pollution—are poverty, inefficiency, subsidies, and waste. Any effective solution, market liberals argue, will require better technology, more economic growth, and what most describe as "sustainable development," understood not as sustainability of the earth itself but as the capacity of the world economy to continue to expand into the near future.

The best way to spur sustainable development and technological innovation, they argue, is through globalization, open markets, international trade, investment, deregulation, privatization, property rights, and the creation of wealth. They feel that market incentives and corporate self-regulation are the most effective ways to govern and that domestic and international laws should minimize regulatory interference and prioritize fair competition.

Understanding technology as a form of power, however, reveals deep flaws in Promethean thinking. Doing so, we can see that market liberals overrate the ability of incentives, private governance, and voluntary pledges to control the long-term consequences of technology for global sustainability. We can see that they underrate the harms arising from economic growth, overconsumption, and new technologies. We can see that they misjudge how often powerful actors repurpose technologies for new, unexpected, and dangerous uses. And we can see that they underestimate the power of technology to destroy the earth, including as weapons of populists, despots, and terrorists.[2]

Market liberals fail as well to account sufficiently for the ways that malicious forces deploy new technologies to suppress activism and attack scientific research.[3] At the same time, they ignore the power of technology to stimulate wasteful and excessive consumption, treating such consumption not as a problem but as a source of economic growth (and thus a solution). They overlook the ecological shadows of technology on distant lands, fragile ecosystems, and future generations. And they downplay the crucial need for precaution and humility when introducing any new technology into the world economy.[4]

Moving toward global sustainability is going to require a far more critical and complex understanding of the ways technology is empowering the forces degrading the earth. At the same time, it is going to require strict controls and constant reminders of the downsides of relying on technology to solve the escalating global environmental crisis. Artificial intelligence is certainly an ingenious technology. And it can be a force of good. But for any chance of a sustainable future, the world is going to need to deploy AI with far stronger safeguards and far less hubris. The last thing the earth needs are more decision makers, no matter how intelligent, who have no moral compass, no sense of humanity, and no caring for others.

What can be done to guide AI toward protecting, rather than destroying, our planet? As we'll see in this chapter, the world is now waking up to the limits and dangers of artificial intelligence. Norms of what constitutes appropriate and inappropriate uses of artificial intelligence are emerging. Industry, government, and civil society groups are starting to cooperate to develop responsibility standards for the deployment of artificial intelligence. And, although environmentalists within organizations such as Greenpeace or Friends of the Earth are still relatively quiet, calls to govern AI for sustainability are growing louder by the day.

TOWARD STATE GOVERNANCE OF AI

All around the world, human rights, labor, peace, and environmental activists are starting to demand stronger controls on the research, development, and deployment of artificial intelligence. Scientists, technologists, entrepreneurs, and academics in every country are joining this chorus of concerned citizens. Governments, too, are increasingly trying to govern artificial intelligence to gain strategic advantages and optimize national benefits, while encouraging responsible research and development.

In 2016, for instance, the Executive Office of US President Barack Obama and the National Science and Technology Council published a pathbreaking report titled *Preparing for the Future of Artificial Intelligence*, and in 2017, the US House of Representatives set up a Congressional Artificial Intelligence Caucus. As is noted in the previous chapter, President Donald Trump went even further in 2019, unveiling the American AI Initiative to accelerate research, development, and the protection of AI technologies across federal agencies. Federal agencies, explains President Trump's executive order creating the initiative, will work to "ensure that technical standards minimize vulnerability to attacks from malicious actors and reflect Federal priorities for innovation, public trust, and public confidence in systems that use AI technologies; and develop international standards to promote and protect those priorities."[5]

Canada has also been developing strategies to govern AI research and development. In 2017, the Canadian government established a Pan-Canadian Artificial Intelligence Strategy. The government followed this up in 2018 by financing an AI-Powered Supply Chains Supercluster to bring together industry and technology sectors to develop "intelligent supply chains" to support export opportunities for small- and medium-sized businesses. That year, Canada also joined with France to form an International Panel on Artificial Intelligence—modeled after the Intergovernmental Panel on Climate Change—with a mission "to support and guide the responsible adoption of AI that is human-centric and grounded in human rights, inclusion, diversity, innovation and economic growth." As part of its duties, the International Panel on Artificial Intelligence will convene an annual conference to facilitate global dialogue on a range of issues, such as data privacy, worker rights, and the governance of machine learning.[6]

The government of Japan, meanwhile, published an Artificial Intelligence Technology Strategy in 2017 and began drafting principles and guidelines for researching and developing AI. That year, the UK government set up an All-Party Parliamentary Group on Artificial Intelligence to advise on the prospects and risks of AI technologies, and the following year, the government announced a Sector Deal for AI to accelerate AI research and development across the country. At the 2018 World Economic Forum in Davos, Switzerland, then UK Prime Minister Theresa May said her government was "establishing the UK as a world leader in artificial intelligence," working "to build a common understanding of how to ensure the safe, ethical, and innovative deployment of artificial intelligence."[7]

State interest in governing artificial intelligence is surging elsewhere, too. In 2017, the Chinese State Council issued a New Generation Artificial Intelligence Plan, with the minister of science and technology announcing the following year that the government was drafting comprehensive guidelines for developing and deploying artificial intelligence. In 2017, France struck a task force to develop a strategy for becoming a leader in artificial intelligence, and in 2018, the French president formerly announced AI for Humanity. Also in 2018, India published a draft of a National Strategy for Artificial Intelligence "to position itself among leaders on the global AI map," while the Group of Seven (G7) countries (Canada, France, Germany, Italy, Japan, the United States, and the United Kingdom) issued the "Charlevoix Common Vision for the Future of Artificial Intelligence," aiming to advance AI technologies that promote "economic growth, societal trust, gender equality and inclusion"—what the common vision calls "human-centric AI."[8] The following year the Organization for Economic Cooperation and Development (OECD) adopted a recommendation setting the first intergovernmental standard to promote "innovation," "trust," and "responsible stewardship" of artificial intelligence.[9]

To varying degrees, all of these government strategies raise the need for ethical guidelines when developing and deploying artificial intelligence. They tend to underscore the need to protect privacy, eliminate bias, and avoid discrimination. They tend to stress the value of regularly auditing machine learning systems for errors, flawed recommendations, and misleading predictions. They also tend to underline the need to enhance public trust, data quality, product safety, and the security of cloud services and the Internet of Things. A few of the strategies highlight the need to democratize access to the benefits and prevent the world's most powerful high-tech corporations from monopolizing the economic value of artificial intelligence. A couple of strategies even note the need to prioritize the goal of advancing sustainability. The emphasis of most of the national strategies, however, is on supporting domestic AI innovation to gain competitive advantages in the world digital economy.[10]

For the most part, these strategies look to the technology industry to self-govern AI through voluntary codes of conduct and industry-wide guidelines. This is hardly surprising given the dominance of market liberal thinking within government circles. There is also a clear risk of industry self-regulation capturing the global governance of artificial intelligence.

Intriguingly, though, some of the loudest voices calling for controls on AI are coming from within the high-tech industry, from entrepreneurs such as Elon Musk to employees at companies such as Google. There are even signs of support for government regulation from the heads of the biggest technology companies. "We don't want to see a commercial race to the bottom," Microsoft president Brad Smith said at a 2019 conference on artificial intelligence. "Law is needed."[11] At the same time, quieter calls for stronger corporate self-governance are coming from analysts within business organizations, such as the international consulting firm PricewaterhouseCoopers.

TOWARD "GOOD" PRIVATE GOVERNANCE OF AI

In 2018, PricewaterhouseCoopers (PwC) published a roadmap for harnessing artificial intelligence as a force of good. Significantly, the report does not shy away from noting the ways that AI can amplify the forces of global harm, and it appeals for principles of "safety," "transparency," and "explainability" to guide research and development of artificial intelligence. Sensibly, the report calls for wide-ranging stakeholder consultations, public-private partnerships, and interdisciplinary conversations as a way of promoting "good governance."[12]

A reasonable overarching goal of good governance of AI, the PwC report says, is to "minimize environmental risks and maximize environmental benefits." Doing so, it notes, is going to require industry to consult widely before implementing AI sustainability solutions; an increase in the amount of private and public financing for environmentally friendly applications; and the development of industry-wide standards and definitions for what would constitute ethical, responsible, and sustainable implementation of artificial intelligence, as well as what would comprise misuse.

The PwC report suggests ways for governments, firms, investors, and researchers to promote good governance of artificial intelligence. For governments, PwC emphasizes the importance of working with civil society and industry to build international and national regulatory structures to guide AI toward supporting the 2030 United Nations Sustainable Development Goals.[13] More specifically, the report recommends the strategic use of government financing to incubate research, leverage corporate funds, and scale up applications toward what it calls "AI for good." It further calls on governments to cooperate with business to construct high-quality data environments to enhance the value and predictability of machine learning. In addition, it recommends the passage of policies to evaluate on an ongoing basis the biases and discriminatory propensities of AI models, especially ones trained from unstructured big data.[14]

For industry, the PwC report recommends establishing ethical baselines as well as corporate advisory bodies to counsel board members and senior executives on the safety and environmental risks of developing and deploying artificial intelligence. It also urges technology firms to develop protocols to ensure data privacy and transparency in algorithms, including, when possible, allowing third-party auditing of data and algorithms to enhance public trust in artificial intelligence.

The PwC report further calls on firms to integrate environmental principles into AI designs and prioritize the development of AI as a tool of sustainability. One exemplary example of corporate social responsibility, the report notes, is Microsoft's AI for Earth. As you may recall from chapter 1, Microsoft set up this program to offer AI services, tools, financing, and technical advice for nongovernmental and community groups working to apply artificial intelligence to advance the environmental management of agriculture, biodiversity, climate change, and water.

As the PwC report predicted, AI for Earth is now facilitating the development of innovative sustainability technologies around the world. In

India, for instance, the program awarded seven grants to environmental entrepreneurs in 2018. These grants include technology training as well as access to Microsoft's cloud computing Azure service and, according to Keshav Dhakad at Microsoft India, are part of a broader effort to expand "Microsoft's commitment to and investment in democratizing AI and advancing sustainability in the country." One project in India is aiming to enhance farm advisory services and pest forecasting; another is working to develop a device that automates the diagnosis of crop diseases by analyzing images on Microsoft Azure. The other projects in India are aiming to develop a wide range of smart sustainability technologies, including ones to document biodiversity, control monkey populations in cities and towns, enhance the efficiency of electrical grids, advance intelligent city management, and distribute water more equitably within megacities.[15]

The PwC report also offers advice for how investors and researchers can promote good governance of artificial intelligence. It calls on institutional investors—including banks, pension funds, insurance companies, and hedge funds—to internalize sustainability principles into AI investment portfolios. And it urges venture capitalists and financiers to build portfolios of companies working to develop AI sustainability technologies, with the goal of accelerating the commercialization of products. For researchers, meanwhile, the report notes the critical need for a deeper understanding of the limits and risks of artificial intelligence for sustainability, including the consequences of algorithmic bias and the dangers for public policy of not fully understanding the underlying principles and criteria of the decisions and recommendations of machine learning technologies.[16]

THE MOVEMENT FOR RESPONSIBLE AI

Around the world activists, scientists, and technologists are also calling for responsible research and development of artificial intelligence. This includes some of the leading experts in deep learning, such as Yoshua Bengio at the University of Montreal, who, along with Yann LeCun and Geoffrey Hinton, received the prestigious 2018 A. M. Turing Award, informally known as the "Nobel Prize of computing." Seeing many dangers ahead, Bengio is urging the global community to negotiate international agreements and impose government regulations to control artificial intelligence. "Self-regulation is not going to work," he said when asked if state regulation of the AI industry was necessary. "Do you think that voluntary taxation works? It doesn't."[17]

Professor Bengio is especially worried about what is happening in the shadows: "in military labs, in security organizations, in private companies providing services to governments or the police." In his home province of Québec, he was instrumental in facilitating a conversation with a cross section of civil society, policymakers, and industry stakeholders to develop a bold set of ethical guidelines for artificial intelligence, known as the Montreal Declaration for Responsible AI Development. The 2018 Declaration contains ten principles, including a commitment to "prudence," which requires that all developers of artificial intelligence systems (AIS) "exercise caution by anticipating, as far as possible, the adverse consequences of AIS use and by taking the appropriate measures to avoid them."[18]

The Declaration includes a "sustainable development" principle, which requires AI developers to work for "strong environmental sustainability of the planet." This principle demands four specific commitments: to build an AI infrastructure, including data centers, that maximizes energy efficiencies and minimizes greenhouse gas emissions; to build a circular economy for AI, where electronic waste flows back into production and consumption; to minimize the ecological costs of extracting natural resources for AI hardware and infrastructure; and finally, to work toward building sustainable global trade and supply chains for artificial intelligence.[19]

Besides developing ethical principles and codes of conduct, large numbers of civil society groups are joining forces to advocate for responsible development of artificial intelligence. One prominent example is the Partnership on AI, which, as is mentioned in chapter 4, was founded in 2016 by Mustafa Suleyman (who cofounded DeepMind) and Eric Horvitz (director of Microsoft Research Labs). This partnership is working to educate the public on both the benefits and risks of artificial intelligence. It sees AI as a powerful tool for advancing knowledge and human well-being, improving healthcare and education, and mitigating climate change, inequality, and food insecurity. It calls on partners, however, to pursue these laudable goals responsibly and sustainably.

The tenets of the Partnership on AI require partners to work to ensure that AI technologies "benefit and empower as many people as possible." They call on partners to pursue these benefits while maintaining a checklist of good practices: public consultation, open research, high accountability, protection of privacy, algorithmic transparency, assurance of personal security, and the trust and cooperation of stakeholders. These tenets further oblige partners to develop "technologies that do no harm" and oppose the "development and use of AI technologies that would violate international conventions or human rights."[20]

More than one hundred partners are involved in the Partnership on AI. These include Amnesty International, the BBC, the Future of Life Institute, the *New York Times*, OpenAI, and the United Nations Development Programme. The partnership also includes many of the world's most influential technology companies, including Amazon, Apple, DeepMind, Facebook, Google, IBM, Microsoft, Samsung, and Sony.

Google and DeepMind, in particular, have been leaders within industry in advocating for responsible research and development of artificial intelligence. Sundar Pichai, the CEO of Alphabet and Google, has spoken out on the need for humility and precaution, and in 2018, he set guiding principles for Google's AI team. These principles require Google's AI researchers to pursue social good, retain scientific integrity, and share discoveries. They require them to prevent bias and protect privacy. And they require them to test for safety and design products to enable accountability.[21]

There is a diversity of views, foci, and strategies within the Partnership on AI. The nonprofit company OpenAI, for instance, is working to democratize access to AI knowledge and software by conducting fundamental research at the frontiers of artificial general intelligence. Elon Musk and Sam Altman (president of Y Combinator, which finances early-stage startups) have personally funded OpenAI, as have companies like Microsoft and Amazon Web Services.

OpenAI is not completely free from the constraints of a for-profit business, even creating a for-profit entity in 2019 that reports to its nonprofit board. That year, OpenAI also took a $1 billion investment from

Microsoft, agreeing to work together to commercialize AI applications on Microsoft's Azure cloud computing service. Still, the researchers and engineers at OpenAI are largely free to present and publish articles, build open-source AI systems, and advocate for safety measures for developing artificial general intelligence. On occasion, OpenAI even holds back on releasing a breakthrough that it deems vulnerable to malicious use. This occurred in 2019, for instance, when OpenAI withheld the full version of a trained AI language model (GPT-2) able to fabricate news stories and mimic the style of even the greatest writers of all time—what the developers describe as "deepfakes for text." In short, OpenAI is striving to expand the benefits and limit the risks of AI, guided by a motto of "discovering and enacting the path to safe artificial general intelligence."[22]

The Future of Life Institute, meanwhile, is calling on the international community to go well beyond voluntary corporate guidelines to govern artificial intelligence. Founded in 2014, this nongovernmental institute aims to raise awareness and support advocacy to confront four existential risks to life on earth: nuclear war, climate change, biotechnology, and artificial intelligence. Like the Partnership on AI and OpenAI, the Future of Life Institute sees great value in artificial intelligence as a way of accelerating medical, environmental, and economic gains. In addition, the Future of Life Institute perceives many ways for governments, citizen groups, and corporations to enhance the benefits from machine learning technologies, such as by creating high-quality, transparent, and standardized datasets. But the Future of Life Institute, like OpenAI, also sees artificial intelligence as presenting grave dangers and is calling for far greater caution as the world marches toward the possibility of one day creating artificial general intelligence, or superintelligence.[23]

The Future of Life Institute sees many ways for the rising power of AI to destabilize politics, societies, and economies. Intelligent automation, the Future of Life Institute argues, has the potential to increase unemployment, intensify inequality, and further concentrate power in the hands of high-tech billionaires. Unless the underlying algorithms are explainable and transparent, the Institute adds, automating management with machine learning systems could end up deepening discrimination, obfuscating accountability, and violating human rights.

The Future of Life Institute worries, too, that AI technologies could empower global criminal networks, intensify cyberwarfare, and subvert democratic processes with fake news, images, and videos. Microtargeting of advertising, messaging, and propaganda, the Future of Life Institute further argues, could empower forces looking to manipulate psychological well-being and destabilize cultures, while the commercialization of artificial intelligence could generate far-reaching risks to consumer safety and online security.

The Future of Life Institute sees "lethal autonomous weapons systems," which kill independently and can gain proficiency with experience, as an especially serious threat. These "killer drones," as chapter 11 documents, appear to be just around the corner. Delegating killing decisions to machines is immoral and unjustifiable, the Future of Life Institute argues, and will offer dictators and despots "powerful instruments of violence and oppression, especially when linked to surveillance and data systems." If these weapons proliferate, the Future of Life Institute further contends, rogue militaries and terrorists are more likely to gain access than has been the case for biological, chemical, or nuclear weapons. Starting to build these weapons in quantity, moreover, could trigger an arms race, which in turn could destabilize regional and international security.

As a first step to combatting these dangers, the Future of Life Institute is working to "stigmatize" these weapons and is calling on governments, technology firms, and individuals to pledge to "neither participate in nor support the development, manufacture, trade, or use of lethal autonomous weapons." The Future of Life Institute is aiming to construct a robust global norm against making, using, or selling these weapons, including an international treaty to ban them.[24] Realistically, as AI expert Toby Walsh correctly notes, "we cannot stop a determined person from building autonomous weapons, just as we cannot stop a determined person from building a chemical weapon. But if we don't want rogue states or terrorists to have easy access to autonomous weapons, we must ensure they are not sold openly by arms companies."[25]

Other nonprofits are campaigning alongside the Future of Life Institute to try to strengthen the norm against lethal autonomous weapons. One example is Article 36, a nonprofit organization founded in the United

Kingdom in 2011 to "prevent the unintended, unnecessary or unacceptable harm caused by certain weapons," including lethal autonomous weapons. Another example is the International Committee for Robot Arms Control, an NGO founded in 2009 by leading security, robotics, and AI experts to campaign for international controls on military robots.

In 2013, nongovernmental organizations from around the world came together to launch the Campaign to Stop Killer Robots. Today this campaign involves one hundred forty nongovernmental organizations from over sixty countries advocating for an international treaty to ban the development of fully autonomous lethal weapons. The steering committee includes Amnesty International, Article 36, Human Rights Watch, and the International Committee for Robot Arms Control, among others.

Jody Williams, who won the 1997 Nobel Peace Prize for her campaign to ban landmines, is one of the activists raising awareness for the Campaign to Stop Killer Robots. "I find the very idea of killer robots more terrifying than nukes," she told NBC News. "Where is humanity going if some people think it's OK to cede the power of life and death of humans over to a machine?" When asked if the sluggish nature of politics and the headlong pace of technology might mean the proliferation of these weapons is unavoidable, she bristled: "People keep saying that it's inevitable. Nothing is inevitable. It's only inevitable if you sit on your butt and don't take action to stop things you think are morally and ethically wrong."[26]

Mary Wareham, a director at Human Rights Watch who is also serving as the coordinator for the Campaign to Stop Killer Robots, is another fiery opponent of weapons that are able to target and kill without human oversight. Like Williams, she is a formidable and tenacious campaigner. "A lot of people dismissed us early on," she said in reference to the Campaign to Stop Killer Robots, "but now they see that we're not going anywhere."[27]

Jody Williams and Mary Wareham, along with countless others, are coordinating opposition, encouraging supporters to lobby politicians, and raising awareness of the potential threat of swarms of miniature "slaughterbots." Like the Future of Life Institute, campaigners like Williams and Wareham are also calling on states to negotiate an international agreement to ban lethal autonomous weapons. One option is to do this along the lines of the 1995 protocol to the 1980 Convention on Certain Conventional Weapons, which preemptively banned the development of "blinding laser weapons" (on the principle that such weapons "are considered to cause unnecessary or unjustifiable suffering to combatants or to affect civilians indiscriminately."[28]

Thousands of AI experts and tens of thousands of citizens have now signed various open letters calling for such a ban. This diffuse, global campaign is gradually gaining governmental support. The European Parliament passed a resolution in 2018 "to work towards an international ban on weapon systems that lack human control over the use of force."[29] The current Secretary General of the United Nations, António Guterres, has endorsed a total ban as well, saying: "For me there is a message that is very clear—machines that have the power and the discretion to take human lives are politically unacceptable, are morally repugnant, and should be banned by international law."[30]

By 2020, thirty countries had at some point called for international legal restrictions on fully autonomous lethal weapons. The vast majority have been developing countries, and France, India, Israel, Russia, South Korea, the United Kingdom, and the United States are notably absent from the list. Pakistan and Brazil are among the states that have called for a ban, and China, while reserving the option to produce and stockpile these weapons, has said it was willing to consider backing an international agreement to restrict their use.[31]

The campaign to prevent an arms race in lethal autonomous weapons has also gained support from some leading technology companies. Google's 2018 AI principles, for instance, allow the company to work with militaries to develop autonomous devices for defensive and nonaggressive purposes, such as to defuse bombs or perform search and rescue. They prevent the company, however, from participating in any projects aiming to build AI weapons, deploy technology or surveillance systems in violation of international law or human rights norms, or design intelligent technologies that "are likely to cause overall harm."[32] These principles did not stop Google executives in 2018 from considering submitting a bid to the US Defense Department for a $10 billion contract to build a cloud computing system known as the Joint Enterprise Defense Infrastructure (JEDI). But they did help convince management to pull out of the competition after Google employees raised concerns that JEDI is going to weaponize machine learning and support "algorithmic warfare."[33]

There is still a long way to go to contain the weaponization of artificial intelligence. Google's hesitancy to build JEDI, for instance, did not stop Amazon, IBM, Microsoft, or Oracle from bidding for the contract (which Microsoft eventually won in 2019). Nor did Amazon's code of conduct and ethics prevent the company from taking on a cloud computing contract a few years ago for the US Central Intelligence Agency worth $600 million.[34]

Still, increasing numbers of technology companies and AI experts are disavowing lethal autonomous weapons and the advancement of algorithmic warfare. Hundreds of organizations and thousands of individuals with AI expertise, for instance, have now signed a petition on the Future of Life Institute's website calling "upon governments and government leaders to create a future with strong international norms, regulations and laws against lethal autonomous weapons."[35]

CONFRONTING AI CAPITALISM

The movement calling for responsible governance of artificial intelligence looks set to keep strengthening over the coming years. Even more nongovernmental organizations are likely to emerge with a core mandate to hold states and firms accountable for developing and deploying AI technologies. Even more workers are likely to challenge the ethical stance on AI of their company, as nearly eight thousand Amazon employees did when signing an open letter in 2019 calling on Jeff Bezos and his board of directors to prioritize climate change and end "all custom solutions specifically designed for oil and gas extraction and exploration."[36] Even more human rights and environmental activists are likely to dedicate resources to campaign for safe, fair, and sustainable applications of machine learning. These activists, too, are likely to continue to coordinate websites, social media, and political lobbying to spotlight new risks of artificial intelligence for global sustainability.

Government policies and business codes of conduct for artificial intelligence also look set to continue to spread. Other jurisdictions seem likely to follow the example of the European Union's General Data Protection Regulation (which, you may recall from chapter 9, went into force in 2018) to do more to safeguard privacy rights and personal data in the digital economy. Companies such as Microsoft and Google seem likely as well to offer even more services and financing to help integrate machine learning into a wide range of conservation and environmental learning tools. At the same time, as access to AI platforms, software, and training democratizes, even more startups, nongovernmental organizations, and researchers will certainly find many new ways to advance environmental research and technologies with machine learning.[37]

Given recent trends, there would also seem to be a good chance that states, high-tech firms, and nonprofits will do even more to try to limit algorithmic bias and discrimination, protect the privacy of citizens, and enhance the transparency of machine learning systems. A global norm against deploying lethal autonomous weapons may even take hold within the state system, along the lines of the taboos against the use of chemical weapons, land mines, biological weapons, and nuclear weapons.[38]

These steps are all vital and necessary for global sustainability. As the analysis in this book reveals, however, the risks of AI for sustainability go even deeper. Those hoping for a more sustainable future are going to need to confront the role of AI in furthering unsustainable production and overconsumption. And they are going to need to stay alert to the ways that artificial intelligence is empowering states and firms to suppress criticism, including criticism of AI itself. The global environmental movement is rightly enthusiastic about the ingenious ways that machine learning is saving energy, forecasting pollution, and fine-tuning climate models. Artificial intelligence is also clearly helping environmental engineers, scientists, and ecologists to protect coral reefs, fight wildlife poachers, track illegal fishing, and prevent illegal logging of tropical rainforests.

As the analysis in *AI in the Wild* underscores, however, moving toward sustainability is going to require environmental activists to do far more to remind the world of the limits of artificial intelligence as a solution for our escalating global environmental crisis. Activist groups such as Greenpeace and Friends of the Earth are going to need to expose the ways that AI is concentrating wealth, empowering big business, intensifying inequality, displacing livelihoods, and revving up the global engine of capitalism. At the same time, the global community is going to need to listen much more attentively to the nonprofits and grassroots movements now advocating for environmental justice and local sustainability.[39]

Artificial intelligence is a highly disruptive, diffuse force, and the more its powers grow, the more it is becoming woven into the fabric of the world order. Strategic state plans and corporate self-governance alone will never be able to prevent this technology from reinforcing the destructive forces of capitalism and militarism. The financial and political stakes are too high. And those who are deploying AI in pursuit of profits and power are too strong and are surfacing from too many different jurisdictions. One day, organizations such as the Partnership on AI, the Campaign to Stop Killer Robots, and the Future of Life Institute may be able to solidify a global norm against the use of lethal autonomous weapons. Let's hope so. But they are not going to stop governments and militaries from deploying artificial intelligence as a tool of unsustainable growth, societal suppression, and global dominance. This is going to require a far bigger uprising of global civil society.

Going forward, those hoping for a more sustainable future will need to keep in mind, too, the ways that vested interests overstate the value and conceal the risks of artificial intelligence. Business and militarized states have powerful incentives to embellish and obfuscate. So do AI startups and researchers. The hype can make it seem as if artificial intelligence is going to resolve the global environmental crisis. Yet as the history of global environmental politics teaches us, technology is not a benign, neutral force. It is an instrument of power, and believing that any technology will save the earth without sweeping political and economic reforms will bring peril, not sustainability.

NOTES

CHAPTER 1

1. The managing director of the Great Barrier Reef Foundation (Anna Marsden) is quoted in "Robot Reef Protector Sees a New Way to Check Great Barrier Reef Health," *Queensland University of Technology News*, August 31, 2018, www.qut.edu .au. Dunbabin is quoted in Marlene Cimons, "This Robot Is Delivering Coral Babies to the Great Barrier Reef," *EcoWatch*, January 13, 2019, www.ecowatch.com. Harrison is quoted in Southern Cross University, "Southern Cross Reef Research a Global TV Hit," *Southern Cross University News*, March 29, 2019, www.scu.edu.au, and in Queensland University of Technology, "Reef RangerBot Becomes 'LarvalBot' to Spread Coral Babies," *PHYS.ORG*, November 1, 2018, https://phys.org.

2. See Rainforest Connection, https://rfcx.org. White is quoted in Devin Coldewey, "Rainforest Connection Enlists Machine Learning to Listen for Loggers and Jaguars in the Amazon," *TechCrunch*, March 23, 2018, https://techcrunch.com. Also see Tracy Ross, "Guardian of the Forest," *snews*, January 11, 2018 (updated January 12, 2018), www.snewsnet.com; Topher White, "What Can Save the Rainforest? Your Used Cell Phone," TED Talk, March 3, 2015, https://www.youtube.com/ watch?v=xPK2Ch90xWo; Topher White, "Better Run World Predicting Illegal Deforestation," video, Rainforest Connection, March 12, 2019, posted at www.youtube .com/watch?v=kI07MVWor6M.

3. Hein is quoted in Lakshmi Sadhu, "AI Robot Lends UBC a Hand in Alternative-Energy Research," *Globe and Mail*, November 29, 2018, A8. The phrases "smarter and faster after every experiment" and "self-driving laboratories" are from Project Ada's website at www.projectada.ca. This robotic platform is named after Ada Lovelace (1815–1852), a pioneer in early computer programming.

4. David Rolnick et al., "Tackling Climate Change with Machine Learning," June 10, 2019, a review article (pp. 1–97) available at https://arxiv.org/pdf/1906.05433.pdf.

5. The quote "putting the power" is from Brad Smith, "Announcing AI for Earth: Microsoft's New Program to Put AI to Work for the Future of Our Planet," *Microsoft: On the Issues*, July 12, 2017, https://blogs.microsoft.com.

6. Lucas Joppa, "AI for Earth with Dr. Lucas Joppa," *Microsoft Podcast*, episode 72, April 17, 2019, www.microsoft.com.

7. See Microsoft, "Project Premonition," established March 2, 2015, www.microsoft .com; AI for Earth, "Project Premonition," www.microsoft.com.

8. Lucas N. Joppa, "The Case for Technology Investments in the Environment," *Nature* 552 (December 21–28, 2017), 325.

9. World Economic Forum (with PwC and the Stanford Woods Institute for the Environment), lead authors Celine Herweijer and Dominic Waughray, *Harnessing Artificial Intelligence for the Earth* (World Economic Forum System Initiative on Shaping the Future of Environment and Natural Resource Security in partnership with PwC and the Stanford Woods Institute for the Environment, 2018).

10. Celine Herweijer, Benjamin Combes, and Jonathan Gillham, *How AI Can Enable a Sustainable Future* (Microsoft in Association with PricewaterhouseCoopers, 2019), 8.

11. Suleyman is quoted in Adam Vaughn, "Google Uses AI to Cut Data Centre Energy Use by 15%," *Guardian*, July 20, 2016, www.theguardian.com. For the estimate of the energy savings from automating the cooling systems of Google's data centers, see Google, *Google Environmental Report 2019* (Google, 2019), 23.

12. Ackerman is quoted in Spencer Soper, "Amazon's Clever Machines Are Moving from the Warehouse to Headquarters," *Bloomberg*, June 13, 2018, www.bloomberg .com.

13. Gore is quoted in Monica Nickelsburg, "Al Gore Predicts Machine Learning and Other Tech Advances Will Usher in a 'Sustainability Revolution,'" *GeekWire*, May 17, 2018, www.geekwire.com.

14. Tay's tweets have been deleted from Twitter. Screenshots of the quoted tweets are available at James Vincent, "Twitter Taught Microsoft's AI Chatbot to be a Racist Asshole in Less than a Day," *The Verge*, March 24, 2016, www.theverge.com.

15. Yampolskiy and Rosenberg are quoted in Hope Reese, "Why Microsoft's 'Tay' AI Bot Went Wrong," *TechRepublic*, March 24, 2016, www.techrepublic.com. As Twitter trolls and racists came to discover, if prompted by "repeat after me," Tay was prone to parroting back even the most heinous words and phrases.

16. Peter Lee, "Learning from Tay's Introduction," *Official Microsoft Blog*, March 25, 2016, https://blogs.microsoft.com. See also Daniel Victor, "Microsoft Created a Twitter Bot to Learn from Users. It Quickly Became a Racist Jerk," *New York Times*, March 25, 2016, http://www.nytimes.com; Elle Hunt, "Tay, Microsoft's AI Chatbot, Gets a Crash Course in Racism from Twitter," *Guardian*, March 24, 2016, www.theguardian .com.

17. A critical political economy lens on the environmental consequences of technology draws insights from six overlapping fields of inquiry: science and technology studies, political economy of the environment, digital security studies, critical technology studies, global environmental politics, and sustainability studies. For a sampling of these literatures, see Further Reading, "Capitalism and Unsustainability," "Global Environmental Crisis," "Global Environmental Politics," "Political Economy of the Environment," "Science and Technology Studies," "Security and Digital Technology," "Sustainability (background)," "Sustainability (and business)," "Sustainability (and environmentalism)," "Sustainability (pathways toward)," "Technology (critiques)," and "Technology and Sustainability."

18. Peter Dauvergne, *Will Big Business Destroy Our Planet?* (Polity, 2018), 5.

19. The quote "screeching acceleration" is from J. R. McNeill, *Something New under the Sun: An Environmental History of the Twentieth-Century World* (W. W. Norton,

2001), 4. At the time of writing, the International Commission on Stratigraphy had not officially declared the Holocene epoch over. Nevertheless, as I do, large numbers of scholars call our current time the "Anthropocene."

20. For a sense of the scale of the global environmental crisis, see Gerardo Ceballos, Paul R. Ehrlich, and Rodolfo Dirzo, "Biological Annihilation via the Ongoing Sixth Mass Extinction Signaled by Vertebrate Population Losses and Declines," *Proceedings of the National Academy of Sciences* 114, no. 30 (2017): E6089–E6096; the Intergovernmental Science-Policy Platform on Biodiversity and Ecosystem Services, www.ipbes.net; and Further Reading, "Global Environmental Crisis."

21. Simon Nicholson and Sikina Jinnah, "Introduction: Living on a New Earth," in *New Earth Politics: Essays from the Anthropocene*, ed. Simon Nicholson and Sikina Jinnah (MIT Press, 2016): 1–16.

22. RT, "Whoever Leads in AI Will Rule the World: Putin to Russian Children on Knowledge Day," *RT*, September 1, 2017, www.rt.com.

23. See Matt McFarland, "Elon Musk: 'With Artificial Intelligence We Are Summoning the Demon,'" *Washington Post*, October 24, 2014. Musk tweeted "potentially more dangerous than nukes" on August 2, 2014.

24. Hawking is quoted in Rory Cellan-Jones, "Stephen Hawking Warns Artificial Intelligence Could End Mankind," *BBC News*, December 2, 2014.

25. See Geoff Mulgan, *Big Mind: How Collective Intelligence Can Change Our World* (Princeton University Press, 2017); Nick Bostrom, *Superintelligence: Paths, Dangers, Strategies* (Oxford University Press, 2014). For a range of perspectives, also see Further Reading, "Artificial Intelligence (optimistic visions)" and "Artificial Intelligence (critiques)."

26. For general overviews of AI, see Further Reading, "Artificial Intelligence (background)." The Further Reading section also offers a sense of the scope and range of recent books on AI, organized under the following headings: "Artificial Intelligence (conservation)," "Artificial Intelligence (culture and education)," "Artificial Intelligence (employment)," "Artificial Intelligence (history)," "Artificial Intelligence (law)," "Artificial Intelligence (weaponization of)," "Business and AI," "Deep Learning," "Driverless Vehicles," "Ethics and AI," "Fourth Industrial Revolution," "Games and AI," "Machine Learning," "Reinforcement Learning," "Robotics," "Singularity," and "Smart Cities."

27. Garry Kasparov, *Deep Thinking: Where Machine Intelligence Ends and Human Creativity Begins* (Public Affairs, 2017).

28. Parts of some books do explore the environmental politics of AI, such as Dain Bolwell, *Governing Technology in the Quest for Sustainability on Earth* (Routledge, 2019); and Fang Fei, Milind Tambe, Bistra Dilkina, and Andrew J. Plumptre, eds., *Artificial Intelligence and Conservation* (Cambridge University Press, 2019).

29. Malcolm Campbell-Verduyn, Marcel Goguen, and Tony Porter, "Big Data and Algorithmic Governance: The Case of Financial Practices," *New Political Economy* 22, no. 2 (2017): 219–236; Nick O'Donovan, "From Knowledge Economy to Automation Anxiety: A Growth Regime in Crisis?," *New Political Economy* (2019): 1–19, https://doi.org/10.1080/13563467.2019.1590326; Leonard Seabrooke, Eleni Tsingou, and Johann Ole Willers, "The Political Economy of Policy Vacuums: The European Commission on Demographic Change," *New Political Economy* (2019): 1–15, https://doi.org/10.1080/13563467.2019.1669549.

30. See, for instance, Elizabeth Thurbon and Linda Weiss, "Economic Statecraft at the Frontier: Korea's Drive for Intelligent Robotics," *Review of International Political*

Economy (2019): 1–25, https://doi.org/10.1080/09692290.2019.1655084; Nick Bernards and Malcolm Campbell-Verduyn, "Understanding Technological Change in Global Finance through Infrastructures," *Review of International Political Economy* 26, no. 5 (2019): 773–789; Marie Langevin, "Big Data for (Not So) Small Loans: Technological Infrastructures and the Massification of Fringe Finance," *Review of International Political Economy* 26, no. 5 (2019): 790–814; Sung-Young Kim, "Hybridized Industrial Ecosystems and the Makings of a New Developmental Infrastructure in East Asia's Green Energy Sector," *Review of International Political Economy* 26, no. 1 (2019): 158–182.

31. Several of these articles are by law and society scholars analyzing the links between "artificial legal intelligence" and power dynamics within societies. See, for instance, Mireille Hildebrandt, "Law as Computation in the Era of Artificial Legal Intelligence: Speaking Law to the Power of Statistics," *University of Toronto Law Journal* 68, supp. 1 (2018): 12–35. For an example of a critical political economy analysis of artificial intelligence, see Clea Bourne, "AI Cheerleaders: Public Relations, Neoliberalism and Artificial Intelligence," *Public Relations Inquiry* 8, no. 2 (2019): 109–125.

32. The quote "what data matters" is from ZDNet editor Larry Dignan, as quoted in Steve Ranger, "What Is the IoT? Everything You Need to Know about the Internet of Things Right Now," *ZDNet*, January 19, 2018, www.zdnet.com.

33. Peter Dauvergne and Jane Lister, *Eco-Business: A Big-Brand Takeover of Sustainability* (MIT Press, 2013).

34. Judy Wajcman, "Automation: Is It Really Different This Time?," *British Journal of Sociology* 68, no. 1 (2017): 123.

35. Jerry Kaplan, as interviewed in *Do You Trust This Computer?*, documentary film, 2018, at http://doyoutrustthiscomputer.org.

36. See Further Reading, "Sustainability (background)," "Sustainability (and environmentalism)," "Sustainability (pathways toward)," "Technology (critiques)," and "Technology and Sustainability."

37. "Autonomous Weapons: An Open Letter from AI & Robotics Researchers," Future of Life Institute, July 28, 2015, https://futureoflife.org/open-letter-autonomous-weapons.

38. "An Open Letter to the United Nations Convention on Certain Conventional Weapons," Future of Life Institute, 2017, https://futureoflife.org/autonomous-weapons-open-letter-2017.

39. Fei-Fei Li was on leave from Stanford University during her time as chief AI scientist for Google Cloud. At the end of 2018, she left Google and returned to Stanford. Portions of her email are reprinted in Scott Shane, Cade Metz, and Daisuke Wakabayashi, "How a Pentagon Contract Became an Identity Crisis for Google," *New York Times*, May 30, 2018, www.nytimes.com.

CHAPTER 2

1. Wang Haifeng is quoted in Owen Churchill, "China's AI Dreams," *Nature*, January 17, 2018, www.nature.com. For an overview of AlphaZero, see David Silver et al., "Mastering Chess and Shogi by Self-Play with a General Reinforcement Learning Algorithm," 2017, https://arxiv.org/pdf/1712.01815.pdf (see p. 4 for the number of hours AlphaZero took to surpass Stockfish's chess ability). Although AlphaZero trained for nine hours, playing 44 million games in total, it did not significantly improve over the last five hours of training (see p. 15).

2. Kenneth Cukier and Viktor Mayer-Schönberger, "The Rise of Big Data," *Foreign Affairs* 92, no. 3 (2013): 27–40.

3. Kenneth Cukier and Viktor Mayer-Schönberger, *Big Data: A Revolution That Will Transform How We Live, Work, and Think* (Houghton Mifflin Harcourt, 2013).

4. Evgeny Morozov, "Digital Technologies and the Future of Data Capitalism," *Social Europe*, June 23, 2015, www.socialeurope.eu; Sarah Myers West, "Data Capitalism: Redefining the Logics of Surveillance and Privacy," *Business & Society* 58, no. 1 (2019): 20–41. See also *Ethics and Legal in AI: Data Capitalism*, All-Party Parliamentary Group on Artificial Intelligence (APPG AI), UK House of Lords, June 26, 2017.

5. Netcraft, "June 2019 Web Server Survey," published by Netcraft Company, available at https://news.netcraft.com.

6. Radicati Group, *Email Statistics Report, 2019–2023* (Radicati Group, 2019), 3.

7. For a sampling of Ashton's writing, see Kevin Ashton, *How to Fly a Horse: The Secret History of Creation, Invention, and Discovery* (Anchor Books, 2015).

8. Knud Lasse Lueth, "State of the IoT 2018: Number of IoT Devices Now at 7B—Market Accelerating," *IOT Analytics*, August 8, 2018, https://iot-analytics.com. Estimating the number of active devices in the Internet of Things is very difficult, and figures vary depending on the definition of the IoT. The figures of the Gartner research firm, for instance, are higher than *IOT Analytics* (for example, Gartner projects that the number of devices in the IoT will reach 25 billion by 2021). See Gartner, "Gartner Identifies Top 10 Strategic IoT Technologies and Trends," *Gartner Newsroom*, November 7, 2018, www.gartner.com. Also see Further Reading, "Internet of Things."

9. For an optimistic vision of the value of the IoT for advancing sustainability, see Jeremy Rifkin, *The Zero Marginal Cost Society: The Internet of Things, the Collaborative Commons, and the Eclipse of Capitalism* (St. Martin's Press, 2014).

10. Glen Whelan, "Born Political: A Dispositive Analysis of Google and Copyright," *Business & Society* 58, no. 1 (2019): 42–73; J. M. Chenou and R. Radu, "The 'Right to Be Forgotten': Negotiating Public and Private Ordering in the European Union," *Business & Society* 58, no. 1 (2019): 74–102. See also Further Reading, "Big Tech (critiques for a general audience)."

11. eMarketer, "US Digital Ad Spending Will Pass Traditional in 2019," *eMarketer*, February 19, 2019, www.emarketer.com; Jasmine Enberg, "Digital Ad Spending 2019," *eMarketer*, March 28, 2019, www.emarketer.com.

12. For consistency, throughout this book I rely on data from the *Fortune* Global 500 list for estimates of corporate revenues (which ranks firms by total revenues for fiscal years ending "on or before March 31").

13. Andrew Marantz, "Mark Zuckerberg's Apology Tour," *New Yorker*, April 16, 2018.

14. For Zuckerberg's testimony, see Senator John Cornyn, "Cornyn Questions Facebook's Zuckerberg on Data Privacy Concerns," Joint Commerce and Judiciary Committee SH-216, www.youtube.com/watch?v=St9GkK5UHwE (published April 10, 2018). Few users read the fine print of "terms and conditions" when downloading apps or joining social media sites like Facebook, Instagram, LinkedIn, Snapchat, Spotify, and YouTube. Most agreements, as a 2018 BBC study revealed, require thirty to sixty minutes to read and a university education to comprehend fully. See Tom Calver and Joe Miller, "Social Site Terms Tougher than Dickens," *BBC News*, July 6, 2018.

15. Facebook, *f newsroom*, "Response to Six4Three Documents," December 4, 2018, https://newsroom.fb.com. See also UK Parliament, "Note by Damian Collins MP,

Chair of the DCMS [Digital, Culture, Media and Sport] Committee, Summary of Key Issues from the Six4Three Files," accessed December 6, 2018, www.parliament.uk (this includes Zuckerberg's email regarding "a few basic thresholds").

16. Jason Murdock, "Facebook Is Tracking You Online, Even If You Don't Have an Account," *Newsweek*, April 17, 2018.

17. SuperData, *2018 Year in Review: Digital Games and Interactive Media* (SuperData: A Nielsen Company, 2019), 7.

18. World Health Organization, 6C51.0 Gaming Disorder, Predominantly Online, *International Classification of Diseases–11*, June 2018, https://icd.who.int.

19. Eyal is quoted in Simone Stolzoff, "The Formula for Phone Addiction Might Double as a Cure," February 1, 2018; see also Nir Eyal, *Hooked: How to Build Habit-Forming Products* (Portfolio/Penguin, 2014). For detailed analysis of "internet addiction," see Christian Montag and Martin Reuter, *Internet Addiction* (Springer, 2017).

20. See Mike Allen, "Sean Parker Unloads on Facebook: 'God Only Knows What It's Doing to Our Children's Brains," *Axios*, November 2017, www.axios.com (this includes a link to a video of Sean Parker making these comments). See also David Kirkpatrick, *The Facebook Effect: The Inside Story of the Company That Is Connecting the World* (Simon & Schuster, 2010).

21. The letter, in conjunction with JANA Partners LLC (like the California State Teachers' Retirement System, an Apple shareholder) is posted on the CalSTRS website, www.calstrs.com.

22. Steyer is quoted in Farhad Manjoo, "It's Time for Apple to Build a Less Addictive iPhone," *New York Times*, January 17, 2018.

23. Simon Kemp, *Digital 2019: Global Digital Overview*, January 31, 2019, https://datareportal.com.

24. See Further Reading, "Security and Digital Technology."

25. Surveillance Camera Commissioner (Tony Porter), *Surveillance Camera Commissioner Annual Report 2016/17*, presented to Parliament pursuant to section 35(1) (b) of the Protection of Freedoms Act 2012, January 2018, 13.

26. Porter is quoted in Matthew Weaver, "UK Public Faces Mass Invasion of Privacy as Big Data and Surveillance Merge," *Guardian*, March 14, 2017.

27. Nigel Inkster, *China's Cyber Power* (Routledge, 2018); Adam Segal, "When China Rules the Web: Technology in Service of the State," *Foreign Affairs* 97, no. 5 (2018): 10–14, 16–18.

28. Chorzempa is quoted in Paul Mozur, "Inside China's Dystopian Dreams: A.I., Shame and Lots of Cameras," *New York Times*, July 8, 2018.

29. McKinsey Global Institute, *Digital Globalization: The New Era of Global Flows* (McKinsey & Company, March 2016). See the summary in brief.

30. Dirk Helbing, Bruno S. Frey, Gerd Gigerenzer, Ernst Hafen, Michael Hagner, Yvonne Hofstetter, Jeroen van den Hoven, Roberto V. Zicari, and Andrej Zwitter, "Will Democracy Survive Big Data and Artificial Intelligence," *Scientific American* 25 (February 2017), www.scientificamerican.com.

31. Comparing a zettabyte (or a trillion gigabytes) to the Library of Congress should be seen as illustrative and in no way definitive. My comparison assumes the library roughly equates to 333 terabytes of data and excludes its archiving of the World Wide Web (such as Twitter) and digital films, audio, and photographs. The estimate is from Tim Fisher, "Terabytes, Gigabytes, & Petabytes: How Big Are They?," *Lifewire*, May 10, 2018, www.lifewire.com. Another way to imagine a zettabyte is to zoom in

on the size of a terabyte, which equates to around 4.5 million 200-page books. The Library of Congress holds around 39 million books and other print materials in its catalogue, but it also contains a vast store of maps, photographs, recordings, sheet music, and other manuscripts.

32. McKinsey Global Institute, *Digital Globalization*, 31. The conversion to Shakespeare's works is from Ben Tarnoff, "Data Is the New Lifeblood of Capitalism: Don't Hand Corporate America Control," *The Guardian*, February 1, 2018.

33. For a political analysis of the global competition to build high-speed 5G mobile networks, see Paul Triolo and Kevin Allison, *Eurasia Group White Paper: The Geopolitics of 5G* (Eurasia Group, November 15, 2018).

34. International Data Corporation (authors David Reinsel, John Gantz, and John Rydning), *Data Age 2025: The Evolution of Data to Life-Critical* (International Data Corporation, April 2017), 3, 7.

CHAPTER 3

1. World Intellectual Property Organization (WIPO), *WIPO Technology Trends: Artificial Intelligence* (WIPO, 2019), 13–14. For an overview of the "deep learning revolution," see Terrence J. Sejnowski, *The Deep Learning Revolution: Artificial Intelligence Meets Human Intelligence* (MIT Press, 2018); for a succinct summary of deep learning, see Yoshua Bengio, "Machines Who Learn," *Scientific American* (June 2016): 46–51.

2. Ng is quoted in E. Kumar Sharma, "AI Is the New Electricity, Says Coursera's Andrew Ng," *Business Today*, March 5, 2018, https://www.businesstoday.in.

3. Lauren deLisa Coleman, "Inside Trends and Forecast for the $3.9T AI Industry," *Forbes*, May 31, 2018, www.forbes.com.

4. Greg Brockman, Ilya Sutskever, and OpenAI, "Introducing OpenAI," December 11, 2015, at https://blog.openai.com/introducing-openai.

5. See International Data Corporation (IDC), *Worldwide Semiannual Cognitive Artificial Intelligence Systems Spending Guide* (IDC, 2019). The estimates of the business value of AI are from the research and consulting firm Gartner as summarized in Charlie Osborne, "Artificial Intelligence Will Be Worth $1.2 Trillion to the Enterprise in 2018," *ZDNet*, April 25, 2018, www.zdnet.com.

6. PricewaterhouseCoopers (PwC) (authors Anand S. Rao and Gerard Verweij), *Sizing the Prize: What's the Real Value of AI for Your Business and How Can You Capitalise?* (PwC, 2017), 1, 4.

7. Heath Terry is quoted in "Two-Faced," *The Economist*, March 31, 2018, 12.

8. PricewaterhouseCoopers, *Sizing the Prize*, 9. PwC sees AI as a driving force of the "Fourth Industrial Revolution." See PwC, *Fourth Industrial Revolution for the Earth: Harnessing Artificial Intelligence for the Earth* (PwC, 2018). Klaus Schwab, the founder of the World Economic Forum, is a leading advocate of the idea that emerging technologies—artificial intelligence, nanotechnology, the IoT, robotics, quantum computing, and biotechnology—are now propelling a "fourth industrial revolution." See Klaus Schwab, *The Fourth Industrial Revolution* (World Economic Forum, 2016).

9. PricewaterhouseCoopers, *Sizing the Prize*, 1–9.

10. CB Insights, "The Race for AI: Google, Intel, Apple in a Rush to Grab Artificial Intelligence Startups," *Research Briefs*, February 27, 2018, www.cbinsights.com.

11. Alexandra Suich Bass, "GrAIt Expectations," *The Economist*, March 31, 2018, 4.

12. John Divine, "Artificial Intelligence Stocks: The 10 Best AI Companies," *U.S. News & World Report*, March 19, 2018.

13. Pichai is quoted in Lauren Goode, "Google CEO Sundar Pichai Compares Impact of AI to Electricity and Fire," *The Verge*, January 19, 2018, www.theverge.com.

14. Google AI, "Under the Hood of the Pixel 2: How AI Is Supercharging Hardware," at https://ai.google/stories/ai-in-hardware.

15. Joe Lawless, "Microsoft and the Future of AI," *MICCSR Case Studies* 12 (2018): 2, https://digitalcommons.tacoma.uw.edu/miccsr_case/12.

16. Microsoft, *The Future Computed: Artificial Intelligence and Its Role in Society* (Microsoft Corporation, 2018), 29.

17. See Microsoft Research AI, "Overview," www.microsoft.com.

18. Microsoft, *The Future Computed*, 41.

19. Alex Webb and Emily Chang, "Tim Cook Says Apple Focused on Autonomous Systems in Cars Push," *Bloomberg Technology*, June 13, 2017, www.bloomberg.com.

20. See Waymo, https://waymo.com; see also Graham Rapier, "Google's Waymo Is Crushing the Competition and Could Be Worth $135 Billion, UBS Says," *Business Insider*, May 11, 2018.

21. Intel and Strategy Analytics (author Roger Lanctot), *Accelerating the Future: The Economic Impact of the Emerging Passenger Economy*, June 2017, 4–5.

22. For details, see Further Reading, "Driverless Vehicles."

23. See Facebook AI Research at https://research.fb.com/category/facebook-ai-research.

24. Zuckerberg is quoted in Drew Harwell, "AI Will Solve Facebook's Most Vexing Problems, Mark Zuckerberg Says. Just Don't Ask When or How," *Washington Post*, April 11, 2018, www.washingtonpost.com.

25. LeCun is quoted in Drew Harwell, "Facebook, Boosting Artificial-Intelligence Research, Says It's 'Not Going Fast Enough,'" *Washington Post*, July 17, 2018.

26. Bezos in quoted in Todd Bishop, "Jeff Bezos Explains Amazon's Artificial Intelligence and Machine Learning Strategy," *GeekWire*, May 6, 2017, www.geekwire.com. See also Further Reading, "Business and AI."

27. The clothing example is from Ralf Herbrich, the director of machine learning at Amazon, as summarized in "In Algorithms We Trust," *The Economist*, March 31, 2018, 5.

28. For details (and the Limp quote), see Steven Levy, "Inside Amazon's Artificial Intelligence Flywheel," *Wired*, February 1, 2018, www.wired.com.

29. Bezos is quoted in Bishop, "Jeff Bezos Explains."

30. The McKinsey figures are summarized in "How AI Is Spreading throughout the Supply Chain," *The Economist*, March 31, 2018.

31. McMillon is quoted in Elaine Low, "Amazon Feud Is 'Absolutely Core' to Walmart-Microsoft Partnership," *Investor's Business Daily*, July 17, 2018, www.investors .com.

32. Li is quoted in Prableen Bajpai, "An In-Depth Look at Baidu's (BIDU) Artificial Intelligence Aspirations," *Nasdaq*, July 25, 2017, www.nasdaq.com.

33. Olivier Maugain and Luo Wang, "How Artificial Intelligence Is Transforming Advertising," *Marketing*, July 23, 2017, www.marketing-interactive.com. See also Greg Williams, "Why China Will Win the Global Race for Complete AI Dominance," *Wired UK*, April 16, 2018, www.wired.co.uk.

34. Bernard Marr, "Artificial Intelligence (AI) in China: The Amazing Ways Tencent Is Driving Its Adoption," *Forbes*, June 4, 2018, www.forbes.com.

35. Philipp Gerbert, Martin Reeves, Sam Ransbotham, David Kiron, and Michael Spira, "Global Competition of AI in Business: How China Differs," *MIT Sloan Management Review*, July 24, 2018, sloanreview.mit.edu.

36. Kai-Fu Lee, *AI Superpowers: China, Silicon Valley, and the New World Order* (Houghton Mifflin Harcourt, 2018), x (p. 4 is the source of my data on venture-capital funding in the China in 2017).

37. John R. Allen and Amir Husain, "The Next Space Race Is Artificial Intelligence," *Foreign Policy*, November 3, 2017, https://foreignpolicy.com. Also see Further Reading, "Artificial Intelligence (weaponization of)."

38. Chris Cornillie, "Finding Artificial Intelligence ˙ Money in the Fiscal 2020 Budget," *Bloomberg Government*, March 28, 2019, https://about.bgov.com.

39. Brent D. Sadler, "Fast Followers, Learning Machines, and the Third Offset Strategy," *Joint Force Quarterly* 83, no. 4 (2016), 13. See also Greg Allen and Taniel Chan, *Artificial Intelligence and National Security*, Harvard Kennedy School, Belfer Center for Science and International Affairs, July 2017.

40. Johnson is quoted in Jay Cassano, "Pentagon's Artificial Intelligence Programs Get Huge Boost in Defense Budget," *Fast Company*, August 15, 2018, www.fastcompany .com.

41. Ecatarina Garcia, "The Artificial Intelligence Race: U.S., Russia and China," *Modern Diplomacy*, April 19, 2018, https://moderndiplomacy.eu. See also Adrian Pecotic, "Whoever Predicts the Future Will Win the AI Arms Race," *Foreign Policy*, March 5, 2019, https://foreignpolicy.com; Michael C. Horowitz, "The Algorithms of August," *Foreign Policy*, September 12, 2018, https://foreignpolicy.com.

42. Elsa Kania, "China's AI Agenda Advances," *The Diplomat*, February 14, 2018, https://thediplomat.com.

43. Government of the People's Republic of China, *State Council Issued Notice of the New Generation Artificial Intelligence Development Plan*, Guofa no. 35, release date July 20, 2017.

44. *Three-Year Action Plan for Promoting Development of a New Generation Artificial Intelligence Industry (2018–2020)*, Chinese Ministry of Industry and Information Technology (MIIT), December 12, 2017, trans. Paul Triolo, Elsa Kania, and Graham Webster, "Translation: Chinese Government Outlines AI Ambitions through 2020," *New America*, January 26, 2018, www.newamerica.org.

45. Kania, "China's AI Agenda Advances"; Jill Dougherty and Molly Jay, "Russia Tries to Get Smart about Artificial Intelligence," *Wilson Quarterly* (Spring) (2018), https://wilsonquarterly.com. See also Gregory C. Allen, *Understanding China's AI Strategy: Clues to Chinese Strategic Thinking on Artificial Intelligence and National Security* (Center for a New American Security, February 2019).

46. Gerasimov is quoted in Sadler, "Fast Followers," 18.

47. Mark Minevich, "These Seven Countries Are in a Race to Rule the World with AI," *Forbes Technology Council*, December 5, 2017, 3, www.forbes.com; Samuel Bendett, "In AI, Russia Is Hustling to Catch Up," *Defense One*, April 4, 2018, www .defenseone.com; Jill Dougherty and Molly Jay, "Russia Tries to Get Smart about Artificial Intelligence," *Wilson Quarterly* (Spring 2018), https://wilsonquarterly.com.

48. Vladimir Putin, "Presidential Address to the Federal Assembly," March 1, 2018, http://en.kremlin.ru/events/president/news/56957.

CHAPTER 4

1. Kai-Fu Lee, *AI Superpowers: China, Silicon Valley, and the New World Order* (Houghton Mifflin Harcourt, 2018), 14.

2. Redfern is quoted in "Using AI to Avert 'Environmental Catastrophe,'" *University of Cambridge Research*, February 21, 2019, www.cam.ac.uk.

3. eBird, "Global Big Day 2019: The Biggest Day in Birding," *eBird News*, May 8, 2019, https://ebird.org.

4. See eBird, https://ebird.org; Steve Kelling et al., "eBird: A Human/Computer Learning Network to Improve Biodiversity Conservation and Research," *AI Magazine* (Spring 2013): 10–20; Brian L. Sullivan et al., "The eBird Enterprise: An Integrated Approach to Development and Application of Citizen Science," *Biological Conservation* 169 (2014): 31–40.

5. Gomes is quoted in Erin Biba, "Three Ways Artificial Intelligence Is Helping to Save the World," *Ensia*, April 26, 2016, https://ensia.com; see also Jim Robbins, "Paying Farmers to Welcome Birds," *New York Times*, April 15, 2014, D1–D2; BirdReturns, The Nature Conservancy, http://birdreturns.org.

6. See EarthCube, www.earthcube.org. For details on the use of AI in the environmental sciences, see Sue Ellen Haupt, Antonello Pasini, and Caren Marzban, eds., *Artificial Intelligence: Methods in the Environmental Sciences* (Springer, 2009).

7. *Living Blue Planet Report: Species, Habitat and Human Well-Being* (WWF International and the Zoological Society of London, 2015), 7; Food and Agriculture Organization (FAO) of the United Nations, *The State of World Fisheries and Aquaculture* (FAO, 2016), 5–6.

8. David A. Kroodsma et al., "Tracking the Global Footprint of Fisheries," *Science* 359, no. 6378 (2018): 904–908.

9. See Global Fishing Watch, http://globalfishingwatch.org.

10. Boerder is quoted and summarized in Cassie Williams, "Artificial Intelligence Shows Unprecedented Detail in Global Fishing Activities," *CBC News*, February 23, 2018, www.cbc.ca.

11. Nate Miller, "Machine Learning and Satellite Data Provide the First Global View of Transshipment Activity," Global Fishing Watch, July 23, 2018, http://globalfishingwatch.org.

12. Food and Agriculture Organization of the United Nations, *Report of the Expert Workshop to Estimate the Magnitude of Illegal, Unreported and Unregulated Fishing Globally*, FAO Fisheries and Aquaculture Report No. 1106, FIRO/R1106 (En), Rome, February 2–4, 2015.

13. For details, see Nathan A. Miller, Aaron Roan, Timothy Hochberg, John Amos, and David A. Kroodsma, "Identifying Global Patterns of Transshipment Behavior," *Frontiers in Marine Science* 5 (2018), https://doi.org/10.3389/fmars.2018.00240; Lacey Malarky and Beth Lowell, *No More Hiding at Sea: Transshipping Exposed*, Oceana Report, February 22, 2017.

14. Kristin Houser, "NASA Is Making a GPS for Space," *World Economic Forum*, August 28, 2018, www.weforum.org; Paul Voosen, "Science Insurgents Plot a Climate Model Driven by Artificial Intelligence," *Science*, July 26, 2018; NASA, Global Climate Change, https://climate.nasa.gov.

15. Ishveena Singh, "The Perfect Storm Called Artificial Intelligence and Geospatial Big Data," *Geoawesomeness*, November 14, 2017, http://geoawesomeness.com.

16. Pedro H. S. Brancalion et al., "Fake Legal Logging in the Brazilian Amazon," *Science Advances* 4, no. 8 (2018): eaat1192; Peter Dauvergne and Jane Lister, *Timber* (Polity, 2011); Peter Dauvergne, *Loggers and Degradation in the Asia-Pacific: Corporations and Environmental Management* (Cambridge University Press, 2001).

17. See Topher White, "The Fight against Illegal Deforestation with TensorFlow," *Google Blog*, March 21, 2018, https://blog.google/technology.

18. Maschler is quoted in Umberto Bacchi, "Artificial Intelligence Can Help Fight Deforestation in Congo: Researchers," *Reuters*, July 27, 2017, www.reuters.com; see also Elizabeth Dow Goldman and Molly Bergen, "How Artificial Intelligence Helped Us Predict Forest Loss in the Democratic Republic of the Congo," *World Resources Institute* (blog), July 26, 2017, www.wri.org. For details, see Elizabeth Goldman, Nancy Harris, and Thomas Maschler, *Predicting Future Forest Loss in the Democratic Republic of the Congo's Carpe Landscapes*, Technical Note (WRI, June 2017).

19. International Union for Conservation of Nature (C. R. Thouless et al.), *African Elephant Status Report: An Update from the African Elephant Database* (IUCN, 2106), 3; World Wide Fund for Nature (WWF), "African Elephant: Strong, Smart, but Vulnerable," WWF, accessed September 26, 2019, www.wwf.org.uk/wildlife/african-elephants.

20. Eric Dinerstein, "Announcing a Tech Breakthrough to Save Elephants and Lions and Much More," *Leonardo DiCaprio Foundation*, February 22, 2019, www.leonardodicaprio.org.

21. See Resolve, "TrailGuard AI," www.resolve.ngo.

22. Christian Nellemann, Rune Henriksen, Patricia Raxter, Neville Ash, Elizabeth Mrema, eds., *The Environmental Crime Crisis: Threats to Sustainable Development from Illegal Exploitation and Trade in Wildlife and Forest Resources* (United Nations Environment Program and GRID-Arendal, 2014), 4.

23. Russo is quoted in Beth Timmins, "Facial Recognition Tool Tackles Illegal Chimp Trade," *BBC News*, January 22, 2019, www.bbc.com.

24. McCormick and Russo are quoted in Nick Webster, "Chimp Facial Recognition Technology to Target Wildlife Traffickers," *The National*, March 3, 2019, www.thenational.ae.

25. Desmond is quoted in Timmins, "Facial Recognition Tool."

26. Russo is quoted in Adele Peters, "Facial Recognition for Chimp Searches the Internet for Stolen Baby Apes," *Fast Company*, January 17, 2019, www.fastcompany.com.

27. Long is quoted in Anne Casselman, "How Artificial Intelligence Is Changing Wildlife Research," *National Geographic*, November 13, 2018. www.nationalgeographic.com.

28. Van Oast is quoted in Casselman, "How Artificial Intelligence."

29. Glenn De'ath, Katharina E. Fabricius, Hugh Sweatman, and Marji Puotinen, "The 27-Year Decline of Coral Cover on the Great Barrier Reef and Its Causes," *Proceedings of the National Academy of Sciences* 109, no. 44 (2012): 17,995–17,999.

30. Terry P. Hughes et al., "Global Warming Transforms Coral Reef Assemblages," *Nature* 556, April 26 (2018): 492–496; Trevor Nace, "Half of the Great Barrier Reef Has Died since 2016," *Forbes*, April 19, 2018, www.forbes.com.

31. De'ath et al., "The 27-Year Decline," 17,995.

32. Jacinta Bowler, "Here's How Scientists Are Mapping the Decline of the Great Barrier Reef with AI," *Science Direct*, September 30, 2017, www.sciencealert.com;

Campbell Kwan, "How AI and Drones Are Trying to Save the Great Barrier Reef," *TechRepublic*, June 26, 2019, www.techrepublic.com.

33. See, for instance, Jonathan Rossiter, "A Robot That Eats Pollution," TEDxWarwick Talk, February 22, 2016, www.ted.com; Bradley Cantrell, Laura J. Martin, and Erle C. Ellis, "Designing Autonomy: Opportunities for New Wildness in the Anthropocene," *Trends in Ecology & Evolution* 32, no. 3 (2017): 156–166.

34. See, for instance, Justin Worland, "Drones Are Helping Catch Poachers Operating under Cover of Darkness," *Time*, March 31, 2018 (including Air Shepherd at https://airshepherd.org); Peter Kohler, "Launching the Marine Litter DRONET," The Plastic Tide (organization announcement), April 22, 2018, www.theplastictide.com; BioCarbon Engineering, www.biocarbonengineering.com.

35. Monga is quoted in Google AI, "AI for Everyone: Inside TensorFlow, Our Open-Source Machine Learning Platform," undated, https://ai.google/stories/tensorflow.

36. Microsoft News Center staff, "Microsoft Expands Artificial Intelligence (AI) Efforts with Creation of New Microsoft AI and Research Group," *Microsoft News Center*, September 29, 2016, https://news.microsoft.com.

37. Donald Kossmann, "Building a Global AI Supercomputer: The 2018 Microsoft Research Faculty Summit," *Microsoft Research Blog*, July 18, 2018, www.microsoft.com.

38. Microsoft News Center staff, "Microsoft Expands Artificial Intelligence."

39. Eric Horvitz and Mustafa Suleyman, "Introduction from the Founding Co-Chairs," *Partnership on AI*, September 28, 2016, www.partnershiponai.org.

40. Brad Smith, "AI for Earth Can Be a Game-Changer for Our Planet," *Microsoft: On the Issues*, December 11, 2017, https://blogs.microsoft.com.

41. See Stuart L. Pimm et al., "The Biodiversity of Species and Their Rates of Extinction, Distribution, and Protection," *Science* 344, no. 6187 (2014), https://doi.org/10.1126/science.1246752.

42. For Joppa's overview of AI for Earth, see Lucas N. Joppa, "The Case for Technology Investments in the Environment," *Nature* 552 (2017): 325–328.

43. Allenby is quoted in Suzanne Choney, "How AI for Earth Can Be a Force Multiplier for Sustainability Solutions," *Microsoft: On the Issues*, January 26, 2018, https://blogs.microsoft.com.

44. "PAWS: Protection Assistant for Wildlife Security," Center for Artificial Intelligence in Society, University of Southern California, accessed September 27, 2019, www.cais.usc.edu/projects/wildlife-security; Elizabeth Lee, "Artificial Intelligence: The New Weapon to Fight Wildlife Poachers," *VOA News*, video, July 10, 2019, www.voanews.com. See also Jackie Snow, "Rangers Use Artificial Intelligence to Fight Poachers," *National Geographic*, June 12, 2016, https://news.nationalgeographic.com.

45. Jonathan Baillie and Lucas Joppa, "Getting Back to Nature with AI," *Microsoft Corporate Blogs*, July 17, 2018, https://blogs.microsoft.com. For background on CSR at Microsoft, see Microsoft, *Microsoft 2018 Corporate Social Responsibility Report* (Microsoft, 2018).

46. For further examples, see Fang Fei, Milind Tambe, Bistra Dilkina, and Andrew J. Plumptre, eds., *Artificial Intelligence and Conservation* (Cambridge University Press, 2019). For a succinct survey of the prospects of advancing sustainability with artificial intelligence, see Tiffany Chen, "Artificial Intelligence as a Solution to Sustainability," in *Sustainable Innovation and Impact*, ed. Cary Krosinsky and Todd Cort (Routledge, 2018), 213–219.

47. The main UN organizing agency of the AI for Good Global Summit is the International Telecommunication Union. See *AI for Good Global Summit: Artificial Intelligence Can Help Solve Humanity's Greatest Challenges*, Conference Report, Geneva, June 7–9, 2017, https://ai.xprize.org; *AI for Good Global Summit: Accelerating Progress toward SDGs*, including webcast archives, Geneva, May 15–17, 2018, www.itu.int.

48. See OpenAI, https://openai.com.

49. WWF (World Wide Fund for Nature), *Living Planet Report 2018: Aiming Higher* (WWF International in collaboration with the Zoological Society of London, 2018), 90.

50. Xiaoxin Wang, Dabang Jiang, and Xianmei Lang, "Climate Change of 4°C Global Warming above Pre-industrial Levels," *Advances in Atmospheric Sciences* 35, no. 7 (2018): 757–770; Patrick T. Brown and Ken Caldeira, "Greater Future Global Warming Inferred from Earth's Recent Energy Budget," *Nature* 552, no. 7683 (2017): 45–50 (plus appendixes). Also see Further Reading, "Global Environmental Crisis."

CHAPTER 5

1. The Walmart and Bayer quotes are from Walmart, "Sustainability," corporate. walmart.com, and Bayer, www.bayer.com. The Google quote is from Google, *Environmental Report: 2017 Progress Update* (Google, October 2017), 6.

2. Kent (who stepped down as Coca-Cola's CEO in 2017) is quoted in Andrew L. Shapiro, "Coca-Cola Goes Green," *Forbes*, January 29, 2010; Nooyi (who stepped down as Pepsi's CEO in 2018) is quoted in PepsiCo, "PepsiCo Launches 2025 Sustainability Agenda Designed to Meet Changing Consumer and Societal Needs," *News Release*, October 17, 2016, www.pepsico.com.

3. See Peter Dauvergne and Jane Lister, *Eco-Business: A Big-Brand Takeover of Sustainability* (MIT Press, 2013); Adrian Parr, *Hijacking Sustainability* (MIT Press, 2012); Adrian Parr, *The Wrath of Capital: Neoliberalism and Climate Change Politics* (Columbia University Press, 2013). Also see Further Reading, "Sustainability (and business)."

4. For a sampling of how CSR and eco-business vary across firms, see Elizabeth Chrun, Nives Dolšak, and Aseem Prakash, "Corporate Environmentalism," *Annual Review of Environment and Resources* 41 (2016): 341–362; Hamish van der Ven, "Socializing the C-Suite," *Business and Politics* 16, no. 1 (2014): 31–63; and Further Reading, "Private Environmental Governance." For analyses of the commitment to sustainability of some corporate executives and middle managers within transnational corporations, see Geoffrey Jones, *Profits and Sustainability: A History of Green Entrepreneurship* (Oxford University Press, 2017); Andrew J. Hoffman, *Finding Purpose: Environmental Stewardship as a Personal Calling* (Greenleaf, 2016).

5. Google, *Environmental Report: 2017 Progress Update*, 3.

6. Anders Andrae's research is summarized (and he is interviewed) in John Vidal (for Climate Home News), "'Tsunami' of Data' Could Consume One Fifth of Global Electricity by 2025," *The Guardian*, December 11, 2017, www.theguardian.com. Andrae is updating earlier research, including Anders S. G. Andrae and Tomas Edler, "On Global Electricity Usage of Communication Technology: Trends to 2030," *Challenges* 6, no. 1 (2015): 117–157. The estimate of the percentage of data centers relying on fossil-fuel electricity is from Gary Cook, a climate and energy researcher with Greenpeace USA.

7. Lotfi Belkhir and Ahmed Elmeligi, "Assessing ICT Global Emissions Footprint: Trends to 2040 & Recommendations," *Journal of Cleaner Production* 177 (2018): 448–463, esp. 461.

8. André Staltz, "The Web Began Dying in 2014: Here's How," *OpenDemocracy*, November 27, 2017, www.opendemocracy.net.

9. Google, *Google Environmental Report 2019* (Google, 2019), 29; Google, *Environmental Report: 2017 Progress Update*, 26; Julia Pyper, "Google Officially Hits Its 100% Renewable Energy Target," *Greentech Media* (GTM), April 5, 2018, www.greentechmedia .com.

10. Gary Cook, "BREAKING: Greenpeace Applauds New Facebook Climate & Clean Energy Commitment," *Greenpeace USA* (news post), August 28, 2018, www.greenpeace .org/usa.

11. Greenpeace, *Doing Bigger Things: The Road to 100% Renewable Energy for Samsung Electronics* (Greenpeace East Asia Seoul office, August 2018), 1.

12. Cook, "BREAKING."

13. Google, "Google Data Centers: Efficiency—How We Do It," undated, www.google .com; Google, *Google Environmental Report 2019*, 19.

14. Adam Vaughn, "Google Uses AI to Cut Data Centre Energy Use by 15%," *The Guardian*, July 20, 2016, www.theguardian.com.

15. Eric Masanet et al., *The Energy Efficiency Potential of Cloud-Based Software: A U.S. Case Study* (Lawrence Berkeley National Laboratory, June 2013), 1, www.osti.gov/ scitech/servlets/purl/1171159.

16. Fuenffinger is quoted in Amanda Gasparik, Chris Gamble, and Jim Gao, "Safety-First AI for Autonomous Data Center Cooling and Industrial Control," *Inside Google*, August 17, 2018, www.blog.google/inside-google.

17. Google, *Environmental Report: 2017 Progress Update*, 23.

18. Hurst is quoted in Neal Karlinsky, "Powering a Clean Future," *The Amazon Blog*, December 5, 2017, https://blog.aboutamazon.com; see also, 3p editors, "Unpacking Corporate Responsibility at Amazon," *TriplePundit: People, Planet, Profit*, March 28, 2018, www.triplepundit.com. After Amazon employees called for greater action to mitigate climate change, in 2019 Amazon became the first company to sign a "Climate Pledge" to reach "net zero carbon" by 2040. CEO Jeff Bezos said his company would achieve this goal by investing in renewable energy, electric fleets, eco-technologies, and carbon offsets. As part of this pledge, he committed his company to achieving 100 percent renewable energy by 2030. See Rachel Siegel and Jay Greene, "Amazon CEO Jeff Bezos Announces New 'Climate Pledge' Ahead of Employee Protests," *Washington Post*, September 19, 2019, www.washingtonpost .com.

19. Lars Landberg and Elizabeth Traige, *Making Renewables Smarter: The Benefits, Risks, and Future of Artificial Intelligence in Solar and Wind Energy*, Group Technology & Research Position Paper, DNV GL, 2017. See also Tom Murray, "Amazon's Big Opportunity: Transparency in Sustainability," *Forbes*, April 2, 2018, www.forbes .com.

20. Peter Holley, "Amazon's One-Day Delivery Service Depends on the Work of Thousands of Robots," *Washington Post*, June 7, 2019, www.washingtonpost.com.

21. Steven Levy, "Inside Amazon's Artificial Intelligence Flywheel," *Wired*, February 1, 2018, www.wired.com.

22. Amazon staff, "5 Things You Don't Know about Amazon Packaging," *The Amazon Blog*, April 17, 2018, https://blog.aboutamazon.com.

23. Steve Banker, Chris Cunnane, and Clint Reiser, "The Amazon Supply Chain: The Most Innovative in the World?," *Logistics Viewpoints*, January 8, 2018, https:// logisticsviewpoints.com.

24. Chris Cunnane, "Amazon Launches Trucking App," *Logistics Viewpoints*, November 29, 2017, https://logisticsviewpoints.com.

25. Andrew Winston, *The Big Pivot: Radically Practical Strategies for a Hotter, Scarcer, and More Open World* (Harvard Business Review Press, 2014). The quote "making better" is from Andrew S. Winston, "Tackling the World's Challenges with Technology," *MIT Sloan Management Review* 58, no. 1 (2016); see also Andrew S. Winston, "Using AI to Help the World Thrive," *MIT Sloan Management Review*, February 1, 2018.

26. Blake Morgan, "How Amazon Has Reorganized around Artificial Intelligence and Machine Learning," *Forbes*, July 16, 2018, www.forbes.com.

27. Matthias Winkenbach, "Remapping the Last Mile of the Urban Supply Chain," *MIT Sloan Management Review* (blog), April 27, 2016, https://sloanreview.mit.edu.

28. Al Naqvi, "How AI and Robotics Can Transform CSR," *Ethical Corporation*, January 18, 2018, www.ethicalcorp.com.

29. See, for instance, DHL and IBM, *Artificial Intelligence in Logistics* (DHL and IBM, 2018).

30. Conor Riffle, "What Artificial Intelligence Means for Sustainability," *GreenBiz*, July 19, 2017, www.greenbiz.com (his article summarizes the research on the 10-K filings).

31. See Riffle, "What Artificial Intelligence Means" (including a summary of the research by the International Energy Agency).

32. Mahoney is quoted in Kevin Bullis, "Smart Wind and Solar Power," *MIT Technology Review* (April 23, 2014).

33. Bullis, "Smart Wind and Solar Power."

34. Bell is quoted in Adam Tucker, "Boston Startup Will Help GE Make Coal-Fired Power Plants Cleaner with Software," *GE Power*, April 19, 2016.

35. Carl Surran, "GE Working on Artificial Intelligence to Make Power Grids $200B More Efficient," *Seeking Alpha*, September 18, 2017, https://seekingalpha.com.

36. Tucker, "Boston Startup."

37. Quoted in Lauren Hepler, "The Sustainable Superpower? 5 Reasons for China's Clean Tech Boom," *GreenBiz*, July 18, 2017, www.greenbiz.com.

38. McKinsey Global Institute (authors Jacques Bughin, Eric Hazan, Sree Ramaswamy, Michael Chui, Tera Allas, Peter Dahlström, Nicolaus Henke, and Monica Trench), *Artificial Intelligence: The Next Digital Frontier?* (McKinsey & Company, 2017), 4.

39. See Celine Herweijer, Benjamin Combes, and Jonathan Gillham, *How AI Can Enable a Sustainable Future* (Microsoft in association with PricewaterhouseCoopers, 2019).

CHAPTER 6

1. Meredith Broussard, *Artificial Unintelligence: How Computers Misunderstand the World* (MIT Press, 2018).

2. World Health Organization, "Road Traffic Injuries," December 7, 2018, www.who.int. Records of traffic fatalities during the twentieth century are incomplete or nonexistent; the estimate of 60 million should be viewed as very rough. See Roberta Pesce, "Death in the 20th Century: The Infographic," *MedCrunch*, April 2, 2013, www.medcrunch.net.

3. Aaron Pressman, "Waymo Reaches 20 Million Miles of Autonomous Driving," *Fortune*, January 6, 2020, www.fortune.com.

4. IHS Markit, *Autonomous Vehicle Sales Forecast and Report* (IHS Markit, 2018).

5. This figure assumes that human error causes 90 percent of fatal collisions. See Michele Bertoncello and Dominik Wee, *Ten Ways Autonomous Driving Could Redefine the Automotive World* (McKinsey & Company, June 2015).

6. See Further Reading, "Driverless Vehicles" and "Electric Vehicles."

7. The United States alone has more than 4 million miles of roads, of which two-thirds are paved (see the Federal Highway of Administration, US Department of Transportation, www.fhwa.dot.gov).

8. Pieter Jan Kole, Ansje J. Löhr, Frank G. A. J. Van Belleghem, and Ad M. J. Ragas, "Wear and Tear of Tyres: A Stealthy Source of Microplastics in the Environment," *International Journal of Environmental Research and Public Health* 14, no. 10 (2017), 1265, https://doi:10.3390/ijerph14101265; Julien Boucher and Damien Friot, *Primary Microplastics in the Oceans: A Global Evaluation of Sources* (International Union for Conservation of Nature and Natural Resources, 2017).

9. International Energy Agency (IEA), *Global EV Outlook 2018* (IEA, 2018), 9–11; Enerdata, "Up to 50% of the Global Car Fleet Could Be Electric in 2050," *Enerdata—EnerFuture*, February 27, 2018, www.enerdata.net.

10. Megan Geuss, "In Shift toward Electric Vehicles, Volkswagen Looking for Cobalt Contracts," *Ars Technica*, September 24, 2017, https://arstechnica.com; Amnesty International, *"This Is What We Die For": Human Rights Abuses in the Democratic Republic of the Congo Power the Global Trade in Cobalt* (Amnesty International, 2016).

11. For a popular account of Tesla and the role of Elon Musk in transforming the electric car industry, see Hamish McKenzie, *Insane Mode: How Elon Musk's Tesla Sparked an Electric Car Revolution to End the Age of Oil* (Dutton, 2018).

12. Joey Gardiner, "The Rise of Electric Cars Could Leave Us with a Big Battery Waste Problem," *The Guardian*, August 10, 2017, www.theguardian.com.

13. Ian Smillie, *Diamonds* (Polity, 2014).

14. Jennifer Clapp, "The Distancing of Waste: Overconsumption in a Global Economy," in *Confronting Consumption*, ed. Tom Princen, Michael Maniates, and Ken Conca (MIT Press, 2002): 155–176; Peter Dauvergne, "The Problem of Consumption," *Global Environmental Politics* 10, no. 2 (2010): 1–10.

15. Rick Carragher, "New Alexa Smart Home Developer Tools Enable Seamless Voice Control of Any Device and Any Feature," *Alexa Blogs* on *Amazon Alexa*, September 20, 2018, https://developer.amazon.com.

16. Jean-Nicolas Louis, Antonio Calo, Kauko Leiviskä, and Eva Pongrácz, "Environmental Impacts and Benefits of Smart Home Automation: Life Cycle Assessment of Home Energy Management System," *IFAC–PapersOnLine* 48, no. 1 (2015): 880–885; Gulnar Mehdi and Mikhal Roshchin, "Electricity Consumption Constraints for Smart-Home Automation: An Overview of Models and Applications," *Energy Procedia* 83 (2015): 60–68.

17. Zion Market Research, *Smart Home Market: Global Industry Perspective, Comprehensive Analysis and Forecast, 2016–2022* (Zion Market Research, 2017). Also see Charlie Wilson, Tom Hargreaves, and Richard Hauxwell-Baldwin, "Benefits and Risks of Smart Home Technologies," *Energy Policy* 103 (2017): 72–83.

18. International Energy Agency, *Digitalization and Energy* (IEA, 2017), 83.

19. Markus Krajewski, "The Great Lightbulb Conspiracy," *Institute of Electrical and Electronics Engineers (IEEE) Spectrum* 51, no. 10 (2014): 56–61; Giles Slade, *Made to Break: Technology and Obsolescence in America* (Harvard University Press, 2006).

20. Joseph Guiltinan, "Creative Destruction and Destructive Creations: Environmental Ethics and Planned Obsolescence," *Journal of Business Ethics* 89, no. 1 (2009): 19–28; Kamila Pope, *Understanding Planned Obsolescence: Unsustainability through Production, Consumption and Waste Generation* (Kogan Page Publishers, 2017).

21. Apple, "Identify Your iPhone Model," November 13, 2019, https://support.apple.com/en-ca/HT201296.

22. Mike Wuerthele, "Apple Grabs 86% of Global Smartphone Profits, iPhone X Alone Seizes 35%," *appleinsider*, April 17, 2018, https://appleinsider.com.

23. Apple, "A Message to Our Customers about iPhone Batteries and Performance," December 28, 2017, www.apple.com.

24. The Apple spokesperson is quoted in Samuel Gibbs, "Apple Admits Slowing Older iPhones Because of Ageing Batteries," *The Guardian*, December 21, 2017, www.theguardian.com.

25. Ala Abdulla, Lance A. Raphael, Sam Mangano, Kirk Pedelty, and Ryan Glaze, plaintiffs, v. Apple, Inc., defendant, United States District Court for the Northern District of Illinois Eastern Division, Civil Action, Case no. 17-cv-9178, filed December 21, 2017, pp. 2–3, 13.

26. The attorney is quoted in Rachel Hinton, "Apple Sued in Chicago for Slowing Down Older iPhones," *Chicago Sun Times*, December 21, 2017, chicago.suntimes.com.

27. Gartner, "Gartner Says Global Smartphone Sales Stalled in the Fourth Quarter of 2018," *Newsroom: Press Releases*, February 21, 2019, www.gartner.com; Statista, "Number of Smartphones Sold to End Users Worldwide from 2007 to 2020 (in Million Units)," Statista, release date August, 2019, www.statista.com.

28. Rick Paulas, "All Good Gadgets Go to Waste," *New York Magazine*, July 31, 2018, http://nymag.com.

29. Mordor Intelligence, *Tantalum Market: Segmented by Products, Application, and Geography—Growth, Trends, and Forecast (2018–2023)* (Mordor Intelligence, April 2018).

30. Daniel Moran, Darian McBain, Keiichiro Kanemoto, Manfred Lenzen, and Arne Geschke, "Global Supply Chains of Coltan: A Hybrid Life Cycle Assessment Study Using a Social Indicator," *Journal of Industrial Ecology* 19, no. 3 (2015): 357–365; Michael Nest, *Coltan* (Polity, 2011); Peter Eichstaedt, *Consuming the Congo: War and Conflict Minerals in the World's Deadliest Place* (Chicago Review Press, 2011).

31. Brian Rohrig, "Smartphones: Smart Chemistry," *ChemMatters* (April–May) (2015): 10–12; Susie Levy, Christine Meisner Rosen, and Alastair Iles, "Mapping the Product Life Cycle: Rare Earth Elements in Electronics," *Case Studies in the Environment* 1, no. 1 (2017): 1–9.

32. Roskill, *Rare Earths: Global Industry, Markets & Outlook* (London: Roskill, 2018); María Victoria Riesgo García, Alicja Krzemień, Miguel Ángel Manzanedo del Campo, Mario Menéndez Álvarez, and Malcolm Richard Gent, "Rare Earth Elements Mining Investment: It Is Not All about China," *Resources Policy* 53 (2017): 66–76; Stefania Massari and Marcello Ruberti, "Rare Earth Elements as Critical Raw Materials: Focus on International Markets and Future Strategies," *Resources Policy* 38, no. 1 (2013): 36–43.

33. Ryan David Kiggins, *The Political Economy of Rare Earth Elements: Rising Powers and Technological Change* (Palgrave Macmillan, 2015).

34. Nawshad Haque, Anthony Hughes, Seng Lim, and Chris Vernon, "Rare Earth Elements: Overview of Mining, Mineralogy, Uses, Sustainability and Environmental Impact," *Resources* 3, no. 4 (2014): 614–635; Saleem H. Ali, "Social and Environmental Impact of the Rare Earth Industries," *Resources* 3, no. 1 (2014): 123–134; Jonathan Kaiman, "Rare Earth Mining in China: The Bleak Social and Environmental Costs," *The Guardian*, March 20, 2014.

35. Koen Binnemans, Peter Tom Jones, Bart Blanpain, Tom Van Gerven, Yongxiang Yang, Allan Walton, and Matthias Buchert, "Recycling of Rare Earths: A Critical Review," *Journal of Cleaner Production* 51 (2013): 1–22.

36. The estimate of eighty electrical devices in an average home is from Federico Magalini, a waste management expert at the sustainability consulting firm Sofies, summarized in Angela Chen, "Why Failing to Recycle Electronics Leaves Gold Mines Untapped," *The Verge*, July 3, 2018, www.theverge.com.

37. C. P. Baldé, V. Forti, V. Gray, R. Kuehr, and P. Stegmann, *The Global E-waste Monitor 2017: Quantities, Flows, and Resources* (United Nations University, International Telecommunication Union, and International Solid Waste Association, 2017), 45, 64.

38. Brian Heater, "Apple Has a New iPhone Recycling Robot Named 'Daisy,'" *TechCrunch*, April 19, 2018, https://techcrunch.com.

39. Michelle Heacock, Carol Bain Kelly, and William A. Suk, "E-Waste: The Growing Global Problem and Next Steps," *Reviews on Environmental Health* 31, no. 1 (2016): 131–135; Peter Dauvergne and Genevieve LeBaron, "The Social Cost of Environmental Solutions," *New Political Economy* 18, no. 3 (2013): 410–430.

40. Baldé et al., *The Global E-waste Monitor 2017* (this study converts annual e-waste into "Eiffel Towers"), 38. The figure for total e-waste in 2018 is from UN Environment, "UN Report: Time to Seize Opportunity, Tackle Challenge of E-Waste," *United Nations Environment Programme Press Release*, January 24, 2019, www.unenvironment .org. The projection of annual e-waste in 2050 is from Kuehr Ruediger, director of the sustainable cycles program at the United Nations University, as summarized in Platform for Accelerating the Circular Economy (PACE), *A New Circular Vision for Electronics: Time for a Global Reboot* (World Economic Forum, January 2019).

41. See Berrin Tansel, "From Electronic Consumer Products to E-Wastes: Global Outlook, Waste Quantities, Recycling Challenges," *Environment International* 98 (2017): 35–45. For an overview of the global politics of the electronics industry, see David S. Abraham, *The Elements of Power: Gadgets, Guns, and the Struggle for a Sustainable Future in the Rare Metal Age* (Yale University Press, 2015).

42. This compares the revenues of the global auto industry with the gross domestic product of countries in 2018. For the estimates of the revenues and employment figures of the global auto industry, see Venkat Sumantran, Charles Fine, and David Gonsalvez, *Faster, Smarter, Greener: The Future of the Car and Urban Mobility* (MIT Press, 2017), x.

43. Kate Crawford and Vladan Joler, *Anatomy of an AI System* (SHARE Foundation and AI Now Institute, 2018), 7, https://anatomyof.ai.

44. Jessica Lyons Hardcastle, "Internet of Things Driving Efficiency Gains across Industries," *Environmental Leader*, January 19, 2017, www.environmentalleader.com.

45. Christopher L. Magee and Tessaleno C. Devezas, "A Simple Extension of Dematerialization Theory," *Technological Forecasting & Social Change* 117 (April 2017): 196–205.

CHAPTER 7

1. United Nations, Department of Economic and Social Affairs, Population Division, *World Urbanization Prospects: The 2018 Revision* (2018); United Nations, Department of Economic and Social Affairs, Population Division, *World Population Prospects: The 2017 Revision, Key Findings and Advance Tables*, Working Paper No. ESA/P/WP/248 (2017), p. 2.

2. This index uses a wide range of variables to compare levels of sustainability, equity, and technological ingenuity. For details, see *IESE Cities in Motion Index* (IESE School of Business, University of Navarra, 2019).

3. International Data Corporation (IDC), *Worldwide Semiannual Smart Cities Spending Guide* (IDC, 2018).

4. For details, see Further Reading, "Smart Cities."

5. Venkat Sumantran, Charles Fine, and David Gonsalvez, *Faster, Smarter, Greener: The Future of the Car and Urban Mobility* (MIT Press, 2017); Andreas Herrmann, Walter Brenner, and Rupert Stadler, *Autonomous Driving: How the Driverless Revolution Will Change the World* (Emerald Publishing, 2018).

6. International Energy Agency (IEA), *World Energy Outlook 2017: Executive Summary* (IEA, 2017), 1–2.

7. Chris Lo, "Smart Cities: Redefining Urban Energy," *Power Technology*, February 8, 2018, www.power-technology.com; Cherrelle Eid, Rudi Hakvoort, and Martin de Jong, "Global Trends in the Political Economy of Smart Grids," in *The Political Economy of Clean Energy Transitions*, ed. Douglas Arent, Channing Arndt, Mackay Miller, Finn Tarp, and Owen Zinaman (Oxford University Press, 2017): 329–348. For a detailed analysis, see Jakob Stoustrup, Anuradha Annaswamy, Aranya Chakrabortty, and Zhihua Qu, eds., *Smart Grid Control: Overview and Research Opportunities* (Springer, 2019).

8. International Energy Agency (IEA), *Electricity Information 2018: Overview* (IEA, 2018).

9. Mircea Eremia, Lucian Toma, and Mihai Sanduleac, "The Smart City Concept in the 21st Century," *Procedia Engineering* 181 (2017): 12–19; Riccardo Bonetto and Michele Rossi, "Smart Grid for the Smart City," in *Designing, Developing, and Facilitating Smart Cities: Urban Design to IoT Solutions*, ed. Vangelis Angelakis, Elias Tragos, Henrich C. Pöhls, Adam Kapovits, and Alessandro Bassi (Springer, 2017): 241–263; Sarvapali D. Ramchurn, Perukrishnen Vytelingum, Alex Rogers, and Nicholas R. Jennings, "Putting the 'Smarts' into the Smart Grid: A Grand Challenge for Artificial Intelligence," *Communications of the ACM* 55, no. 4 (2012): 86–97.

10. See IBM, "Green Horizons," accessed March 12, 2019, www.research.ibm.com/green-horizons; Heather Clancy, "Artificial Intelligence Gets Smarter," *GreenBiz*, May 8, 2018, www.greenbiz.com.

11. Frost & Sullivan (an international consulting firm), "Frost & Sullivan Experts Announce Global Smart Cities to Raise a Market of Over $2 Trillion by 2025," April 4, 2018, https://ww2.frost.com.

12. Du Yifei, "Hangzhou Growing 'Smarter' Thanks to AI Technology," *People's Daily*, October 20, 2017, http://en.people.cn (Zheng Yijiong is quoted in this article); Xinhua, "AI-Driven Technology Reshaping City Traffic in China," *Xinhuanet*, March 10, 2018, www.xinhuanet.com.

13. Vincent Mao, "Wonders Develops Diverse Smart City Solutions with New Techs," *DigiTimes*, September 12, 2018, www.digitimes.com.

14. Chia Jie Lin, "Five Chinese Smart Cities Leading the Way," *GovInsider*, July 10, 2018, https://govinsider.asia.

15. Huawei, "IoT, Driving Verticals to Digitalization: Smart Parking," accessed March 12, 2019, www.huawei.com/minisite/iot/en/smart-parking.html.

16. Ren Xiaojin, "New Smart City to Serve as Model for Future Construction," *China Daily Europe*, June 9, 2017, www.chinadaily.com.cn.

17. Cai Chaolin is quoted in Chia Jie Lin, "Five Chinese Smart Cities."

18. For a balanced assessment of the advantages and disadvantages of smart cities, see Angelakis, Tragos, Pöhls, Kapovits, and Bassi, *Designing, Developing, and Facilitating Smart Cities*. Also see Further Reading, "Smart Cities."

19. William E. Rees, "Ecological Footprints and Appropriated Carrying Capacity: What Urban Economics Leaves Out," *Environment and Urbanization* 4, no. 2 (1992): 121–130. See also Mathis Wackernagel and William Rees, *Our Ecological Footprint: Reducing Human Impact on the Earth* (New Society Publishers, 1998).

20. Peter Dauvergne, *The Shadows of Consumption: Consequences for the Global Environment* (MIT Press, 2008); Joan Martínez-Alier, "Scale, Environmental Justice, and Unsustainable Cities," *Capitalism Nature Socialism* 14, no. 4 (2003): 43–63.

21. Thomas Princen, *Treading Softly: Paths to Ecological Order* (MIT Press, 2010); Jennifer Clapp and Doris A. Fuchs, eds., *Corporate Power in Global Agrifood Governance* (MIT Press, 2009); Jennifer Clapp, "The Distancing of Waste: Overconsumption in a Global Economy," in *Confronting Consumption*, ed. Thomas Princen, Michael Maniates, and Ken Conca (MIT Press, 2002): 155–176.

22. Peter Dauvergne, *Will Big Business Destroy Our Planet?* (Polity, 2018), 12.

23. As the International Energy Agency reminds us, smart appliances, electronics, and internet devices are set to be core sources of the rising demand for electricity over the next few decades. International Energy Agency, *World Energy Outlook 2017*, 2–3.

24. William Rees and Mathis Wackernagel, "Urban Ecological Footprints: Why Cities Cannot Be Sustainable—and Why They Are a Key to Sustainability," *Environmental Impact Assessment Review* 16, no. 4–6 (1996), 223.

25. See Further Reading, "Capitalism and Unsustainability."

26. Edoardo Croci, Sabrina Melandri, and Tania Molteni, "Comparing Mitigation Policies in Five Large Cities: London, New York City, Milan, Mexico City, and Bangkok," in *Cities and Climate Change: Responding to An Urgent Agenda*, ed. Daniel Hoornweg, Mila Freire, Marcus J. Lee, Perinaz Bhada-Tata, and Belinda Yuen (World Bank, 2011), 55.

27. Hugo Valin et al., "The Future of Food Demand: Understanding Differences in Global Economic Models," *Agricultural Economics* 45, no. 1 (2014): 51–67.

28. See Further Reading, "Smart Agriculture." For a succinct overview, see Kumba Sennaar, "AI in Agriculture: Present Applications and Impact," *TechEmergence*, September 16, 2018, www.techemergence.com.

29. S. Fuentes et al., "Automated Grapevine Cultivar Classification Based on Machine Learning Using Leaf Morpho-Colorimetry, Fractal Dimension and Near-Infrared Spectroscopy Parameters," *Computers and Electronics in Agriculture* 151 (2018): 311–318. Fuentes is quoted in Catriona May, "Five Ways Technology Is Changing the Ways We Drink," *Pursuit*, July 20, 2018, https://pursuit.unimelb.edu.au.

30. See Connecterra, www.connecterra.io. Yasir Khokhar is quoted in Victor Tangermann, "'Cow FitBits' Won't Make Cows Happier Because They're Not Milk Robots," *Futurism*, April 13, 2018, https://futurism.com.

31. Parmy Olson, "This Startup Built a Treasure Trove of Crop Data by Putting A.I. in the Hands of Indian Farmers," *Forbes*, October 15, 2018, www.forbes.com.

32. Rupavatharam is quoted in John H. Tibbetts, "From Identifying Plant Pests to Picking Fruit, AI Is Reinventing How Farmers Produce Your Food," *Ensia*, January 10, 2018, https://ensia.com.

33. See the video at the Blue River Technology, "Introducing See & Spray: Precisely Spraying Herbicides Only Where Needed," accessed October 11, 2019, http://smartmachines.bluerivertechnology.com.

34. See Harvest CROO Robotics, "About," accessed October 15, 2019, https://harvestcroo.com.

35. See Small Robot Company, accessed October 12, 2019, www.smallrobotcompany.com; Lauren James, "UK Robotics Start-Ups Using AI to Solve Pressing World Problems Show Their Ideas in Hong Kong," *South China Morning Post*, April 15, 2018, www.scmp.com.

36. Quoted in Mike Wilson and Ben Potter, "4 Ways Tech Will Transform Your Farm," *Farm Futures*, September 26, 2018, www.farmfutures.com.

37. Quoted in Grant Gerlock, "Farmers Look for Ways to Circumvent Tractor Software Locks," *National Public Radio*, April 9, 2017, www.npr.org.

38. See, for instance, Jennifer Clapp, *Food*, 3rd ed. (Polity, 2020); Nora McKeon, *Food Security Governance: Empowering Communities, Regulating Corporations* (Routledge, 2015); Colin K. Khoury et al., "Increasing Homogeneity in Global Food Supplies and the Implications for Food Security," *Proceedings of the National Academy of Sciences* 111, no. 11 (2014): 4001–4006; Matias E. Margulis, "The Regime Complex for Food Security: Implications for the Global Hunger Challenge," *Global Governance: A Review of Multilateralism and International Organizations* 19, no. 1 (2013): 53–67.

39. For a sampling of this literature, see Jennifer Clapp, "Mega-Mergers on the Menu: Corporate Concentration and the Politics of Sustainability in the Global Food System," *Global Environmental Politics* 18, no. 2 (2018): 12–33; Jennifer Clapp, Peter Newell, and Zoe W. Brent, "The Global Political Economy of Climate Change, Agriculture and Food Systems," *The Journal of Peasant Studies* 45, no. 1 (2018): 80–88; Peter Dauvergne, "The Global Politics of the Business of 'Sustainable' Palm Oil," *Global Environmental Politics* 18, no. 2 (2018): 34–52; Jennifer Clapp, "The Tradeification of the Food Sustainability Agenda," *Journal of Peasant Studies* 44, no. 2 (2017): 335–353; Philip Howard, *Concentration and Power in the Food System: Who Controls What We Eat?* (Bloomsbury Publishing, 2016).

40. Lucas Joppa, "AI Can Be a Game-Changer for the World's Forests. Here's How," *World Economic Forum*, September 11, 2018, www.weforum.org.

41. John Robert McNeill, *Something New under the Sun: An Environmental History of the Twentieth-Century World* (W. W. Norton, 2001); Dolly Jørgensen, Finn Arne Jørgensen, and Sara B. Pritchard, eds., *New Natures: Joining Environmental History with Science and Technology Studies* (University of Pittsburgh Press, 2013). See also Joseph Murphy, ed., *Governing Technology for Sustainability* (Earthscan, 2007); Victor Galaz, *Global Environmental Governance, Technology and Politics: The Anthropocene Gap* (Edward Elgar, 2014).

42. John Asafu-Adjaye et al., *An Ecomodernist Manifesto*, www.ecomodernist.org, April 2015 (the quote "a good . . ." is on p. 6).

43. Rosemary-Claire Collard, Jessica Dempsey, and Juanita Sundberg, "The Moderns' Amnesia in Two Registers," *Environmental Humanities* 7 (2015): 227–232; Bronislaw Szerszynski, "Getting Hitched and Unhitched with the Ecomodernists,"

Environmental Humanities 7 (2015): 239–244; Anne Fremaux and John Barry, "The 'Good Anthropocene' and Green Political Theory: Rethinking Environmentalism, Resisting Ecomodernism," in *Anthropocene Encounters: New Directions in Green Political Thinking*, ed. Frank Biermann and Eva Lövbrand (Cambridge University Press, 2019), 4.

CHAPTER 8

1. PricewaterhouseCoopers (PwC) (authors Anand S. Rao and Gerard Verweij), *Sizing the Prize: What's the Real Value of AI for Your Business and How Can You Capitalise?* (PwC, 2017), 5.

2. PricewaterhouseCoopers, *Sizing the Prize*, 7.

3. Wesley Charnock, "Artificial Intelligence: The New Cyber Crime Threat," *IFSEC Global*, June 21, 2018, www.ifsecglobal.com. Artificial intelligence, as this article mentions, is also proving to be a powerful tool in fighting cybercrime.

4. The concept of "fair earth share" is from William E. Rees and Jennie Moore, "Ecological Footprints, Fair Earth-Shares and Urbanization," in *Living within a Fair Share Ecological Footprint*, ed. Robert Vale and Brenda Vale (Routledge 2013): 3–32.

5. Global Footprint Network, "Data and Methodology" and "Open Data Platform," accessed January 17, 2020, http://data.footprintnetwork.org. See also David Lin et al., "Ecological Footprint Accounting for Countries: Updates and Results of the National Footprint Accounts, 2012–2018," *Resources* 7, no. 58 (2018), https://doi.org/10.3390/resources7030058.

6. Oxfam International, *Extreme Carbon Inequality*, Oxfam Media Briefing, December 2, 2015, 1.

7. *Forbes* tracks the wealth of the world's billionaires at www.forbes.com/billionaires. See also Kerry A. Dolan and Luisa Kroll, "*Forbes* Billionaires 2018: Meet the Richest People on the Planet," *Forbes*, March 6, 2018, www.forbes.com.

8. Angel Au-Yeung, "Meet the World's Richest Tech Billionaires in 2018," *Forbes*, March 6, 2018, www.forbes.com.

9. Oxfam International, *An Economy for the 99%* (Oxfam International, 2017), 2.

10. Credit Suisse Research Institute, *Global Wealth Report 2017* (Credit Suisse, 2017).

11. Chuck Collins and Josh Hoxie, *Billionaire Bonanza: The Forbes 400 and the Rest of Us* (Institute for Policy Studies, 2017), 2.

12. This estimate is from a UK House of Commons library study, as summarized in Michael Savage, "Richest 1% on Target to Own Two-Thirds of All Wealth by 2030," *The Guardian*, April 7, 2018, www.theguardian.com.

13. Oxfam International, *Reward Work, Not Wealth* (Oxfam International, 2018), 10; Macías and Byanyima are quoted in Reuters, "The World's Richest 1% Took Home 82% of Wealth Last Year, Oxfam Says," *Fortune*, January 22, 2018, http://fortune.com.

14. McKinsey Global Institute (authors James Manyika, Michael Chui, Mehdi Miremadi, Jacques Bughin, Katy George, Paul Willmott, and Martin Dewhurst), *A Future That Works: Automation, Employment, and Productivity* (McKinsey & Company, 2017).

15. Kai-Fu Lee, *AI Superpowers: China, Silicon Valley, and the New World Order* (Houghton Mifflin Harcourt, 2018), 19.

16. McKinsey Global Institute (authors Jacques Bughin, Eric Hazan, Sree Ramaswamy, Michael Chui, Tera Allas, Peter Dahlström, Nicolaus Henke, and Monica

Trench), *Artificial Intelligence: The Next Digital Frontier?* (McKinsey & Company, 2017).

17. McKinsey Global Institute (authors Dominic Barton, Jonathan Woetzel, Jeong-min Seong, and Qinzheng Tian), *Artificial Intelligence: Implications for China* (McKinsey & Company, 2017).

18. Karen Harris, Austin Kimson, and Andrew Schwedel, *Labor 2030: The Collision of Demographics, Automation and Inequality* (Bain & Company, 2018), 4.

19. Morgan R. Frank, Lijun Sun, Manuel Cebrian, Hyejin Youn, and Iyad Rahwan, "Small Cities Face Greater Impact from Automation," *Journal of the Royal Society Interface* 15 (2018), 20170946, https://doi.org/10.1098/rsif.2017.0946.

20. James Vincent, "Robots and AI Are Going to Make Social Inequality Even Worse, Says New Report," *Verge*, July 13, 2017, www.theverge.com; see also Boston Consulting Group, *The State of Social Mobility in the UK* (Sutton Trust, 2017).

21. Anton Korinek and Joseph E. Stiglitz, "Artificial Intelligence and Its Implications for Income Distribution and Unemployment," first published in December 2017 as a paper for a National Bureau of Economic Research Conference, republished in *The Economics of Artificial Intelligence: An Agenda*, ed. Ajay K. Agrawal, Joshua S. Gans, and Avi Goldfarb (University of Chicago Press, 2019).

22. Lee, *AI Superpowers*, 146.

23. Lee, *AI Superpowers*, 172. For an analysis of the potential positive and negative consequences of artificial intelligence for development in the poorer regions of the global South, see International Development Research Centre (IDRC) (authors Matthew L. Smith and Sujaya Neupane), *Artificial Intelligence and Human Development* (IDRC, 2018).

24. Jennifer Wang, "The Richest Women in the World in 2018," *Forbes*, March 6, 2018, www.forbes.com.

25. Valentina Zarya, "Female Founders Got 2% of Venture Capital Dollars in 2017," *Fortune*, January 31, 2018, http://fortune.com.

26. Tom Simonite, "AI Is the Future—But Where Are the Women?," *Wired*, August 17, 2018, www.wired.com.

27. The Google employee is quoted in Matthew Weaver, Alex Hern, Victoria Bekiempis, Lauren Hepler, and Jose Fermoso, "Google Walkout: Global Protests after Sexual Misconduct Allegations," *The Guardian*, November 1, 2018, www.theguardian.com.

28. Jeffrey Dastin, "Amazon Scraps Secret AI Recruiting Tool That Showed Bias against Women," *Reuters*, October 9, 2018, www.reuters.com; Simonite, "AI Is the Future."

29. Google, *Google Diversity Annual Report 2018* (Google, 2018), 5, 9; Facebook, "Facebook Diversity Update," 2018, www.facebook.com/careers/diversity-report.

30. Fei-Fei Li and Melinda Gates were speaking to Jessi Hempel; the transcripts are reprinted in Jessi Hempel, "Melinda Gates and Fei-Fei Li Want to Liberate AI from 'Guys with Hoodies,'" *Wired*, May 4, 2017, www.wired.com.

31. Meredith Broussard, *Artificial Unintelligence: How Computers Misunderstand the World* (MIT Press, 2018).

32. Anandkumar is quoted in Simonite, "AI Is the Future."

33. See AI4ALL at http://ai-4-all.org.

34. Bettina Büchel, "Artificial Intelligence Could Reinforce Society's Gender Equality Problems," *The Conversation*, March 1, 2018, https://theconversation.com. See

also Jesse Emspak, "How a Machine Learns Prejudice," *Scientific American*, December 29, 2016, www.scientificamerican.com.

35. For a summary of Amazon's struggles to create a smart hiring tool, see Dastin, "Amazon Scraps Secret AI Recruiting Tool" (which includes Shah's quote).

36. Julia Angwin, Jeff Larson, Surya Mattu, and Lauren Kirchner, "Machine Bias," *ProPublica*, May 23, 2016, www.propublica.org.

37. Whittaker is quoted in Randy Rieland, "Artificial Intelligence Is Now Used to Predict Crime. But Is It Biased?," *Smithsonian.com*, March 5, 2018, www.smithsonianmag.com.

38. Julia Dressel and Hany Farid, "The Accuracy, Fairness, and Limits of Predicting Recidivism," *Science Advances* 4, no. 1 (2018): eaao5580. Other studies confirm the potential for systemic algorithmic bias in predictive policing tools. See, for instance, Alexander Babuta and Marion Oswald, *Data Analytics and Algorithmic Bias in Policing* (Royal United Services Institute for Defence and Security Studies, Briefing Paper, 2019).

39. Azadzoy is quoted in Erin Brodwin, "The Startup behind a Tool Designed to Save You a Doctor's Visit Has Partnered with Bill and Melinda Gates," *Business Insider*, October 10, 2018, www.businessinsider.com.

40. For details, see Ada Health, "About Ada," accessed January 13, 2020, https://ada.com/about.

41. Brian Wahl, Aline Cossy-Gantner, Stefan Germann, and Nina R Schwalbe, "Artificial intelligence (AI) and Global Health: How Can AI Contribute to Health in Resource-Poor Settings?," *BMJ Global Health* 3 (2018): e000798.

42. Lee, *AI Superpowers*, 112–113 (the quote is on p. 113); see also Smart Finance, www.smartfinancegroup.com.

43. Paul Nemitz, "Constitutional Democracy and Technology in the Age of Artificial Intelligence," *Philosophical Transactions of the Royal Society A* 376 (2018), 20180089, https://doi.org/10.1098/rsta.2018.0089 (the quotes are on p. 2).

44. For details, see Joshua A. Kroll, "The Fallacy of Inscrutability," *Philosophical Transactions of the Royal Society A* 376 (2018), 20180084, https://doi.org/10.1098/rsta.2018.0084.

45. Schultz is quoted in Rieland, "Artificial Intelligence."

46. For thoughtful reflections on possible ways to move toward "ethical," "responsible," and "sustainable" governance of artificial intelligence and intelligent robots, see Corinne Cath, "Governing Artificial Intelligence: Ethical, Legal, and Technical Opportunities and Challenges," *Philosophical Transactions of the Royal Society A* 376 (2018), 20180080, https://doi.org/10.1098/rsta.2018.0080; Alan F. T. Winfield and Marina Jirotka, "Ethical Governance Is Essential to Building Trust in Robotics and Artificial Intelligence Systems," *Philosophical Transactions of the Royal Society A* 376 (2018), 20180085, https://doi.org/10.1098/rsta.2018.0085; Chris Reed, "How Should We Regulate Artificial Intelligence?," *Philosophical Transactions of the Royal Society A* 376 (2018), 20170360, https://doi.org/10.1098/rsta.2017.0360; Ugo Pagallo, "Apples, Oranges, Robots: Four Misunderstandings in Today's Debate on the Legal Status of AI Systems," *Philosophical Transactions of the Royal Society A* 376 (2018), 20180168, https://doi.org/10.1098/rsta.2018.0168; Luciano Floridi, "Soft Ethics, the Governance of the Digital and the General Data Protection Regulation," *Philosophical Transactions of the Royal Society A* 376 (2018), 20180081, https://doi.org/10.1098/rsta.2018.0081; Vidushi Marda, "Artificial Intelligence Policy in India: A Framework for Engaging the Limits of Data-Driven Decision-Making," *Philosophical Transactions of the Royal Society A* 376 (2018), 20180087, https://doi.org/10.1098/rsta.2018.0087.

CHAPTER 9

1. Shindell is quoted in Deborah Zabarenko, "2005 Was Warmest Year on Record: NASA," *Reuters*, January 25, 2006.

2. Even a rise of 1.5°C to 2.0°C is going to cause widespread global environmental change. See Intergovernmental Panel on Climate Change (IPCC), *Global Warming of 1.5°C: Summary for Policymakers* (IPCC, 2018), www.ipcc.ch.

3. This estimate is based on data from the Copernicus Climate Change Service. See Copernicus Climate Change Service, "Last Four Years Have Been the Warmest on Record—and CO2 Continues to Rise," *Copernicus Communication—European Centre for Medium-Range Weather Forecasts*, January 7, 2018, https://climate.copernicus.eu.

4. Laure Zanna, Samar Khatiwala, Jonathan M. Gregory, Jonathan Ison, and Patrick Heimbach, "Global Reconstruction of Historical Ocean Heat Storage and Transport," *Proceedings of the National Academy of Sciences* 116, no. 4 (2019): 1126–1131.

5. António Guterres, "Secretary General's Address to the General Assembly," *United Nations Secretary General*, September 25, 2018, http://webtv.un.org. See also Yann Robiou du Pont and Malte Meinshausen, "Warming Assessment of the Bottom-Up Paris Agreement Emissions Pledges," *Nature Communications* 9, no. 1 (2018).

6. See Corinne Le Quéré et al., "Global Carbon Budget 2018," *Earth System Science Data* 10, no. 4 (2018): 2143, https://doi.org/10.5194/essd-10-2141-2018; Rebecca Lindsey, "Climate Change: Atmospheric Carbon Dioxide," *Climate.gov* (National Oceanic and Atmospheric Administration), September 19, 2019, www.climate.gov.

7. See National Oceanic and Atmospheric Administration, "Carbon Dioxide Levels Hit Record Peak in May," *Earth System Research Laboratory: Global Monitoring Division* (National Oceanic and Atmospheric Administration), June 4, 2019, www.esrl.noaa.gov.

8. See Le Quéré et al., "Global Carbon Budget 2018," 2141–2194. Reay is quoted in Damian Carrington, "'Brutal News': Global Carbon Emissions Jump to All-Time High in 2018," *Guardian*, December 5, 2018, www.theguardian.com.

9. International Energy Agency (IEA), *Oil 2018: Analysis and Forecasts to 2023: Executive Summary* (Organization for Economic Co-operation and Development and IEA, 2018), 3, for the quote; International Energy Agency, *Oil 2019: Analysis and Forecasts to 2024: Executive Summary* (Organization for Economic Co-operation and Development and IEA, 2019), esp. 2. Also see Christophe McGlade and Paul Ekins, "The Geographical Distribution of Fossil Fuels Unused When Limiting Global Warming to 2°C," *Nature* 517, no. 7533 (2015): 187–193.

10. BP, *BP Statistical Review of World Energy* (BP, 2019), 16, 32, 44. For a projection of when global coal production will peak, see Minqi Li, "World Coal 2018–2050: World Energy Annual Report (Part 4)," posted on *Peak Oil Barrel*, September 20, 2018, http://peakoilbarrel.com. For data on investments in coal production, see Urgewald and BankTrack, Media Briefing, "COP24: New Research Reveals the Banks and Investors Financing the Expansion of the Global Coal Plant Fleet," *Coalexit.org*, December 5, 2018, https://coalexit.org.

11. Nicola Jones, "Machine Learning Tapped to Improve Climate Forecasts," *Nature* 548 (August 24, 2017): 379–380.

12. Evan Patrick, "Artificial Intelligence Has Its Sights Set on America's Oil and Gas Fields. Here's What to Expect," *Environmental Defense Fund Blog*, August 1, 2018, www.edf.org/blog.

13. Oil analyst Florian Thaler made this prediction, as quoted in Irina Slav, "The Future of Artificial Intelligence in Oil and Gas," *OilPrice*, December 22, 2018, https://oilprice.com.

14. McKinsey Global Institute (authors Michael Chui, James Manyika, Mehdi Mire-madi, Nicolaus Henke, Rita Chung, Pieter Nel, and Sankalp Malhotra), *Notes from the AI Frontier: Insights from Hundreds of Use Cases* (McKinsey Global Institute, April 2018), 18. See also International Data Corporation (IDC), *2018 Oil & Gas Predictions Report* (IDC, 2018).

15. MarketsandMarkets, *AI in Oil & Gas Market by Type (Hardware, Software, Services), Application (Upstream, Midstream, Downstream), Function (Predictive Maintenance, Production Planning, Field Service, Material Movement, Quality Control), and Region—Global Forecast to 2022* (MarketsandMarkets, December 2017).

16. Scott Kimbleton and John Matson, "Cognitive Computing: Augmenting Human Intelligence to Improve Oil and Gas Outcomes," *Journal of Petroleum Technology* 70, no. 4 (2018).

17. Geoffrey Cann, "The Three Ways AI Will Impact Oil and Gas," *Energy Now Media*, August 6, 2018, https://energynow.ca. See also Geoffrey Cann and Rachael Goydan, *Bits, Bytes, and Barrels: The Digital Transformation of Oil and Gas* (MADCann Press, 2019).

18. See Kumba Sennaar, "Artificial Intelligence in Oil and Gas: Comparing the Applications of 5 Oil Giants," *Emerj*, December 12, 2018, https://emerj.com.

19. Brian Merchant, "How Google, Microsoft, and Big Tech Are Automating the Climate Crisis," *Gizmodo*, February 21, 2019, https://gizmodo.com.

20. "Rockwell Automation and Schlumberger Enter Joint Venture Agreement to Create Sensia, the Oil and Gas Industry's First Fully Integrated Automation Solutions Provider," *Business Wire*, February 19, 2019, www.businesswire.com. For details on Huawei, see "Huawei Joins Hands with PCITC to Embrace Smart Factory 2.0," *PR Newswire* (Cision), November 13, 2017, www.prnewswire.com.

21. Tony Paikeday, "NVIDIA and Baker Hughes, a GE Company, Pump AI into Oil & Gas Industry," *NVIDIA Blog*, January 29, 2018, https://blogs.nvidia.com.

22. Reprinted in Karen Weise, "Employees Push Amazon to Do More on Climate," *New York Times*, April 11, 2019, B3. For details on the machine learning products designed by Amazon Web Services for the oil and gas industry, see https://aws.amazon.com/oil-and-gas.

23. Mann is quoted in Brian Merchant, "Amazon Is Aggressively Pursuing Big Oil as It Stalls Out on Clean Energy," *Gizmodo*, April 8, 2019, https://gizmodo.com.

24. Dale Schilling, Julian King, Rohin Wood, and Tom Vogt, "Mining Value in AI," *Mining Journal*, June 23, 2017, www.mining-journal.com.

25. Heidi Vella, "The Fourth Industrial Revolution: Bringing AI to Mining," *Mining Journal*, December 19, 2017, www.mining-journal.com.

26. Bernard Marr, "The 4th Industrial Revolution: How Mining Companies Are Using AI, Machine Learning and Robots," *Forbes*, September 7, 2018, www.forbes.com.

27. Parker is quoted in Ry Crozier, "Rio Tinto to Build New 'Intelligent' Mines," *iTnews*, June 19, 2018, www.itnews.com.au.

28. Christopher L. Magee and Tessaleno C. Devezas, "A Simple Extension of Dematerialization Theory," *Technological Forecasting & Social Change* 117 (April 2017): 196–205.

29. See United Nations, Sustainable Development Goals, "Goal 12: Responsible Consumption and Production," accessed January 18, 2019, www.un.org/sustainabledevelopment/sustainable-consumption-production.

30. WWF and Institute of Zoology, *Living Planet Report 2018: Aiming Higher (Summary)* (WWF and Zoological Society of London, 2018), 18; Krista Greer et al., "Global

Trends in Carbon Dioxide (CO2) Emissions from Fuel Combustion in Marine Fisheries from 1950 to 2016," *Marine Policy* 107 (September 2019), https://doi.org/ 10.1016/j.marpol.2018.12.001; Food and Agriculture Organization of the United Nations (FAO), *The State of Food Security and Nutrition in the World: Building Climate Resilience and Food Security and Nutrition* (FAO, 2018), 2 (for the figure on chronic malnutrition); FAO, *Global Food Losses and Food Waste: Extent, Causes and Prevention* (FAO, 2011).

31. Calculated from 2016 data from the Global Footprint Network, "Open Data Platform," accessed January 20, 2020, http://data.footprintnetwork.org.

32. Credit Suisse Research Institute, *Global Wealth Report 2017* (Credit Suisse, 2017); Oxfam, *Extreme Carbon Inequality*, Oxfam Briefing, December 2, 2015.

33. For an analysis of the cultural political economy of the automobile, see Matthew Paterson, *Automobile Politics: Ecology and Cultural Political Economy* (Cambridge University Press, 2007).

34. The estimate of how much oil goes into making plastics is from World Economic Forum, *The New Plastics Economy: Rethinking the Future of Plastics* (World Economic Forum, January 2016), 7. The estimate of global plastic production until 2019 and the projection until 2060 are extrapolated from data in Jenna R. Jambeck, Roland Geyer, Chris Wilcox, Theodore R. Siegler, Miriam Perryman, Anthony Andrady, Ramani Narayan, and Kara Lavender Law, "Plastic Waste Inputs from Land into the Ocean," *Science* 347, no. 6223 (2015): 768–771.

35. United Nations Environment Program (UNEP), *Marine Plastic Debris and Microplastics—Global Lessons and Research to Inspire Action and Guide Policy Change* (UNEP, 2016), 38.

36. Julien Boucher and Damien Friot, *Primary Microplastics in the Oceans: A Global Evaluation of Sources* (International Union for Conservation of Nature and Natural Resources, 2017). The estimate of the percentage of plastic waste that is recycled is from Roland Geyer, Jenna R. Jambeck, and Kara Lavender Law, "Production, Use, and Fate of All Plastics Ever Made," *Science Advances* 3, no. 7 (2017), 1. The estimate of tire pollution is from P. J. Kole, A. J. Löhr, F. G. Van Belleghem, and A. M. Ragas, "Wear and Tear of Tyres: A Stealthy Source of Microplastics in the Environment," *International Journal of Environmental Research and Public Health* 14, no. 10 (2017), 1265, https://doi:10.3390/ijerph14101265.

37. Laurent Lebreton et al., "Evidence That the Great Pacific Garbage Patch Is Rapidly Accumulating Plastic," *Scientific Reports* 8, no. 1 (2018): 1–15.

38. Boris Worm, Heike K. Lotze, Isabelle Jubinville, Chris Wilcox, and Jenna Jambeck, "Plastic as a Persistent Marine Pollutant," *Annual Review of Environment and Resources* 42, no. 1 (2017): 1–26; N. M. Hall, K. L. E. Berry, L. Rintoul, and M. O. Hoogenboom, "Microplastic Ingestion by Scleractinian Corals," *Marine Biology* 162, no. 3 (2015): 725–732. Also see Peter Dauvergne, "Why Is the Global Governance of Plastic Failing the Oceans?," *Global Environmental Change* 51 (July 2018): 22–31; Peter Dauvergne, "The Power of Environmental Norms: Marine Plastic Pollution and the Politics of Microbeads," *Environmental Politics* 27, no. 4 (2018): 579–597.

39. Mikaela Weisse and Elizabeth Dow Goldman, "2017 Was the Second-Worst Year on Record for Tropical Tree Cover Loss," *World Resources Institute Blog*, June 26, 2018, www.wri.org. "Tree cover loss" includes the canopy loss of both natural forests and plantations.

40. For an analysis of the global environmental politics of the palm oil industry, see Peter Dauvergne, "The Global Politics of the Business of 'Sustainable' Palm Oil," *Global Environmental Politics* 18, no 2 (2018): 34–52. Also see Rachel D. Garrett et

al., "Criteria for Effective Zero-Deforestation Commitments," *Global Environmental Change* 54 (2019): 135–147.

41. Statista, "Global Advertising Spending from 2014 to 2021 (in Billion U.S. Dollars)," Statista, last updated June 17, 2019, www.statista.com.

42. McKinsey Global Institute, *Notes from the AI Frontier*, 18.

43. Michael Brenner, "How to Use Artificial Intelligence to Boost Sales," Concured, January 10, 2019, www.concured.com. See also Michael Brenner, "How Deep Learning Will Drive the Future of Marketing," Marketing Insider Group, January 16, 2019, https://marketinginsidergroup.com; Tom Chavez, Chris O'Hara, and Vivek Vaidya, *Data Driven: Harnessing Data and AI to Reinvent Customer Engagement* (McGraw-Hill Education, 2018).

44. NtechLab, https://ntechlab.com; "Russian Startup Will Implement a Facial Recognition System in the Domestic Shopping Malls," *Scienews*, April 13, 2018, http://scienews.com.

45. Ian MacKenzie, Chris Meyer, and Steve Noble, "How Retailers Can Keep Up with Consumers," *McKinsey & Company Retail* (online), October 2013, www.mckinsey.com; Blake Morgan, "How Amazon Has Reorganized around Artificial Intelligence and Machine Learning," *Forbes,* July 16, 2018, www.forbes.com.

46. Galagher Jeff is quoted in Mike O'Brien, "How Walmart Is Going All in on Artificial Intelligence," *ClickZ,* January 22, 2019, www.clickz.com. For a sense of how some Walmart employees and customers are reacting to robotic staff, see Drew Harwell, "Meet Your New Co-Worker," *Washington Post,* June 9, 2019, G01. (As Harwell shows, some customers seem to enjoy taunting and occasionally kicking the robots.)

47. Pichai is quoted in Jillian D'Onfro, "Google's CEO Is Looking to the Next Big Thing beyond Smartphones," *Business Insider,* April 21, 2016, www.businessinsider.com.

48. Stat Counter, "Search Engine Market Share Worldwide: Dec 2017–Dec 2018," *GlobalStats,* accessed January 22, 2018, http://gs.statcounter.com; Statista, "Advertising Revenue of Google from 2001 to 2018 (in Billion U.S. Dollars)," Statista, last updated April 29, 2019, www.statista.com.

49. Matthew Johnston, "How Facebook Makes Money: Advertising Dominates Revenue, But Growth is Slowing," *Investopedia,* updated January 12, 2020, www.investopedia.com.

50. Quiñonero Candela is quoted in Steven Levy, "Inside Facebook's AI Machine," *Wired,* February 23, 2017, www.wired.com. See also Further Reading, "Social Media (industry and politics)" and "Big Tech (critiques for a general audience)."

51. Kai-Fu Lee, *AI Superpowers: China, Silicon Valley, and the New World Order* (Houghton Mifflin Harcourt, 2018), 68–69; Wang Chen, "Food Delivery Apps Skewered for Creating Plastic Waste," *chinadialogue,* October 3, 2018, www.chinadialogue.net; Cheng Yu, "Nation's Taste for Online Food Delivery Grows," *China Daily,* May 25, 2018, www.chinadaily.com.cn.

52. Mark Purdy and Paul Daugherty, *How AI Boosts Industry Profitability and Innovation* (Accenture Research, 2017), 10–16 (data), 8 (the quote "holds vast"), 16 (the quote "offers unprecedented"). Accenture is a leading consulting and information technology company, with revenues in fiscal year 2019 (ending August 31) of $43 billion.

53. For details, see Further Reading, "Capitalism and Unsustainability" and "Global Environmental Crisis."

CHAPTER 10

1. See Global Witness, *Honduras: The Deadliest Place to Defend the Planet* (Global Witness, 2017); Global Witness, *Enemies of the State* (Global Witness, 2019).

2. See China Development Brief, "English Translation of China's New Law on Overseas NGOs," *China Development Brief*, May 3, 2016, www.chinadevelopmentbrief .cn. For an overview of environmental NGOs in China, see Dan Guttman et al., "Environmental Governance in China: Interactions between the State and 'Nonstate Actors,'" *Journal of Environmental Management* 220 (2018): 126–135.

3. Miriam Matejova, Stefan Parker, and Peter Dauvergne, "The Politics of Repressing Environmentalists as Agents of Foreign Influence," *Australian Journal of International Affairs* 72, no. 2 (2018): 145–162; Diana Fu and Greg Distelhorst, "Grassroots Participation and Repression under Hu Jintao and Xi Jinping," *The China Journal* 79, no. 1 (2018): 100–122; Kendra E. Dupuy, James Ron, and Aseem Prakash, "Hands Off My Regime! Governments' Restrictions on Foreign Aid to Non-Governmental Organizations in Poor and Middle Income Countries," *World Development* 84 (2016): 299–311; Kendra E. Dupuy, James Ron, and Aseem Prakash, "Who Survived? Ethiopia's Regulatory Crackdown on Foreign-Funded NGOs," *Review of International Political Economy* 22, no. 2 (2015): 419–456.

4. Maria Tysiachniouk, Svetlana Tulaeva, and Laura A. Henry, "Civil Society under the Law 'On Foreign Agents': NGO Strategies and Network Transformation," *Europe-Asia Studies* 70, no. 4 (2018): 615–637; Jo Crotty, Sarah Marie Hall, and Sergej Ljubownikow, "Post-Soviet Civil Society Development in the Russian Federation: The Impact of the NGO Law," *Europe-Asia Studies* 66, no. 8 (2014): 1253–1269.

5. Peter Dauvergne and Genevieve LeBaron, *Protest Inc.: The Corporatization of Activism* (Polity, 2014); Adrian Parr, *Hijacking Sustainability* (MIT Press, 2012); Lisa Ann Richey and Stefano Ponte, *Brand Aid: Shopping Well to Save the World* (University of Minnesota Press, 2011).

6. See Peter Dauvergne, *Environmentalism of the Rich* (MIT Press, 2016).

7. Rob Nixon, *Slow Violence and the Environmentalism of the Poor* (Harvard University Press, 2011); Joan Martinez-Alier, *The Environmentalism of the Poor: A Study of Ecological Conflicts and Valuation* (Edward Elgar, 2003); Ramachandra Guha and Joan Martinez-Alier, *Varieties of Environmentalism: Essays North and South* (Earthscan, 1997).

8. Robin Broad and Julia Fischer-Mackey, "From Extractivism towards Buen Vivir: Mining Policy as an Indicator of a New Development Paradigm Prioritising the Environment," *Third World Quarterly* 38, no. 6 (2017): 1327–1349; Rose J. Spalding, "From the Streets to the Chamber: Social Movements and the Mining Ban in El Salvador," *European Review of Latin American and Caribbean Studies* (106) (July–December 2018): 47–74.

9. Global Witness, *At What Cost* (Global Witness, 2018, including a revision in January 2019), 8, 13.

10. Jordan G. Teicher, "Gazing Back at the Surveillance Cameras That Watch Us," *New York Times*, August 13, 2018, www.nytimes.com; the UK estimate of license plate recordings is from Surveillance Camera Commissioner (Tony Porter), *Surveillance Camera Commissioner Annual Report 2017/18*, presented to Parliament pursuant to section 35(1)(b) of the Protection of Freedoms Act 2012, January 2019, p. 32.

11. "Keep an Eye Out: Russia's Video Surveillance Market," *Securika Moscow*, July 26, 2018, www.securika-moscow.ru.

12. For an analysis of the global culture of surveillance, see David Lyon, *The Culture of Surveillance* (Polity, 2018). See also, Further Reading, "Surveillance."

13. For an overview of the growing importance of artificial intelligence for surveillance technologies in the United States, see Jay Stanley, *The Dawn of Robot Technologies: AI, Video Analytics, and Privacy* (American Civil Liberties Union, 2019).

14. Research and Markets, *Video Surveillance Market to 2025: Global Analysis and Forecasts by Platform, Industries and Services* (Research and Markets, 2018). See also Nikki Gladstone, "How Facial Recognition Technology Permeated Everyday Life," *Centre for International Governance and Innovation*, September 19, 2018, www.cigionline .org; Ravindra Das, *The Science of Biometrics: Security Technology for Identity Verification* (Routledge, 2018).

15. Ji Feng is quoted in Rob Schmitz, "Facial Recognition in China Is Big Business as Local Governments Boost Surveillance," *National Public Radio*, April 3, 2018, www.npr .org.

16. Zhang is quoted in Nathan Vanderklippe, "Chinese School Installs Cameras to Monitor Students," *Globe and Mail*, June 2, 2018, A3.

17. Jiang is quoted in Vanderklippe, "Chinese School Installs," A3.

18. Paul Mozur, "Inside China's Dystopian Dreams: A.I., Shame and Lots of Cameras," *New York Times*, July 8, 2018.

19. Human Rights Watch, *China's Algorithms of Repression: Reverse Engineering a Xinjiang Police Mass Surveillance App* (Human Rights Watch, May 2019). For a fuller understanding of China's treatment of the Uyghur people, see Nick Holdstock, *China's Forgotten People: Xinjiang, Terror and the Chinese State* (I. B. Tauris, 2015); James A. Millward, *Eurasian Crossroads: A History of Xinjiang* (Columbia University Press, 2007).

20. James Vincent, "Artificial Intelligence is Going to Supercharge Surveillance," *Verge*, January 23, 2018, www.theverge.com.

21. Raymond Zhong, "At China's Internet Conference, a Darker Side of Tech Emerges," *New York Times*, November 8, 2018; Charles Rollet, "Dahua and Hikvision Win over $1 Billion in Government-Backed Projects in Xinjiang," *IPVM*, April 23, 2018, https://ipvm.com.

22. Paul Mozur, "Facial Scans Tighten China's Grip on a Minority," *New York Times*, April 15, 2019, A1 (this includes CloudWalk's website quote).

23. Xie Yinan is quoted in Schmitz, "Facial Recognition in China"; the description of SenseTime's business was made by June Jin, SenseTime's head of marketing, as summarized in Schmitz.

24. Zak Doffman, "Why We Should Fear China's Emerging High-Tech Surveillance State," *Forbes*, October 28, 2018, www.forbes.com.

25. Simon Denyer, "Beijing Bets on Facial Recognition in a Big Drive for Total Surveillance," *Washington Post*, January 7, 2018, www.washingtonpost.com. See also David Curtis Wright, *'Eyes as Bright as Snow': Facial Recognition Technology and Social Control in China* (Canadian Global Affairs Institute, June 2018); Xiao Qiang, "The Road to Digital Unfreedom: President Xi's Surveillance State," *Journal of Democracy* 30, no. 1 (2019): 53–67.

26. Stephen Chen, "How Tensions with the West Are Putting the Future of China's Skynet Mass Surveillance System at Stake," *South China Morning Post*, October 4, 2018, www.scmp.com; IDIS, *The Video Surveillance Report 2018* (IDIS, March 2018).

27. Scott N. Romaniuk and Tobias Burgers, "How China's AI Technology Exports Are Seeding Surveillance Societies Globally," *The Diplomat*, October 18, 2018,

https://thediplomat.com; Ven Rathavong, "China to Help Install Security Cameras," *Khmer Times*, May 12, 2018, www.khmertimeskh.com.

28. Charles Rollet, "Ecuador's All-Seeing Eye Is Made in China," *Foreign Policy*, August 9, 2018, https://foreignpolicy.com.

29. Amy Hawkins, "Beijing's Big Brother Tech Needs African Faces," *Foreign Policy*, July 24, 2018, https://foreignpolicy.com; Shan Jie, "China Exports Facial ID Technology to Zimbabwe," *Global Times*, April 12, 2018, www.globaltimes.cn.

30. Miles Brundage et al., *The Malicious Use of Artificial Intelligence: Forecasting, Prevention, and Mitigation* (Future of Humanity Institute, University of Oxford, Centre for the Study of Existential Risk, University of Cambridge, Center for a New American Security, Electronic Frontier Foundation, and OpenAI, February, 2018); Elaine Kamarck, "Malevolent Soft Power, AI, and the Threat to Democracy," *Brookings*, November 29, 2018, www.brookings.edu.

31. Gary King, Jennifer Pan, and Margaret E. Roberts, "Reverse-Engineering Censorship in China: Randomized Experimentation and Participant Observation," *Science* 345 (6199) (2014), 891.

32. Freedom House, *Freedom on the Net 2018: The Crisis of Social Media* (Freedom House, October 2019), 5, 24–25.

33. Chen Yong is quoted in Zhong, "At China's Internet Conference."

34. State Council of the People's Republic of China, "Planning Outline for the Construction of Social Credit System (2014–2020)," *China Copyright and Media*, posted and edited by Rogier Creemers on June 14, 2014, updated on April 25, 2015, https://chinacopyrightandmedia.wordpress.com.

35. Li Yingyun is quoted in Rachel Botsman, "Big Data Meets Big Brother as China Moves to Rate Its Citizens," *Wired*, October 21, 2017, www.wired.co.uk.

36. See Rachel Botsman, *Who Can You Trust? How Technology Brought Us Together and Why It Might Drive Us Apart* (Portfolio Penguin, 2017); Simina Mistreanu, "Life inside China's Social Credit Laboratory," *Foreign Policy*, April 3, 2018, https://foreignpolicy.com; Yongxi Chen and Anne S. Y. Cheung, "The Transparent Self under Big Data Profiling: Privacy and Chinese Legislation on the Social Credit System," *Journal of Comparative Law* 12, no. 2 (2017): 356–378; Christina Zhou and Bang Xiao, "China's Social Credit System is Pegged to Be Fully Operational by 2020—But What Will It Look Like?," *ABC News*, Australian Broadcasting Corporation, updated January 1, 2020, www.abc.net.au.

37. Fan Liang, Vishnupriya Das, Nadiya Kostyuk, and Muzammil M. Hussain, "Constructing a Data-Driven Society: China's Social Credit System as a State Surveillance Infrastructure," *Policy & Internet* 10, no. 4 (2018): 415–453.

38. Steven Feldstein, "The Road to Digital Unfreedom: How Artificial Intelligence Is Reshaping Repression," *Journal of Democracy* 30, no. 1 (2019), 41.

39. Nawal Al-Maghafi, *Weapons of Mass Surveillance*, British Broadcasting Corporation (BBC) documentary, 2017, www.bbc.com; Maaike Goslinga, Dimitri Tokmetzis, Sebastian Gjerding, and Lasse Skou Andersen, "How European Spy Technology Falls into the Wrong Hands," *de Correspondent*, February 23, 2017, https://thecorrespondent.com; Machiko Kanetake, "The EU's Export Control of Cyber Surveillance Technology: Human Rights Approaches," *Business and Human Rights Journal* 4, no. 1 (2019): 155–162; and Further Reading, "Security and Digital Technology."

40. Costigan and Zelazney are quoted in Stacy Cowley, "Banks and Retailers Are Tracking How You Type, Swipe and Tap," *New York Times*, August 13, 2018.

41. Cowley, "Banks and Retailers Are Tracking." Also see BioCatch, www.biocatch .com.

42. The CEO of BioCatch is quoted in "Behavioral Biometrics Leader BioCatch Closes $30M New Investment," *BioCatch Press Release*, March 12, 2018, www.biocatch.com.

43. Lynch is quoted in Cowley, "Banks and Retailers Are Tracking." The estimate of the market value of behavioral biometrics is from MarketsandMarkets, *Behavioral Biometrics Market by Component (Software & Services), Application (Identity & Access Management, Risk & Compliance Management, Fraud Detection & Prevention Management), Deployment Model, Organization Size, and Vertical: Global Forecast to 2023* (MarketsandMarkets, July 2018).

44. Global Witness, *At What Cost*, 15.

CHAPTER 11

1. John Winthrop, *Winthrop Papers, 1631–1637* (Massachusetts Historical Society, 1943, III), 167, quoted in Alfred W. Crosby, *Ecological Imperialism: The Biological Expansion of Europe, 900–1900*, new ed. (Cambridge University Press, 2004), 208.

2. Milton Leitenberg, *Deaths in Wars and Conflicts in the 20th Century*, 3rd ed. (Cornell University Peace Studies Program, Occasional Paper no. 29, 2006), 9.

3. My estimates of the number of deaths under the Khmer Rouge and during the Rwandan genocide are in the middle range. See Patrick Heuveline, "The Boundaries of Genocide: Quantifying the Uncertainty of the Death Toll during the Pol Pot Regime in Cambodia (1975–79)," *Population Studies* 69, no. 2 (2015): 201–218; David Yanagizawa-Drott, "Propaganda and Conflict: Evidence from the Rwandan Genocide," *Quarterly Journal of Economics* 129, no. 4 (2014): 1947–1994.

4. Michael C. Horowitz, "Artificial Intelligence, International Competition, and the Balance of Power," *Texas National Security Review* 1, no. 3 (2018): 36–57.

5. Work is quoted in Sydney J. Freedberg Jr., "War without Fear: DepSecDef Work on How AI Changes Conflict," *Breaking Defense*, May 31, 2017, https://breakingdefense .com.

6. Kenneth Payne, *Strategy, Evolution, and War: From Apes to Artificial Intelligence* (Georgetown University Press, 2018).

7. Paul Scharre, *Army of None: Autonomous Weapons and the Future of War* (W. W. Norton, 2018).

8. The phrase "environmental blowback" is from Joshua Pearce and David Denkenberger, "A National Pragmatic Safety Limit for Nuclear Weapon Quantities," *Safety* 4, no. 2 (2018): 1–17. The estimate of America's stockpile of active nuclear weapons is from the US Department of Energy (declassified for the year 2017).

9. See Stockholm International Peace Institute (SIPRI), *SIPRI Military Expenditure Database*, 2019, www.sipri.org/databases/milex. These figures are in constant 2017 US dollars.

10. Brian Glyn Williams, "The CIA's Covert Predator Drone War in Pakistan, 2004–2010: The History of an Assassination Campaign," *Studies in Conflict & Terrorism* 33, no. 10 (2010): 871–892; Derek Gregory, "From a View to a Kill: Drones and Late Modern War," *Theory, Culture & Society* 28, no. 7–8 (2011): 188–215.

11. Moseley is quoted in "'Reaper' Moniker Given to MQ-9 Unmanned Aerial Vehicle," *U.S. Airforce News*, September 14, 2006, www.af.mil/News/story.

12. Garrett Reim, "USAF Auto-Lands MQ-9 Block 5 Reaper for First Time," *FlightGlobal*, September 19, 2018, flightglobal.com.

13. OUTREACH@DARPA.MIL, "ACTUV 'Sea Hunter' Prototype Transitions to Office of Naval Research for Further Development," DARPA, January 30, 2018.

14. Northrop Grumman, MQ-4C, www.northropgrumman.com.

15. Work is quoted in Julian Turner, "Sea Hunter: Inside the US Navy's Autonomous Submarine Tracking Vessel," *Naval Technology*, May 3, 2018, www.naval-technology.com.

16. Scurry is quoted in Mike Gross, "How a Triton Mishap Might Boost Confidence in Autonomous Vehicles," *C4ISRNET*, February 15, 2019, www.c4isrnet.com.

17. Peter Lee, "Drones Will Soon Decide Who to Kill," *The Conversation*, April 11, 2018, https://theconversation.com. For details on the research project, see Department of Defense (Army), "Automatic Target Recognition of Personnel and Vehicles from an Unmanned Aerial System Using Learning Algorithms," *Small Business Innovation Research Program*, closing date, February 7, 2018, www.sbir.gov/sbirsearch/detail/1413823.

18. President of the United States, *National Security Strategy of the United States of America*, December 2017, 20.

19. US Department of Defense, *Summary of the 2018 National Defense Strategy of the United States of America: Sharpening the American Military's Competitive Edge* (Department of Defense, 2018), 7; US Department of Defense, Summary of the *Department of Defense Artificial Intelligence Strategy: Harnessing AI to Advance Our Security and Prosperity* (Department of Defense, 2018), 4.

20. Mattis is quoted in Aaron Mehta, "AI Makes Mattis Question 'Fundamental' Beliefs about War," *C4ISRNET*, February 17, 2018, www.c4isrnet.com.

21. White House, "Artificial Intelligence for the American People," Briefing Statement, Issued on May 10, 2018, www.whitehouse.gov.

22. Shanahan is quoted in "DoD Officially Establishes Joint Artificial Intelligence Center," *MeriTalk*, July 2, 2018, www.meritalk.com.

23. President Donald J. Trump, "Executive Order on Maintaining American Leadership in Artificial Intelligence," Executive Orders of the White House, February 11, 2019, www.whitehouse.gov, 1–2.

24. Chris Cornillie, "Pentagon Bridge Artificial Intelligence's 'Valley of Death'?," *Bloomberg Government*, September 14, 2018, https://about.bgov.com.

25. Steve Andriole, "Trump's AI Initiative: Everything but Money," *Forbes*, February 12, 2019, www.forbes.com.

26. Government of the People's Republic of China, *State Council Issued Notice of the New Generation Artificial Intelligence Development Plan*, Guofa No. 35, release date July 20, 2017.

27. Stephen Chen, "China Takes Surveillance to New Heights with Flock of Robotic Doves, but Do They Come in Peace?," *South China Morning Post*, June 28, 2018, www.scmp.com.

28. Yi-Zheng Lian, "China, the Party-Corporate Complex," *New York Times*, February 12, 2017, www.nytimes.com. For an analysis of the militarization of commercial technologies in China, see *Fortifying China: The Struggle to Build a Modern Defense Economy* (Cornell University Press, 2008). For an analysis of why China is gaining ground in the commercialization of AI technologies, see Kai-Fu Lee, *AI Superpowers: China, Silicon Valley, and the New World Order* (Houghton Mifflin Harcourt, 2018).

29. Liu Guozhi is quoted in Michael C. Horowitz, Gregory C. Allen, Elsa B. Kania, and Paul Scharre, *Strategic Competition in an Era of Artificial Intelligence* (Center for a New American Security, July 2018), 13.

30. Elsa B. Kania, *Battlefield Singularity: Artificial Intelligence, Military Revolution, and China's Future Military Power* (Center for a New American Security, November 2017); Sophie-Charlotte Fischer, "Artificial Intelligence: China's High-Tech Ambitions," *Center for Security Studies (CSS) Analyses in Security Policy* 220 (February 2018): 1–4; Tom Upchurch, "How China Could Beat the West in the Deadly Race for AI Weapons," *Wired*, August 8, 2018, www.wired.co.uk; Kristin Huang, "The Drones That Have Become Part of China's Military Strategy," *South China Morning Post*, September 29, 2018, www.scmp.com.

31. Alina Polyakova, "Weapons of the Weak: Russia and AI-Driven Asymmetric Warfare," *Brookings Report*, November 15, 2018, www.brookings.edu; Samuel Bendett, "Russia: Expect a National AI Roadmap by Midyear," *Defense One*, January 8, 2019, www.defenseone.com.

32. Sharkey is quoted in Mark Smith, "Is 'Killer Robot' Warfare Closer Than We Think?," *BBC*, August 25, 2017, www.bbc.com.

33. Associated Press, "Putin: Leader in Artificial Intelligence Will Rule World," *CNBC*, September 4, 2017, www.cnbc.com.

34. Walsh is quoted in Smith, "Is 'Killer Robot' Warfare Closer."

35. Aude Fleurant, Alexandra Kuimova, Nan Tian, Pieter D. Wezeman, and Siemon T. Wezeman, "The SIPRI Top 100 Arms-Producing and Military Services Companies, 2017," *SIPRI Fact Sheet*, December 2018, www.sipri.org.

36. M. L. Cummings, Heather M. Roff, Kenneth Cukier, Jacob Parakilas, and Hannah Bryce, *Artificial Intelligence and International Affairs Disruption Anticipated* (Royal Institute of International Affairs, 2018), 15.

37. See Lockheed Martin, www.lockheedmartin.com.

38. Ulrike Esther Franke, "A European Approach to Military Drones and Artificial Intelligence," *European Council on Foreign Relations*, June 23, 2017, www.ecfr.eu.

39. Navarro is quoted in Sharon Weinberger, "China Has Already Won the Drone Wars," *Foreign Policy*, May 10, 2018, https://foreignpolicy.com.

40. Burt is quoted in Jamie Doward, "Britain Funds Research into Drones That Decide Who They Kill, Says Report," *The Guardian*, November 10, 2018, www.theguardian .com; see also Peter Burt, *Off the Leash: The Development of Autonomous Military Drones in the UK* (Drone Wars UK, November 2018); Drone Wars UK, https://dronewars.net; and Further Reading, "Drone Warfare."

41. Ian G. R. Shaw, "Robot Wars: US Empire and Geopolitics in the Robotic Age," *Security Dialogue* 48, no. 5 (2017): 451–470.

42. Michael E. O'Hanlon, "The Role of AI in Future Warfare," *Brookings Report*, November 29, 2018, www.brookings.edu. See also Michael E. O'Hanlon, *The Senkaku Paradox: Risking Great Power War over Small Stakes* (Brookings Institution Press, 2019).

43. Roper is quoted in Chris Baraniuk, "US Military Tests Swarm of Mini-Drones Launched from Jets," *BBC News*, January 10, 2017, www.bbc.com.

44. Cornachio is quoted in Gina Harkins, "Marines Test New Drone Swarms a Single Operator Can Control," *Defense Tech*, July 23, 2018, www.military.com.

45. Williamson is quoted in Dan Sabbagh, "UK Will Deploy Drone Squadron after Brexit, Says Defence Secretary," *The Guardian*, February 11, 2019, www.theguardian .com. See also Joanna Frew, *Drone Wars: The Next Generation* (Drone Wars UK, May 2018).

46. "Unmanned 'Shark Swarm' to Be Used in Sea Battles, Military Patrols," *Global Times*, June 6, 2018, http://en.people.cn; Jeffrey Lin and P. W. Singer, "China Is

Making 1,000-UAV Drone Swarms Now," *Popular Science*, January 8, 2018, www.popsci .com.

47. Ivan Semeniuk, "International Scientists Urge UN to Ban Lethal Robots," *Globe and Mail*, February 16, 2019, A10. The estimate of commercial drone sales is from Grand View Research, Commercial Drone Market Size, Share, & Trends (Grand View Research, June 2019); Gartner, "Gartner Says Almost 3 Million Personal and Commercial Drones Will Be Shipped in 2017," *Gartner Newsroom*, February 9, 2017, www .gartner.com.

48. Wilby is quoted in Brian Wheeler, "Terrorists Certain to Get Killer Robots, Says Defence Giant," *BBC News*, November 30, 2017, www.bbc.com.

49. Miller is quoted in "U.S. Army Will Blast UAVs out of the Sky Using Microwave Weapons," *Defence Blog*, August 11, 2018, https://defence-blog.com.

50. Jeremy Straub, "Artificial Intelligence Is the Weapon of the Next Cold War," *The Conversation*, January 29, 2018, https://theconversation.com. See also Further Reading, "Artificial Intelligence (weaponization of)."

51. Michael Carl Haas and Sophie-Charlotte Fischer, "The Evolution of Targeted Killing Practices: Autonomous Weapons, Future Conflict, and the International Order," *Contemporary Security Policy* 38, no. 2 (2017): 281–306.

52. Ronald C. Arkin, "The Case for Ethical Autonomy in Unmanned Systems," *Journal of Military Ethics* 9, no. 4 (2010): 332–341.

53. Chris Cole, *Drone Wars: Out of Sight, out of Mind, out of Control* (Drone Campaign Network, October 2016); Pavel Sharikov, "Artificial Intelligence, Cyberattack, and Nuclear Weapons: A Dangerous Combination," *Bulletin of the Atomic Scientists* 74, no. 6 (2018): 368–373.

54. Nuland's quote is on the back cover of Amir Husain, John Rutherford Allen, Robert O. Work, August Cole, Paul Scharre, Bruce Porter, Wendy R. Anderson, and Jim Townsend, *Hyperwar: Conflict and Competition in the AI Century* (SparkCognition Press, 2018). Allen is quoted in "SparkCognition Releases 'Hyperwar: Conflict and Competition in the AI Century' at Time Machine 2018," *CISION PR Newswire*, November 6, 2018, www.prnewswire.com.

CHAPTER 12

1. See John S. Dryzek, *The Politics of the Earth: Environmental Discourses*, 3rd ed. (Oxford University Press, 2013), 26, 52–72.

2. For an overview of market liberal thinking, see Jennifer Clapp and Peter Dauvergne, *Paths to a Green World: The Political Economy of the Global Environment*, 2nd ed. (MIT Press, 2011).

3. For an analysis of how industry constructs "doubt" to sabotage science, see Naomi Oreskes and Erik M. Conway, *Merchants of Doubt: How a Handful of Scientists Obscured the Truth on Issues from Tobacco Smoke to Global Warming* (Bloomsbury, 2011). For an analysis of the backlash and strategic undermining of the idea of "limits to growth," see Kerryn Higgs, *Collision Course: Endless Growth on a Finite Planet* (MIT Press, 2014).

4. See Further Reading, "Global Environmental Governance" and "Global Environmental Politics."

5. President Donald J. Trump, "Executive Order on Maintaining American Leadership in Artificial Intelligence," Executive Orders of the White House, February 11, 2019, www.whitehouse.gov, 3.

6. See Government of Canada, Office of the Prime Minister, "Mandate for the International Panel on Artificial Intelligence," *News*, December 6, 2018, https://pm.gc.ca; Government of Canada, Office of the Prime Minister, "Prime Minister Announces Investment in Artificial Intelligence to Create over 16,000 Jobs for Canadians," *News*, December 6, 2018, https://pm.gc.ca. Also see the Canadian Institute for Advanced Research (CIFAR), "Pan-Canadian Artificial Intelligence Strategy," www.cifar.ca/ai/pan-canadian-artificial-intelligence-strategy.

7. Theresa May, "Theresa May's Davos Address in Full," *World Economic Forum*, January 25, 2018, www.weforum.org.

8. National Institution for Transforming India (NITI Aayog), *National Strategy for Artificial Intelligence*, Discussion Paper, NITI Aayog, June 2018, 5; Group of Seven (G7), "Charlevoix Common Vision for the Future of Artificial Intelligence," Charlevoix, Québec, 2018, 2, https://g7.gc.ca. For the French "AI for Humanity" plan, see Cédric Villani, *For a Meaningful Artificial Intelligence: Towards a French and European Strategy*, A Parliamentary Mission from 8th September 2017 to 8th March, 2018, aiforhumanity.fr.

9. Organization for Economic Co-operation and Development (OECD), *Recommendation of the Council on Artificial Intelligence*, OECD/LEGAL/0449, 2019, 3.

10. For a summary overview, see Jeff Loucks, Susanne Hupfer, David Jarvis, and Timothy Murphy, "Future in the Balance? How Countries Are Pursuing an AI Advantage," *Deloitte Insights*, May 1, 2019.

11. Smith is quoted in Cade Metz, "Is Ethical A.I. Even Possible?," *New York Times*, March 1, 2019, www.nytimes.com.

12. PricewaterhouseCoopers (PwC) (lead authors Celine Herweijer, Benjamin Combes, Pia Ramchandani, and Jasnam Sidhu), *Fourth Industrial Revolution for the Earth: Harnessing Artificial Intelligence for the Earth* (PwC, 2018), 26.

13. See United Nations, Sustainable Development Goals, https://sustainabledevelopment.un.org.

14. PricewaterhouseCoopers, *Fourth Industrial Revolution for the Earth*, 27.

15. Microsoft News Center India staff, "Microsoft Announces AI for Earth Grant Recipients from India and Deepens Commitment to Sustainability in the Country," *Microsoft News Center India*, September 4, 2018, https://news.microsoft.com (this includes the quote by Microsoft India's Keshav Dhakad). For analyses of how CSR can advance sustainability, see Further Reading, "Private Environmental Governance."

16. PricewaterhouseCoopers, *Fourth Industrial Revolution for the Earth*, 26–28.

17. Bengio is quoted in Davide Castelvecchi, "AI Pioneer: 'The Dangers of Abuse Are Very Real,'" *Nature*, April 4, 2019, www.nature.com.

18. Bengio is quoted in Castelvecchi, "AI Pioneer"; the prudence principle is at *Montreal Declaration for Responsible AI Development*, 2018 (Université de Montréal), 13. For a thoughtful case for why the study of machine learning should involve a wide range of academic disciplines, see Iyad Rahwan et al., "Machine Behavior," *Nature* 568 (April 25, (2019): 477–486.

19. *Montreal Declaration for Responsible AI Development*, 15.

20. See Partnership on AI, "Tenets," accessed January 13, 2020, www.partnershiponai.org.

21. Sundar Pichai, "AI at Google: Our Principles," *Google*, June 7, 2018, https://blog.google/technology/ai/ai-principles.

22. OpenAI, "About OpenAI," accessed March 6, 2019, https://openai.com/about. For an overview of the language model GPT-2, see "Better Language Models and Their Implications," *OpenAI Blog*, February 14, 2019, https://blog.openai.com. For a summary of why OpenAI withheld its "deepfakes for text," see Alex Hern, "New AI Fake Text Generator May Be Too Dangerous to Release, Say Creators," *The Guardian*, February 14, 2019, www.theguardian.com.

23. Nick Bostrom, a professor of philosophy at Oxford University who authored *Superintelligence: Paths, Dangers, Strategies*, is on the scientific advisory board of the Future of Life Institute. Max Tegmark, a professor of physics at the Massachusetts Institute of Technology who authored *Life 3.0: Being Human in the Age of Artificial Intelligence*, is one of five founders of the Future of Life Institute.

24. Future of Life Institute, "About the Lethal Autonomous Weapons Systems (Laws) Pledge," accessed March 6, 2019, https://futureoflife.org.

25. Walsh is quoted in Ian Sample, "Thousands of Leading AI Researchers Sign Pledge against Killer Robots," *The Guardian*, July 18, 2018, www.theguardian.com. See also Toby Walsh, *It's Alive: Artificial Intelligence from the Logic Piano to Killer Robots* (La Trobe University Press, 2017); and Toby Walsh, *2062: The World That AI Made* (La Trobe University Press, 2018).

26. Williams is quoted in Keith Wagstaff, "Jody Williams Helped Ban Landmines. Can She Stop Killer Robots?," *NBC News*, April 15, 2015, www.nbcnews.com.

27. Wareham is quoted in Rebecca Kheel, "Fighting the Rise of the Machines," *The Hill*, March 6, 2018, https://thehill.com.

28. United Nations Office at Geneva, The Convention on Certain Conventional Weapons, amended December 21, 2001, www.unog.ch.

29. European Parliament, Report on a European Parliament Recommendation to the Council on the 73rd session of the United Nations General Assembly (2018/2040(INI), Committee on Foreign Affairs, June 27, 2018.

30. Guterres was speaking at a "Web Summit" in Lisbon, Portugal; his remarks are reprinted at António Guterres, "Machines with Power, Discretion to Take Human Life Politically Unacceptable, Morally Repugnant, Secretary-General Tells Lisbon 'Web-Summit,'" *United Nations Press Release*, November 5, 2018, www.un.org.

31. Campaign to Stop Killer Robots, "Country Views on Killer Robots," October 25, 2019, www.stopkillerrobots.org.

32. Pichai, "AI at Google: Our Principles."

33. Ben Tarnoff, "Weaponised AI is Coming: Are Algorithmic Forever Wars Our Future?," *The Guardian*, October 11, 2018, www.theguardian.com; Naomi Nix, "Google Drops Out of Pentagon's $10 Billion Cloud Competition," *Bloomberg Technology*, October 8, 2018, www.bloomberg.com.

34. David Meyer, "Oracle Claimed That Bidding for the Pentagon's Massive Cloud Contract Favors Amazon: The Government Is Unconvinced," *Fortune*, November 15, 2018, http://fortune.com.

35. Future of Life Institute, "Lethal Autonomous Weapons Pledge," accessed January 21, 2020, https://futureoflife.org/lethal-autonomous-weapons-pledge.

36. Open letter to Jeff Bezos and the Amazon Board of Directors, April 10, 2019, https://medium.com.

37. Amazon, Google, and Microsoft, for instance, all now offer free online courses in machine learning. See Nick Heath, "Google, Amazon, Microsoft: How Do Their

Free Machine-Learning Courses Compare?," *TechRepublic*, November 28, 2018, www
.techrepublic.com.

38. Richard M. Price, *The Chemical Weapons Taboo* (Cornell University Press, 1997);
Richard M. Price, "Reversing the Gun Sights: Transnational Civil Society Targets
Land Mines," *International Organization* 52, no. 3 (1998): 61–644; Nina Tannenwald,
The Nuclear Taboo: The United States and the Non-Use of Nuclear Weapons since 1945
(Cambridge University Press, 2007).

39. See Further Reading, "Sustainability (background)," "Sustainability (and business),"
"Sustainability (and environmentalism)," and "Sustainability (pathways toward)."

FURTHER READING

ARTIFICIAL INTELLIGENCE (BACKGROUND)

Chace, Calum. *Surviving AI: The Promise and Peril of Artificial Intelligence*. Threes Cs, 2015.

Domingos, Pedro. *The Master Algorithm: How the Quest for the Ultimate Learning Machine Will Remake Our World*. Basic Books, 2015.

Ford, Martin. *Architects of Intelligence: The Truth about AI from the People Building It*. Packt Publishing, 2018.

Frankish, Keith, and William M. Ramsey, eds. *The Cambridge Handbook of Artificial Intelligence*. Cambridge University Press, 2014.

Lee, Kai-Fu. *AI Superpowers: China, Silicon Valley, and the New World Order*. Houghton Mifflin Harcourt, 2018.

Levesque, Hector J. *Common Sense, the Turing Test, and the Quest for Real AI*. MIT Press, 2017.

Marcus, Gary, and Ernest Davis. *Rebooting AI: Building Artificial Intelligence We Can Trust*. Pantheon, 2019.

Mitchell, Melanie. *Artificial Intelligence: A Guide for Thinking Humans*. Farrar, Straus and Giroux, 2019.

Nourbakhsh, Illah Reza, and Jennifer Keating. *AI and Humanity*. MIT Press, 2020.

Reese, Bryon. *The Fourth Age: Smart Robots, Conscious Computers, and the Future of Humanity*. Atria Books, 2018.

Tegmark, Max. *Life 3.0: Being Human in the Age of Artificial Intelligence.* Alfred A. Knopf, 2017.

Walsh, Toby. *Machines That Think: The Future of Artificial Intelligence.* Prometheus Books, 2018.

Walsh, Toby. *2062: The World That AI Made.* La Trobe University Press, 2018.

ARTIFICIAL INTELLIGENCE (CONSERVATION)

Fei, Fang, Milind Tambe, Bistra Dilkina, and Andrew J. Plumptre, eds. *Artificial Intelligence and Conservation.* Cambridge University Press, 2019.

ARTIFICIAL INTELLIGENCE (CRITIQUES)

Barnhizer, David, and Daniel Barnhizer. *The Artificial Intelligence Contagion: Can Democracy Withstand the Imminent Transformation of Work, Wealth and the Social Order?* Clarity Press, 2019.

Barrat, James. *Our Final Invention: Artificial Intelligence and the End of the Human Era.* St. Martin's Press, 2013.

Bostrom, Nick. *Superintelligence: Paths, Dangers, Strategies.* Oxford University Press, 2014.

Broussard, Meredith. *Artificial Unintelligence: How Computers Misunderstand the World.* MIT Press, 2018.

Collins, Harry. *Artifictional Intelligence: Against Humanity's Surrender to Computers.* Polity, 2018.

Perlas, Nicanor. *Humanity's Last Stand: The Challenge of Artificial Intelligence. A Spiritual-Scientific Response.* Temple Lodge Publishing, 2018.

Smith, Brian Cantwell. *The Promise of Artificial Intelligence: Reckoning and Judgment.* MIT Press, 2019.

ARTIFICIAL INTELLIGENCE (CULTURE AND EDUCATION)

Aoun, Joseph E. *Robot-Proof: Higher Education in the Age of Artificial Intelligence.* MIT Press, 2017.

Bentley, R. Alexander, and Michael J. O'Brien. *The Acceleration of Cultural Change: From Ancestors to Algorithms.* MIT Press, 2017.

ARTIFICIAL INTELLIGENCE (EMPLOYMENT)

Cameron, Nigel M. de S. *Will Robots Take Your Job? A Plea for Consensus.* Polity, 2017.

Daugherty, Paul R., and H. James Wilson. *Human + Machine: Reimagining Work in the Age of AI.* Harvard Business Review Press, 2018.

Ford, Martin. *Rise of the Robots: Technology and the Threat of a Jobless Future*. Basic Books, 2015.

ARTIFICIAL INTELLIGENCE (HISTORY)

Crevier, Daniel. *AI: The Tumultuous History of the Search for Artificial Intelligence*. Basic Books, 1993.

Nilsson, Nils J. *The Quest for Artificial Intelligence*. Cambridge University Press, 2009.

ARTIFICIAL INTELLIGENCE (LAW)

Ashley, Kevin D. *Artificial Intelligence and Legal Analytics: New Tools for Law Practice in the Digital Age*. Cambridge University Press, 2017.

Chinen, Mark. *Law and Autonomous Machines: The Co-evolution of Legal Responsibility and Technology*. Edward Elgar, 2019.

Collins, Ronald K. L., and David M. Skover. *Robotica: Speech Rights and Artificial Intelligence*. Cambridge University Press, 2018.

ARTIFICIAL INTELLIGENCE (OPTIMISTIC VISIONS)

Brynjolfsson, Erik, and Andrew McAfee. *The Second Machine Age: Work, Progress, and Prosperity in a Time of Brilliant Technologies*. W. W. Norton, 2014.

Husain, Amir. *The Sentient Machine: The Coming Age of Artificial Intelligence*. Simon & Schuster, 2017.

Kasparov, Garry. *Deep Thinking: Where Machine Intelligence Ends and Human Creativity Begins*. Public Affairs, 2017.

Kurzweil, Ray. *How to Create a Mind: The Secret of Human Thought Revealed*. Penguin, 2013.

Lovelock, James, with Bryan Appleyard. *Novacene: The Coming Age of Hyperintelligence*. Allen Lane, 2019.

Malone, Thomas W. *Superminds: The Surprising Power of People and Computers Thinking Together*. Little, Brown, 2018.

Miller, Arthur I. *The Artist in the Machine: The World of AI-Powered Creativity*. MIT Press, 2019.

Mulgan, Geoff. *Big Mind: How Collective Intelligence Can Change Our World*. Princeton University Press, 2017.

Topol, Eric. *Deep Medicine: How Artificial Intelligence Can Make Healthcare Human Again*. Basic Books, 2019.

ARTIFICIAL INTELLIGENCE (WEAPONIZATION OF)

Freedman, Lawrence. *The Future of War: A History*. PublicAffairs, 2017.

Latiff, Robert H. *Future War: Preparing for the New Global Battlefield*. Alfred A. Knopf, 2017.

Payne, Kenneth. *Strategy, Evolution, and War: From Apes to Artificial Intelligence*. Georgetown University Press, 2018.

Scharre, Paul. *Army of None: Autonomous Weapons and the Future of War*. W. W. Norton, 2018.

Schwarz, Elke. *Death Machines: The Ethics of Violent Technologies*. Manchester University Press, 2018.

Welsh, Sean. *Ethics and Security Automata: Policy and Technical Challenges of the Robotic Use of Force*. Routledge, 2017.

BIG DATA

Cukier, Kenneth, and Viktor Mayer-Schönberger. *Big Data: A Revolution That Will Transform How We Live, Work, and Think*. Houghton Mifflin Harcourt, 2013.

Eagle, Nathan, and Kate Greene. *Reality Mining: Using Big Data to Engineer a Better World*. MIT Press, 2014.

Kelleher, John D., and Brendan Tierney. *Data Science*. MIT Press, 2018.

Marr, David. *Data Strategy: How to Profit from a World of Big Data, Analytics and the Internet of Things*. Kogan Page, 2017.

Mayer-Schönberger, Viktor, and Thomas Ramgee. *Reinventing Capitalism in the Age of Big Data*. Basic Books, 2018.

Pomerantz, Jeffrey. *Metadata*. MIT Press, 2015.

Sadowski, Jathan. *Too Smart: How Digital Capitalism Is Extracting Data, Controlling Our Lives, and Taking Over the World*. MIT Press, 2020.

Schneier, Bruce. *Data and Goliath: The Hidden Battles to Collect Your Data and Control Your World*. W. W. Norton, 2015.

Sugimoto, Cassidy R., Hamid R. Ekbia, and Michael Mattioli, eds. *Big Data Is Not a Monolith*. MIT Press, 2016.

BIG TECH (CRITIQUES FOR A GENERAL AUDIENCE)

Pasquale, Frank. *The Black Box Society: The Secret Algorithms That Control Money and Information*. Harvard University Press, 2015.

Taplin, Jonathan. *Move Fast and Break Things: How Google, Facebook and Amazon Cornered Culture and Undermined Democracy*. Little, Brown, 2018.

Webb, Amy. *The Big Nine: How the Tech Titans and Their Thinking Machines Could Warp Humanity*. PublicAffairs, 2019.

BUSINESS AND AI

Agrawal, Ajay, Joshua Gans, and Avi Goldfarb, eds. *The Economics of Artificial Intelligence: An Agenda*. University of Chicago Press, 2019.

Agrawal, Ajay, Joshua Gans, and Avi Goldfarb. *Prediction Machines: The Simple Economics of Artificial Intelligence*. Harvard Business Review Press, 2018.

Castrounis, Alex. *AI for People and Business: A Framework for Better Human Experiences and Business Success*. O'Reilly Media, 2019.

Chavez, Tom, Chris O'Hara, and Vivek Vaidya. *Data Driven: Harnessing Data and AI to Reinvent Customer Engagement*. McGraw-Hill Education, 2018.

Davenport, Thomas H. *The AI Advantage: How to Put the Artificial Intelligence Revolution to Work*. MIT Press, 2018.

Davenport, Thomas H., and Julie Kirby. *Only Humans Need Apply: Winners and Losers in the Age of Smart Machines*. HarperBusiness, 2016.

Finlay, Steven. *Artificial Intelligence and Machine Learning for Business: A No-Nonsense Guide to Data Driven Technologies*. 2nd ed. Relativistic, 2017.

Marr, Bernard, with Matt Ward. *Artificial Intelligence in Practice: How 50 Successful Companies Used Artificial Intelligence to Solve Problems*. Wiley, 2019.

McAfee, Andrew, and Erik Brynjolfsson. *Machine, Platform, Crowd: Harnessing Our Digital Future*. W. W. Norton, 2017.

Sahota, Neil, and Michael Ashley. *Own the A.I. Revolution: Unlock Your Artificial Intelligence Strategy to Disrupt Your Competition*. McGraw-Hill Education, 2019.

Skilton, Mark, and Felix Hovsepian. *The 4th Industrial Revolution: Responding to the Impact of Artificial Intelligence on Business*. Palgrave Macmillan, 2017.

CAPITALISM AND UNSUSTAINABILITY

Klein, Naomi. *This Changes Everything: Capitalism vs. the Climate*. Simon and Schuster, 2015.

Mazzucato, Mariana. *The Value of Everything: Making and Taking in the Global Economy*. PublicAffairs, 2018.

Moore, Jason W. *Capitalism in the Web of Life: Ecology and the Accumulation of Capital*. Verso Books, 2015.

Wright, Christopher, and Daniel Nyberg. *Climate Change, Capitalism, and Corporations*. Cambridge University Press, 2015.

CLOUD COMPUTING

Hu, Tung-Hui. *A Prehistory of the Cloud*. MIT Press, 2015.

Mosco, Vincent. *To the Cloud: Big Data in a Turbulent World*. Paradigm Publishers, 2014.

Ruparelia, Nayan B. *Cloud Computing*. MIT Press, 2016.

DEEP LEARNING

Goodfellow, Ian, Yoshua Bengio, and Aaron Courville. *Deep Learning*. MIT Press, 2016.

Graupe, Daniel. *Deep Learning Neural Networks: Design and Case Studies*. World Scientific Publishing, 2016.

Kelleher, John D. *Deep Learning*. MIT Press, 2019.

Patterson, Josh, and Adam Gibson. *Deep Learning: A Practitioner's Approach*. O'Reilly Media, 2017.

Sejnowski, Terrence J. *The Deep Learning Revolution: Artificial Intelligence Meets Human Intelligence*. MIT Press, 2018.

DRIVERLESS VEHICLES

Burns, Lawrence D., with Christopher Shulgan. *Autonomy: The Quest to Build the Driverless Car—and How It Will Reshape Our World*. HarperCollins, 2018.

Herrmann, Andreas, Walter Brenner, and Rupert Stadler. *Autonomous Driving: How the Driverless Revolution Will Change the World*. Emerald Publishing, 2018.

Lipson, Hod, and Melba Kurman. *Driverless: Intelligent Cars and the Road Ahead*. MIT Press, 2016.

Meyboom, AnnaLisa. *Driverless Urban Futures: A Speculative Atlas for Autonomous Vehicles*. Routledge, 2019.

Simoudis, Evangelos. *The Big Data Opportunity in Our Driverless Future*. Corporate Innovators, 2017.

Sumantran, Venkat, Charles Fine, and David Gonsalvez. *Faster, Smarter, Greener: The Future of the Car and Urban Mobility*. MIT Press, 2017.

DRONE WARFARE

Chamayou, Grégoire. *A Theory of the Drone*. Translated by Janet Lloyd. New Press, 2015.

Gusterson, Hugh. *Drone: Remote Control Warfare*. MIT Press, 2015.

Kreuzer, Michael P. *Drones and the Future of Air Warfare: The Evolution of Remotely Piloted Aircraft*. Routledge, 2016.

Lee, Peter. *Reaper Force: Inside Britain's Drone Wars*. John Blake, 2018.

Williams, Brian Glyn. *Predators: The CIA's Drone War on al Qaeda*. Potomac Books, 2013.

ELECTRIC VEHICLES

McKenzie, Hamish. *Insane Mode: How Elon Musk's Tesla Sparked an Electric Car Revolution to End the Age of Oil*. Dutton, 2018.

Mom, Gijs. *The Electric Vehicle: Technology and Expectations in the Automobile Age*. Johns Hopkins University Press, 2012.

ETHICS AND AI

Boddington, Paula. *Towards a Code of Ethics for Artificial Intelligence*. Springer, 2017.

Coeckelbergh, Mark. *AI Ethics*. MIT Press, 2020.

Gunkel, David J. *The Machine Question: Critical Perspectives on AI, Robots, and Ethics*. MIT Press, 2012.

Gunkel, David J. *Robot Rights*. MIT Press, 2018.

Lin, Patrick, and Keith Abney, eds. *Robot Ethics 2.0: From Autonomous Cars to Artificial Intelligence*. Oxford University Press, 2017.

FOURTH INDUSTRIAL REVOLUTION

Schwab, Klaus. *The Fourth Industrial Revolution*. World Economic Forum, 2016.

Schwab, Klaus, with Nicolas Davis. *Shaping the Fourth Industrial Revolution*. World Economic Forum, 2018.

GAMES AND AI

Sadler, Matthew, and Natasha Regan. *Game Changer: AlphaZero's Groundbreaking Chess Strategies and the Promise of AI*. New In Chess, 2019.

Togelius, Julian. *Playing Smart: On Games, Intelligence and Artificial Intelligence*. MIT Press, 2019.

GLOBAL ENVIRONMENTAL CRISIS

Angus, Ian. *Facing the Anthropocene: Fossil Fuel Capitalism and the Crisis of the Earth System*. NYU Press, 2016.

Barnosky, Anthony D. *Dodging Extinction: Power, Food, Money, and the Future of Life on Earth*. University of California Press, 2014.

Higgs, Kerryn. *Collision Course: Endless Growth on a Finite Planet*. MIT Press, 2014.

Kolbert, Elizabeth. *The Sixth Extinction: An Unnatural History*. Henry Holt, 2014.

Lewis, Simon L., and Mark A. Maslin. *The Human Planet: How We Created the Anthropocene*. Penguin, 2018.

McKibben, Bill. *Falter: Has the Human Game Begun to Play Itself Out?* Henry Holt, 2019.

Wallace-Wells, David. *The Uninhabitable Earth: Life after Warming*. Tim Duggan Books, 2019.

Woodwell, George M. *A World to Live In: An Ecologist's Vision for a Plundered Planet*. MIT Press, 2016.

GLOBAL ENVIRONMENTAL GOVERNANCE

Baber, Walter F., and Robert V. Bartlett. *Consensus and Global Environmental Governance: Deliberative Democracy in Nature's Regime*. MIT Press, 2015.

Biermann, Frank. *Earth System Governance: World Politics in the Anthropocene*. MIT Press, 2014.

Conca, Ken. *An Unfinished Foundation: The United Nations and Global Environmental Governance*. Oxford University Press, 2015.

Durant, Robert F., Daniel J. Fiorino, and Rosemary O'Leary, eds. *Environmental Governance Reconsidered: Challenges, Choices, and Opportunities*. 2nd ed. MIT Press, 2017.

Gordon, David J. *Cities on the World Stage: The Politics of Global Urban Climate Governance*. Cambridge University Press, 2020.

Park, Susan, and Teresa Kramarz, eds. *Global Environmental Governance and the Accountability Trap*. MIT Press, 2019.

Steinberg, Paul F. *Who Rules the Earth? How Social Rules Shape Our Planet and Our Lives*. Oxford University Press, 2015.

Young, Oran R. *Governing Complex Systems: Social Capital for the Anthropocene*. MIT Press, 2017.

GLOBAL ENVIRONMENTAL POLITICS

Chasek, Pamela S., David L. Downie, and Janet Welsh Brown. *Global Environmental Politics*. 7th ed. Westview Press, 2017.

Corry, Olaf, and Hayley Stevenson, eds. *Traditions and Trends in Global Environmental Politics: International Relations and the Earth*. Routledge, 2018.

Dauvergne, Peter, and Justin Alger, eds. *A Research Agenda for Global Environmental Politics*. Edward Elgar, 2018.

DeSombre, Elizabeth R. *What Is Environmental Politics?* Polity, 2020.

Detraz, Nicole. *Gender and the Environment*. Polity, 2017.

Latour, Bruno. *Down to Earth: Politics in the New Climatic Regime.* Translated by Catherine Porter. Polity, 2018.

Newell, Peter. *Global Green Politics.* Cambridge University Press, 2020.

Nicholson, Simon, and Sikina Jinnah, eds. *New Earth Politics: Essays from the Anthropocene.* MIT Press, 2016.

Nicholson, Simon, and Paul Wapner, eds. *Global Environmental Politics: From Person to Planet.* Routledge, 2014.

O'Neill, Kate. *The Environment and International Relations.* 2nd ed. Cambridge University Press, 2017.

Stevenson, Hayley. *Global Environmental Politics: Problems, Policy and Practice.* Cambridge University Press, 2017.

Stoett, Peter J., with Shane Mulligan. *Global Ecopolitics: Crisis, Governance, and Justice.* 2nd ed. University of Toronto Press, 2019.

Vig, Norman J., and Michael E. Kraft, eds. *Environmental Policy: New Directions for the Twenty-First Century.* 10th ed. CQ Press, 2019.

INTERNET OF THINGS

Greengard, Samuel. *The Internet of Things.* MIT Press, 2015.

Rifkin, Jeremy. *The Zero Marginal Cost Society: The Internet of Things, the Collaborative Commons, and the Eclipse of Capitalism.* St. Martin's Press, 2014.

Sinclair, Bruce. *IoT Inc.: How Your Company Can Use the Internet of Things to Win in the Outcome Economy.* McGraw-Hill Education, 2017.

MACHINE LEARNING

Alpaydin, Ethem. *Machine Learning: The New AI.* MIT Press, 2016.

Gerrish, Sean. *How Smart Machines Think.* MIT Press, 2018.

ONLINE ADDICTION

Carr, Nicholas. *The Shallows: What the Internet Is Doing to Our Brains.* W. W. Norton, 2011.

Eyal, Nir. *Hooked: How to Build Habit-Forming Products.* Portfolio/Penguin, 2014.

Montag, Christian, and Martin Reuter. *Internet Addiction.* Springer, 2017.

ONLINE GAMING

Taylor, T. L. *Play between Worlds: Exploring Online Game Culture.* MIT Press, 2011.

Taylor, T. L. *Raising the Stakes: E-Sports and the Professionalization of Computer Gaming.* MIT Press, 2015.

ONLINE RETAIL INDUSTRY

Stone, Brad. *The Everything Store: Jeff Bezos and the Age of Amazon.* Random House, 2013.

POLITICAL ECONOMY OF THE ENVIRONMENT

Clapp, Jennifer, and Peter Dauvergne. *Paths to a Green World: The Political Economy of the Global Environment.* 2nd ed. MIT Press, 2011.

Frey, R. Scott, Paul K. Gellert, and Harry F. Dahms, eds. *Ecologically Unequal Exchange: Environmental Injustice in Comparative and Historical Perspective.* Palgrave Macmillan, 2019.

Katz-Rosene, Ryan, and Matthew Paterson. *Thinking Ecologically about the Global Political Economy.* Routledge, 2018.

Newell, Peter. *Globalization and the Environment: Capitalism, Ecology and Power.* Polity, 2012.

PRIVATE ENVIRONMENTAL GOVERNANCE

Auld, Graeme. *Constructing Private Governance: The Rise and Evolution of Forest, Coffee, and Fisheries Certification.* Yale University Press, 2014.

Balboa, Cristina M. *The Paradox of Scale: How NGOs Build, Maintain, and Lose Authority in Environmental Governance.* MIT Press, 2018.

Green, Jessica F. *Rethinking Private Authority: Agents and Entrepreneurs in Global Environmental Governance.* Princeton University Press, 2013.

van der Ven, Hamish. *Beyond Greenwash: Explaining Credibility in Transnational Eco-Labeling.* Oxford University Press, 2019.

REINFORCEMENT LEARNING

Sutton, Richard S., and Andrew G. Barto. *Reinforcement Learning: An Introduction.* 2nd ed. MIT Press, 2018.

ROBOTICS

Danaher, John, and Neil McArthur, eds. *Robot Sex: Social and Ethical Implications.* MIT Press, 2017.

Ford, Martin. *The Rise of Robots: Technology and the Threat of a Jobless Future.* Basic Books, 2015.

Jordan, John. *Robots.* MIT Press, 2016.

Lee, Mark H. *How to Grow a Robot: Developing Human-Friendly, Social AI.* MIT Press, 2020.

Mindell, David A. *Our Robots, Ourselves: Robotics and the Myths of Autonomy*. Viking, 2015.

Murphy, Robin R. *Introduction to AI Robotics*. 2nd ed. MIT Press, 2018.

SCIENCE AND TECHNOLOGY STUDIES

Felt, Ulrike, Rayvon Fouché, Clark A. Miller, and Laurel Smith-Doerr, eds. *The Handbook of Science and Technology Studies*. 4th ed. MIT Press, 2016.

Godin, Benoît. *Models of Innovation: The History of an Idea*. MIT Press, 2017.

Hess, David J. *Undone Science: Social Movements, Mobilized Publics, and Industrial Transition*. MIT Press, 2016.

Kaplan, David, ed. *Philosophy, Technology, and the Environment*. MIT Press, 2017.

Oliveira, Arlindo. *The Digital Mind: How Science Is Redefining Humanity*. MIT Press, 2017.

SECURITY AND DIGITAL TECHNOLOGY

Choucri, Nazli, and David D. Clark. *Cyberspace and International Relations: The Co-Evolution Dilemma*. MIT Press, 2018.

Deibert, Ronald J. *Black Code: Inside the Battle for Cyberspace*. Signal, 2013.

Mitnick, Kevin D. *The Art of Invisibility: The World's Most Famous Hacker Teaches You How to Be Safe in the Age of Big Brother and Big Data*. Little, Brown, 2017.

Morozov, Evgeny. *The Net Delusion: The Dark Side of Internet Freedom*. Public Affairs, 2012.

Schneier, Bruce. *Click Here to Kill Everybody: Security and Survival in a Hyper-connected World*. W. W. Norton, 2018.

Singer, P. W., and Allan Friedman. *Cybersecurity and Cyberwar: What Everyone Needs to Know*. Oxford University Press, 2014.

SINGULARITY

Callaghan, Vic, James Miller, Roman Yampolskiy, and Stuart Armstrong, eds. *The Technological Singularity: Managing the Journey*. Springer, 2017.

Kurzweil, Ray. *The Singularity Is Near: When Humans Transcend Biology*. Viking Press, 2005.

Shanahan, Murray. *The Technological Singularity*. MIT Press, 2015.

SMART AGRICULTURE

Billingsley, John, ed. *Robotics and Automation for Improving Agriculture*. Burleigh Dodds Science Publishing, 2019.

Nhamo, Nhamo, David Chikoye, and Therese Gondwe, eds. *Smart Technologies for Sustainable Smallholder Agriculture: Upscaling in Developing Countries*. Academic Press, 2017.

Zhang, Qin, ed. *Precision Agriculture Technology for Crop Farming*. CRC Press, 2016.

SMART CITIES

Angelakis, Vangelis, Elias Tragos, H. Pöhls, Adam Kapovits, and Alessandro Bassi, eds. *Designing, Developing, and Facilitating Smart Cities: Urban Design to IoT Solutions*. Springer, 2017.

Green, Ben. *The Smart Enough City: Putting Technology in Its Place to Reclaim Our Urban Future*. MIT Press, 2019.

Halegoua, Germaine. *Smart Cities*. MIT Press, 2020.

McLaren, Duncan, and Julian Agyeman. *A Case for Truly Smart and Sustainable Cities*. MIT Press, 2015.

Townsend, Anthony M. *Smart Cities: Big Data, Civic Hackers, and the Quest for a New Utopia*. W. W. Norton, 2013.

SOCIAL MEDIA (INDUSTRY AND POLITICS)

Kirkpatrick, David. *The Facebook Effect: The Inside Story of the Company That Is Connecting the World*. Simon & Schuster, 2010.

Singer, P. W., and Emerson T. Brooking. *LikeWar: The Weaponization of Social Media*. Eamon Dolan/Houghton Mifflin Harcourt, 2018.

Vaidhyanathan, Siva. *Antisocial Media: How Facebook Disconnects Us and Undermines Democracy*. Oxford University Press, 2018.

SURVEILLANCE

Lyon, David. *The Culture of Surveillance*. Polity, 2018.

Schneier, Bruce. *Data and Goliath: The Hidden Battles to Collect Your Data and Control Your World*. W. W. Norton, 2015.

Zuboff, Shoshana. *The Age of Surveillance Capitalism: The Fight for a Human Future at the New Frontier of Power*. Public Affairs, 2018.

SUSTAINABILITY (BACKGROUND)

Caradonna, Jeremy L. *Sustainability: A History*. Oxford University Press, 2014.

Curren, Randall, and Ellen Metzger. *Living Well Now and in the Future: Why Sustainability Matters*. MIT Press, 2017.

Portney, Kent E. *Sustainability*. MIT Press, 2015.

Robertson, Margaret. *Sustainability: Principles and Practice*. Routledge, 2014.

Thiele, Leslie. *Sustainability*. 2nd ed. Polity, 2016.

SUSTAINABILITY (AND BUSINESS)

Bloomfield, Michael John. *Dirty Gold: How Activism Transformed the Jewelry Industry*. MIT Press, 2017.

Dauvergne, Peter. *Will Big Business Destroy Our Planet?* Polity, 2018.

Dauvergne, Peter, and Jane Lister. *Eco-Business: A Big-Brand Takeover of Sustainability*. MIT Press, 2013.

Jones, Geoffrey. *Profits and Sustainability: A History of Green Entrepreneurship*. Oxford University Press, 2017.

Nemetz, Peter N. *Business and the Sustainability Challenge: An Integrated Perspective*. Routledge, 2013.

Ponte, Stefano. *Business, Power and Sustainability in a World of Global Value Chains*. Zed Books, 2019.

Winston, Andrew. *The Big Pivot: Radically Practical Strategies for a Hotter, Scarcer, and More Open World*. Harvard Business Review Press, 2014.

SUSTAINABILITY (AND ENVIRONMENTALISM)

Dauvergne, Peter. *Environmentalism of the Rich*. MIT Press, 2016.

Dauvergne, Peter, and Genevieve LeBaron. *Protest Inc.: The Corporatization of Activism*. Polity, 2014.

Parr, Adrian. *Birth of a New Earth: The Radical Politics of Environmentalism*. Columbia University Press, 2018.

Wapner, Paul. *Living through the End of Nature: The Future of American Environmentalism*. MIT Press, 2010.

SUSTAINABILITY (PATHWAYS TOWARD)

Cohen, Maurie J. *The Future of Consumer Society: Prospects for Sustainability in the New Economy*. Oxford University Press, 2017.

Dryzek, John S., and Pickering, Jonathan. *The Politics of the Anthropocene*. Oxford University Press, 2019.

Harrison, Neil E. *Sustainable Capitalism and the Pursuit of Well-Being*. Routledge, 2014.

Klein, Naomi. *On Fire: The Case for a Green New Deal*. Simon & Schuster, 2019.

Litfin, Karen T. *Ecovillages: Lessons for Sustainable Community*. Polity, 2013.

Maniates, Michael. *Does Living Green Make a Difference?* Polity, 2020.

Rudel, Thomas K. *Shocks, States, and Sustainability: The Origins of Radical Environmental Reforms*. Oxford University Press, 2019.

Smith, Zachary A., and Heather M. Farley. *Sustainability: If It's Everything, Is It Nothing?* Routledge, 2013.

Wapner, Paul. *Is Wildness Over?* Polity, 2020.

TECHNOLOGY (CRITIQUES)

Bridle, James. *New Dark Age: Technology and the End of the Future*. Verso, 2018.

Eubanks, Virginia. *Automating Inequality: How High-Tech Tools Profile, Police, and Punish the Poor*. St. Martin's Press, 2018.

Golding, Edward L. *A History of Technology and Environment: From Stone Tools to Ecological Crisis*. Routledge, 2017.

Noble, Safiya Umoja. *Algorithms of Oppression: How Search Engines Reinforce Racism*. New York University Press, 2018.

Smith, Robert Elliot. *Rage inside the Machine: The Prejudice of Algorithms, and How to Stop the Internet Making Bigots of Us All*. Bloomsbury Business, 2019.

TECHNOLOGY AND SUSTAINABILITY

Bolwell, Dain. *Governing Technology in the Quest for Sustainability on Earth*. Routledge, 2019.

Galaz, Victor. *Global Environmental Governance, Technology and Politics: The Anthropocene Gap*. Edward Elgar, 2014.

INDEX

Ackerman, Neil, 6
Acquisitions and mergers, 38
Activism, 161–162
  environmental, 148–151, 194–196
  murders of activists, 150–151,
    162
  online, 157
Ada Health, 129
Ada robotic platform, 3
Addictive technology, 29–31
Advertising, 17
  AI-enhanced, 143–144
  digital, 27, 145
  expenditures, 142
  online revenues, 145
  targeted, 28
Africa, 59–60, 151
African Americans, 128
Agribusiness, 111–113, 151
Agriculture, 16, 102. *See also* Smart
  farming
AI4ALL, 127
AI for Earth, 4–5, 54, 65–67, 113,
  186–187
AI for Earth Innovation, 66–67
AI for Good, 67

AI-Powered Supply Chains Supercluster,
  183
Airbus, 58
Alexa, 26, 42, 90, 144
Algorithmic governance, 32, 157
Alibaba, 44–45, 105, 122, 145
Allen, John R., 46, 177
Allenby, Jeffrey, 66
All-Party Parliamentary Group on
  Artificial Intelligence, 184
Alphabet, 27, 38–39
AlphaGo, 47
AlphaZero, 23
Altman, Sam, 189
Amazon, 6, 10
  AI applications, 42–43
  Alexa, 26, 42
  Amazon Echo, 26
  Amazon Fresh, 43
  Amazon Go, 26–27, 42, 144
  biased hiring tool, 127–128
  CIA contract, 194
  delivery drones, 27
  eco-business, 76–79
  employee open letter, 194
  fulfillment centers, 77

Amazon Web Services (AWS), 77,
    137–138
American AI Initiative, 168, 183
American Express, 161
Analytics, AI, 36–37
Anandkumar, Anima, 127
Andrae, Anders, 73–74
Andriole, Steve, 169
Animals
    decrease of populations, 140
    health, 109
    identification of, 61
    poaching, 66
    tracking, 55
    trafficking, 60–61
Anthropocene, 9
Apple, 30, 38–39
    AI research, 40
    Daisy robot, 96
    gender/racial inequality, 126
    iPhone performance, 25, 92–93
    market capitalization value, 40
Arms industry, 172–173. *See also*
    Weapons, AI
Article 36, 191–192
Artificial intelligence (AI). *See also*
    Machine learning
    criticisms of, 8
    dangers of, 119–120, 130–131,
        190–191
    development of, 35–36, 48–49, 179
    and environmental issues, 12,
        179–180
    political uses of, 10–11
    unsustainable uses of, 10, 195
    writing about, 11–13
Artificial Intelligence Technology
    Strategy, 183
*Artificial Unintelligence: How Computers
    Misunderstand the World,* 85
Ashton, Kevin, 26
Aspuru-Guzik, Alán, 3
Audubon Society, 55

Aurora Innovation, 87
Australia, 173
Authoritarian governments, 160
Auto industry, 41, 87, 97–98, 140–141
Automatic identification system (AIS),
    56–57
Autonomous weapons, 167, 191–193
Azadzoy, Hila, 129
Azure cloud computing, 5, 64, 187

BAE Systems, 173
Baidu, 44–45, 47, 145
Baihe, 159
Bank fraud, 161
Bank loans, 130
Battery packs, automobile, 89
Bayer, 71, 102
Behavioral biometric software, 160–161
BehavioSec, 160
Bell, Ganesh, 81
Bengio, Yoshua, 187–188
Berlinguette, Curtis, 3
Bezos, Jeff, 42, 121–122, 194
Bias, 10, 16
Big data, 23–24
Big Data: A Revolution, 24
Big Pivot, The, 78
Billionaires, 121–122, 125
Bill & Melinda Gates Foundation,
    129
BioCatch, 160–161
Bird tracking, 55
Blinding laser weapons, 177, 193
Blue River Technology, 110
Boerder, Kristina, 57
Bolivia, 156
Brazil, 31, 142
Brenner, Michael, 143
Brin, Sergey, 122
Broussard, Meredith, 85
Buffet, Warren, 122
Burt, Peter, 173
Business partnerships, 64–65, 68

Business value of AI, 37, 65
Byanyima, Winnie, 122

Cáceres, Berta, 149
Cai Chaolin, 106
Cambodia, 155
Cambridge Analytica, 27
Cambridge University, 54
Camera trap technology, 60
Campaign to Stop Killer Robots, 192
Canada, 183
Cann, Geoffrey, 137
Capitalism, global, 195–196
Car batteries, 89
Carbon emissions, 58
  ICT industry, 73–74
  increase of, 134–135
Carbon footprint, 121
Cell phones, 25, 58–59, 67
Central Intelligence Agency (CIA), 31
Charlevoix Common Vision for the
    Future of Artificial Intelligence, 184
Chen Yong, 158
Chesapeake Conservancy, 66
ChimpFace, 60–61
China, 10, 30
  advertising and marketing, 145
  armed drones, 173, 175
  BAT, 44–46
  billionaires, 122
  and developing countries, 124–125
  eco-business, 81–82
  food delivery, 145
  and foreign NGOs, 149
  job loss, 123
  loan repayment, 130
  military applications, 47, 170
  military spending, 165
  online censorship, 157–160
  potential GDP increase, 38
  poverty, 120
  rare earth elements, 94–95
  smart cities, 105–108

  social credit system, 158–159
  surveillance technology, 17, 32, 151–
    156, 159, 169
  weapons, 169–170
China Electronics Technology Group
    Corporation, 175
Chorzempa, Martin, 32
Clausewitz, Carl von, 165
Clearpath Robotics, 175
Climate change, 134–138. *See also*
    Carbon emissions; Environmental
    management
  and cities, 108
  fossil-fuel emissions, 135
  global warming, 69, 134–135
  research, 3
  satellite imaging, 57–58
  tracking, 56
Closed-circuit television (CCTV), 32, 151
Cloud computing, 5, 64, 75, 187
CloudWalk Technology, 154, 156
Coal-fired electricity, 82
Coal production, 135
Cobalt, 89
Coca-Cola, 71–72
Cognitive CSR, 79
Colonialism, 163
Coltan, 93–94
Columbia, 31, 140
Commercial AI, 36–38
  and big tech, 38–40, 44–46
  deep learning, 37
  retail industry, 42–44
  self-driving market, 41
  and social media, 41–42
Commodifying data, 25, 27–29
Competition for AI supremacy, 35, 37–
    38, 46–47, 49, 185
Connecterra, 109
Conservation, global, 53–54. *See also*
    Environmental management
  bird tracking, 55
  political economy of, 67–69

Conservation X Labs, 60
Consumerism, 141–145
Consumer products, 15–17, 85–86,
    140–141. *See also* Smart products
Consumption, 133–134, 139–145
  and advertising, 142–143
  and ecological footprint, 140
  global sustainability of, 85–86
  overconsumption, 107–108
  personal, 121
  plastics, 141–142
  urban, 107–108
Convention on Certain Conventional
    Weapons protocol of 1995, 193
Cook, Gary, 75
Cook, Tim, 40
Coral reefs, 1–2, 69
Cornachio, Matt, 174
Cornell University, 55
Corporate social responsibility (CSR)
    programs, 14, 79–82, 186
Corporate sustainability, 5
Corporations. *See* Transnational
    corporations
Correctional Offender Management
    Profiling for Alternative Sanctions
    (COMPAS), 128
Cortana, 39
Costigan, Neil, 160
CrackBerry, 30
Crawford, Kate, 98
Criminal justice predictions, 128
Cross-selling, 143
Crown-of-thorns starfish, 1, 62–63
Cukier, Kenneth, 24
Cybersecurity industry, 31
Cybersurveillance, 157–160

Dahua, 153, 155
Daimler, 41
Daisy robot, 96
Data
  and addiction, 29–31
  big data, 23–24

commodifying, 25, 27–29
digitalization of, 24–25
and energy efficiency, 74
environmental, 54–55
and security, 31–32
value of, 13
world production of, 33
Data capitalism, 25
Data centers, 74–76
Datafication, 24–25
Datasphere, 33
Daugherty, Paul, 146
Deepfakes for text, 190
Deep learning, 4, 37, 54, 58, 142–143
DeepMind, 5–6, 23, 39, 189
*Deep Thinking: Where Machine
    Intelligence Ends and Human Creativity
    Begins*, 12
Defense Advanced Research Projects
    Agency (DARPA), 166, 169
Deforestation, 58–59, 69, 142
Delivery systems, 78–79
Democratic Republic of the Congo, 59–
    60, 89, 94, 138
Department of Defense (DoD), 168
Descartes Labs, 58
Desmond, Jenny, 61
Developing countries, 124–125, 129,
    193
Dhakad, Keshav, 187
Digital advertising, 27–28, 145
Digital fingerprints, 160–161
DigitalGlobe, 58
Digitalization, 24–25
Digital traces, 25, 27
Dilkina, Bistra, 66
Dinerstein, Eric, 60
Discrimination, 10, 16, 120
  gender inequality, 119, 125–126
  and machine bias, 127–128
  racial, 126, 128
Diversity, 126–127
Divine, John, 38
Doffman, Zak, 155

Driverless vehicles, 6, 36, 40–41, 85–89, 97–98
Drones
  agricultural uses, 108–109
  armed, 172–175, 191
  coral bleaching, 63
  Predator/Reaper, 165–166
  tracking poachers, 4
Dryzek, John S., 181

EarthCube, 55–56
Earth-imaging companies, 58
Earth shares, 120–122
eBird, 55
Eco-business, 14–15, 71–83. *See also*
  Transnational corporations
  acceleration of, 82–83
  Amazon, 76–79
  and CSR, 79–82
  Google, 73–76
  rebound effects, 73
  and sustainability, 71–72, 82–83
  utility companies, 80–81
  Xcel Energy, 80
Ecological footprint, 107, 121, 140
Ecomodernist Manifesto, An, 114
Economic growth, 146
Economic uses of AI, 36
Ecosystems management, 14, 53–54, 58.
  See also Environmental management
Ecuador, 156
EHang, 175
Electricity, 82, 103–104
Electric self-driving vehicles, 41, 88–89
Electronics industry, 94
Elephants, 59–60
Ellison, Larry, 122
El Salvador, 150
Email, 25
Emotient, 40
Employment opportunities, 123
Enerdata, 89
Energy consumption, 103–104
Energy efficiency, 74–76, 91, 98

Environmental datasets, 54–56
Environmental inequality, 120
Environmentalism
  market liberal, 181
  suppressing, 148–151
Environmental management, 1–4, 53.
  See also Climate change
  bird tracking, 55
  and business partnerships, 64–65, 68
  data, 54–55
  Great Barrier Reef, 62–64
  overfishing, 56–57
  and plastics, 88, 141–142
  political economy of, 67–69
  rainforests, 58–59
  and urban consumption, 107
  wildlife, 59–62
Eritrea, 140
Ethical principles of development, 188
Ethiopia, 155
European Parliament resolution of 2018
  on lethal autonomous weapons, 193
European Union's General Data
  Protection Regulation, 130, 195
ExxonMobil, 10
Eyal, Nir, 30

Facebook, 25
  acquisitions, 28–29, 42
  advertising, 28, 145
  as data generator, 27
  design goals, 30
  gender/racial inequality, 126
  and renewable energy, 75
  revenues, 27
  and user data, 27–28
Facial expression technology, 148, 152–154
Facial recognition, 40, 60, 143–144, 153–154
Fair earth shares, 120–122
Farming, 15, 101. *See also* Smart farming
Feldstein, Steven, 159
Financial systems, 43

Fish consumption, 140
Fishing fleets, tracking, 56–58
Fitbit for cows, 109
Food
  delivery, 145
  demand, 108
  waste, 140
Fossil-fuel emissions, 135
Fossil-fuel power plants, 80
France, 30, 183–184
Free Basics app, 28
Free-to-play gaming, 29
Freeware, 29
Fuenffinger, Dan, 76
Fuentes, Sigfredo, 109
Future of Life Institute, 190–191, 194

Gaming disorder, 29
Garcia, Ecatarina, 47
Gariepy, Ryan, 175
Gas industry, 136–139
Gates, Bill, 121–122
Gates, Melinda, 126
GE Digital, 81
Gender inequality, 119, 125–126
General Atomics MQ-1 Predator drone,
  165–166
General Atomics MQ-9 Reaper drone,
  166
General Electric, 81
General Motors, 41
Geoanalytics, 58
GE Power, 80–81
Gerasimov, Valery, 47–48
Giraffes, 61
Global capitalism, 195–196
Global Fishing Watch, 56–57
Global sustainability, 6, 8, 10, 16
  and business partnerships, 64–65
  and colonialism, 163
  of consumption, 85–86
  and investment, 187
  limits of, 114–115

and politics, 14, 180
and private governance, 185–186
and smart cities, 106–108
and smart products, 86, 97–98
sustainable development principles,
  188
and technocratic thinking, 181
and technology, 181–182, 196
and war, 164
Global warming, 69, 134–135
Global Witness, 150–151
Gomes, Carla, 55
Google, 5, 38–39, 71, 122
  advertising, 145
  AI consumer products, 39
  AIS, 56
  eco-business, 73–76
  energy efficiency, 75–76
  Google Search, 27
  JEDI, 193–194
  machine bias, 127
  Project Maven, 19
  and renewable energy, 74
  responsible R&D, 189
  self-driving cars, 41, 87
  sexual harassment/discrimination,
    125–126
  TensorFlow, 2, 64
  user profiles, 27
  Voice Search, 76
  weapons projects, 193–194
Gore, Al, 6
Government
  authoritarian, 160
  and competitive advantage, 185
  funding, 67, 186
  and global capitalism, 195–196
  regulation, 130–131, 182–185, 195
  state power, 147–151, 162
Great Barrier Reef, 62–64, 67
Great Pacific Garbage Patch, 141
Green Horizons, 104
Greenhouse gases, 5, 74, 80, 85

Greenpeace, 150
Gross domestic product (GDP), 5, 38
Group of Seven (G7), 184
Guangzhou, 106
Guterres, António, 134, 193

Habit-forming products, 30
Hangzhou, 105
Harop kamikaze drone, 172
Harrison, Peter, 2
Harvest CROO Robotics, 110–111
Hassabis, Demis, 18
Hawking, Stephen, 11, 18
Health applications, 129
Hein, Jason, 3
Hikvision, 153, 155
Hinton, Geoffrey, 187
Home automation, 90–91, 98, 103
Honduras, 148–149
Hon Hai Precision Industry, 39
Honour of Kings, 30–31
*Hooked: How to Build Habit-Forming
    Products*, 30
Horvitz, Eric, 65, 188
Household products, 90–93
Huawei, 105–106, 137, 155
Human evolution, 9
Hurst, Kara Hartnett, 77

IBM's cognitive computing, 104
IBM Watson AI XPRIZE, 67
Identity theft, 161
iFlyTek, 45
Income inequality, 119
India, 110, 140, 165, 184, 187
Inequality, 119–128
  developing countries, 124–125
  and diversity, 126–127
  earth shares, 120–122
  and ecological footprints, 121
  gender, 119, 125–126
  and increased productivity, 119–120,
    124

and machine bias, 127–128
  social, 10, 16, 123–127
  wealth distribution, 121–122, 124
Infectious diseases, 4
Information and communications
    technology (ICT) industry, 73–74
Instagram, 28, 42
Intelligence operations, 46–47
Intelligent automation, 5–6, 10
Intelligent mines, 139
International Committee for Robot
    Arms Control, 192
International Panel on Artificial
    Intelligence, 183
Internet
  growth of, 25
  increasing use, 31
  search engine market, 145
Internet of Things (IoT), 26–27,
    104
Internet.org, 28
Inventory management, 43
Investment, AI, 38
  government, 67, 186
  smart city technology, 102
  and sustainability, 187
iPhones, 25, 92–93
IrisKing, 153–154
Iris recognition, 153–154
Israel Aerospace Industries, 172
Ivory poaching, 60

Japan, 183
Jeff, Galagher, 144
Jiang Xueqin, 153
Jinnah, Sikina, 9
Job loss, 120, 123, 125
John Deere, 110
Johnson, Theodore, 47
Joint Enterprise Defense Infrastructure
    (JEDI), 193–194
Joler, Vladan, 98
Joppa, Lucas, 4–5, 65–66, 113

Kalashnikov, 171
Kaplan, Jerry, 17
Kasparov, Garry, 12
Keely, Mac, 111
Kent, Muhtar, 71
Khokhar, Yasir, 109
Killer drones, 191
Korinek, Anton, 124
Kossmann, Donald, 64
Krajewski, Markus, 91
Kroodsma, David A., 56

LarvalBot, 1–2, 63
LeCun, Yann, 42, 187
Lee, Kai-Fu, 46, 54, 123–124, 130
Lee, Peter, 7, 167
Lee Sedol, 47
Li, Fei-Fei, 19, 126–127
Li, Robin, 45, 47
Liberia Chimpanzee Rescue and
    Protection, 61
Limp, David, 43
LinkedIn, 127
Lithium-ion batteries, 89
Liu Guozhi, 170
Li Yingyun, 158–159
Loans, repayment of, 130
Lockheed Martin, 172–173, 175
Long, Robert, 61
Longline fishing, 57
Lynch, Jennifer, 161

Ma, Jack, 122
Machine bias, 10, 127–128
Machine learning, 3–4
    and bias, 10, 127–128
    and big data, 24
    energy efficiency of, 76
    inventory management, 43
    and marketing, 143
    patents, 35
    tracking species, 55
Macías Aymar, Iñigo, 122

Made to Break: Technology and
    Obsolescence, 91
Maduro, Nicolás, 175
Magic Pony Technology, 42
Mahoney, William, 80
Ma Huateng, 122
Malaysia, 155
Mann, Michael, 138
Manufacturing, 43
Marine plastic pollution, 141
Marketing, 16–17, 143–145
Market liberal environmentalism,
    181–182
Martin, Steven, 81
Maschler, Thomas, 59
Mattis, James, 168
May, Theresa, 184
Mayer-Schönberger, Viktor, 24
McCormick, Colin, 60–61
McDonald's, 71
McMillon, Doug, 44
Meat consumption, 142
Megvii, 154
Meituan, 145
Merchant, Brian, 137
Messaging apps, 25
Microfinancing, 129–130
Microsoft, 4, 38–39, 44, 71
    AI for Earth, 4–5, 54, 65–67, 113,
        186–187
    Azure cloud computing, 5, 64,
        187
    Cortana, 39
    gender/racial inequality, 126
    and OpenAI, 190
    Tay chatbot, 7
Microsoft Research AI, 39–40
Military-industrial complex, AI, 46–48,
    164–165. See also Weapons, AI
Military spending, 165
Miller, Daniel, 175
Miller, Nate, 57
Mining, 93–95, 138–139

Mobile phones, 25
Monga, Rajat, 64
Mongolia, 155
Monopolies, 124
Monsanto, 102
Montreal Declaration for Responsible AI
    Development, 188
Morgan, Blake, 79
Moseley, T. Michael, 166
Mosquitoes, 4–5
Mozur, Paul, 154
Murders of activists, 150–151, 162
Musk, Elon, 11, 18, 185, 189

Nadella, Satya, 39
Naqvi, Al, 79
National Aeronautics and Space
    Administration (NASA), 57
National Geographic Society, 66
National Science Foundation, 56
Natural resources, 16–17
Nature Conservancy, 55
Navarro, Peter, 173
Nemitz, Paul, 130–131
Nerekhta, 171
Nestlé, 71
NeuCo, 81
Neural networks, artificial, 80
Nicholson, Simon, 9
Nig, Andrew, 36
Nike, 71
Nitrous oxide, 80
Nongovernmental organizations
    (NGOs), 149–150, 192
Nonprofits partnerships, 65–65,
    68
Nooyi, Indra, 72
North America GDP increase, 38
Northrop Grumman MQ-4C Triton
    aircraft, 166–167
NtechLab, 143–144
Nuland, Victoria, 177
NVIDIA, 137

Obama, Barack, 183
Obsolescence, planned, 91
Oceana, 56
Oceanalpha, 175
Off the Leash: The Development of
    Autonomous Military Drones in the
    UK, 173
O'Hanlon, Michael, 174
Oil production, 135–139
Online addiction, 30–31
Online gaming, 29–31
Online security, 161
Online surveillance, 157–160
OpenAI, 37, 68, 189–190
Oracle, 122
Orbital Insight, 58
Organization for Economic Cooperation
    and Development (OECD), 184
Overconsumption, 107–108
Overfishing, 56–58, 140

Packaging, 77–78
Page, Larry, 122
Paikeday, Tony, 137
Palm oil consumption, 142
Pan-Canadian Artificial Intelligence
    Strategy, 183
Parker, Kellie, 139
Parker, Sean, 30
Partnership on AI, 65, 188–189
Patents, 35
Paulas, Rick, 93
Payne, Kenneth, 165
Pentagon, U.S., 11
People's Liberation Army, 170
PepsiCo, 72
Perdix drones, 174
Philippines, 31
Pichai, Sundar, 39, 144, 188
Ping An, 105
Planet, 58
Planned obsolescence, 91
Plantix, 109–110

Plastics, 88, 141–142
Platform-M combat robot, 171
Platform services, 25
Poaching, 66
Political economy perspective, 7–13
  agricultural conglomerates, 112–113
  AI downsides, 180
  environmental management, 67–69
  smart products, 97–99
Pollution
  e-waste, 95–98
  forecasting, 104
  plastics, 88, 141–142
Population, world, 101
Porter, Tony, 32
Poseidon drone, 171
Poverty, 120, 129–130, 133
Predictive analytics, 136–138, 143
Predix, 81
*Preparing for the Future of Artificial
  Intelligence,* 183
PricewaterhouseCoopers (PwC),
  185–186
Privacy, 120, 161
Private governance, 185–187
Procter & Gamble, 71
Production, 133–134
  coal/oil production, 135–136
  gas industry, 136–139
  plastics, 141–142
Productivity, 133
Profitability, 146
Project Maven, 19
Project Premonition, 4–5
ProPublica, 128
Protection Assistant for Wildlife Security
  (PAWS), 66
Public safety, 156–157
Purdy, Mark, 146
Putin, Vladimir, 10–11, 48, 149, 171

Qi Lu, 81–82
Quiñonero Candela, Joaquin, 145

Racial discrimination, 126, 128
Rainforest Connection, 2–3, 58–59
Rainforests, 58–59
RangerBot, 1, 63
Rare earth elements, 94–95
RealFace, 40
Reay, David, 135
Recommendation engines, 144
Recycling, 95–96
Redfern, Simon, 54
Rees, William E., 107
Refrigerants, 86
Regulation
  government, 130–131, 182–185,
    195
  private, 185–187
  self-regulation, 186, 188
Relay, 78
Renewable energy, 74–77, 104
Resolve, 60
Responsible research and development,
  187–194
Retail industry, 42–44, 78–79,
  142–144
Ride-sharing, 88
Riffle, Conor, 79–80
Rio Tinto, 10, 138–139
Road infrastructure, 88
Robots, 1–2, 4
  Amazon fulfillment centers, 77
  environmental management, 63
  farming tools, 110–111
Rockwell Automation, 137
Roper, William, 174
Rosenberg, Louis, 7
Royal Bank of Scotland, 161
Royal Dutch Shell, 10
Rupavatharam, Srikanth, 110
Russia, 10–11, 47–48
  arms manufacturers, 172
  foreign agents law, 149
  military spending, 165
  oil production, 135

surveillance, 151–152, 155
weapons, 170–171
Russo, Alexandra, 60–61

Sadler, Brent D., 46
Samsung, 39, 75
Samsung SGR-A1 sentry gun, 172
Satellite imaging, 57–58
Saudi Arabia, 135, 165
Scenario modeling, 59
Scharre, Paul, 165
Schlumberger, 137
Schultz, Jason, 131
Scurry, Bryan, 167
Sea Hunter, 166
Search engine market, 145
Security
  datafying, 31–32
  online, 161
  personal, 120
  surveillance, 154
"See and spray" machine, 110
Seine fishing, 57
Self-driving industry, 6, 36, 40–41, 85–
  89, 97–98
Self-driving laboratories, 3
Self-regulation, 186, 188
Semeniuk, Ivan, 175
SenseTime, 154
Sensia, 137
Sensors, 26
Serengeti National Park, 59–60
Sesame Credit, 158–159
Shah, Nihar, 128
Shanahan, Patrick, 168
Shanghai, 106
Shaw, Ian, 173
Shenzhen, 154
Shindell, Drew, 134
Shipping, 77–78
SkyTruth, 56–57
Slade, Giles, 91
Small Robot Company, 111

Smart appliances, 4
Smart cities, 101–108
  in China, 105–106
  electricity grids, 103–104
  features of, 102–103
  limitations of, 106–108
  traffic management, 105–106
Smart farming, 108–113
  equipment, 110–111
  and global food production, 112
  and industrial agriculture, 112–113
  risks of, 111–113
  small farms, 114
Smart Finance, 130
Smart homes, 90–91, 98, 103
Smartphones, 25
  addiction to, 30
  farming apps, 114
  iPhones, 25, 92–93
  and rare earth elements, 94
Smart products, 85–99. *See also*
  Smartphones
  driverless and electric vehicles, 6, 36,
    40–41, 85–89, 97–98
  e-waste, 95–97
  household, 90–93
  mining for, 93–95
  political economy of, 97–99
  and sustainability, 86, 89
Smith, Brad, 185
Snapchat, 42
Social inequality, 10, 16, 123–127
Social media, 25
  addiction to, 30
  and commercial AI, 41–42
Social sustainability, 129–131
South Korea, 30, 172
Soybean consumption, 142
SpaceKnow, 58
Spatial mapping, 59
Spyware, 160
Starfish, 1, 62–63
Startups, AI, 38

State governance, 182–185
State power, 147–151, 162, 196. *See also*
    Surveillance
Steyer, James, 31
Stiglitz, Joseph E., 124
Strategy, Evolution, and War, 165
Straub, Jeremy, 175–176
Suleyman, Mustafa, 5–6, 18, 65, 188
Supercharging hardware, 39
Supercomputer, AI, 64
Supply chains, 43, 183
Surveillance, 17, 31–32, 143–144,
    151–160
  behavioral biometrics, 160–161
  closed-circuit television (CCTV), 32,
    151
  drones, 173
  facial expression technology, 148,
    152–153
  facial recognition, 40, 60, 143–144,
    153–154
  globalization of, 148, 155–156
  online, 157–160
  security systems, 154
  technology sales, 159–160
Sustainability. *See also* Global
    sustainability
  corporate, 5, 76
  and eco-business, 71–72, 82–83
  and global capitalism, 72
  social, 129–131
Sustainable development, 181, 188
Swarm wars, 174–175
Synthetics, 141

T-14 Armata battle tank, 171
Tallinn, Jaan, 18
Tantalum, 93–94
Targeted advertising, 28
Tay.ai chatbot, 7
Technology
  addictive, 29–31
  companies, 38–40, 44–46, 54

  downsides of, 182
  embrace of, 114
  and global sustainability, 181–182,
    196
  "in the wild," 13
  oil and gas production, 137–138
  and power, 196
  self-regulation, 185
  smart city, 102
  surveillance, 17, 31–32
  telecommunication, 58, 155
  unsustainable uses of, 10, 114–115
Telecommunications, 58, 155
Temperature, average global, 134
Tencent, 30, 105, 122, 145
  revenues, 44–45
  state censorship, 157–158
TensorFlow, 2, 64, 109
Tensor processor unit (TPU), 76
TerraLoupe, 58
Terry, Heath, 37
Tesla, 89
Text messaging, 25
Thailand, 31
Thales, 175
Toxic waste, 95
Toyota, 41, 87
Traffic accidents, 86–87
TrailGuard AI, 60
Transnational corporations, 38–40,
    44–46
  addictive technology, 30
  and agriculture, 102
  and automation, 33, 38
  competition for data, 27
  and eco-business, 71–72, 82–83
  investment, 81
  and mining, 94, 139
  monopolies, 124
  and NGOs, 150
  profitability, 146
  and regulation, 186, 188
  and sustainability partnerships, 65

Transportation, 45
Transshipments, 57
Transsion Holdings, 155
Tropical rainforests, 58–59, 69, 142
Trump, Donald, 46, 167–169, 183
Tsing Capital, 81
Tucker, Adam, 81
Twitter, 41–42

Uber, 41, 87
Unilever, 71
United Kingdom, 31–32, 184
  armed drones, 173
  elite education in, 123–124
  job loss, 124
  surveillance, 151–152
  swarming weapons, 174
United Nations, 67
United States
  AI military budget, 169
  arms manufacturers, 172
  billionaires, 122
  and Chinese AI industry, 45–46
  and developing countries, 124–125
  ecological footprint, 121, 140
  job loss, 123
  military spending, 165
  oil production, 135
  and superpower competition,
    46–47
  surveillance, 151
  weapons, 165–169, 173–175
UPS, 26
Uran-9, 171
Urban living, 15, 107–108
Urban transportation, 45
User profiles, 27
Utility companies, 80–81
Uyghur people, 153–154

Venture capital, 46, 125
Video surveillance. See Surveillance
Vincent, James, 153

Vineyard management, 108–109
Volkswagen, 41

Wackernagel, Mathis, 107–108
Wajcman, Judy, 16
Walmart, 10, 43–44, 71, 79, 144
Walsh, Toby, 172, 191
Wang Haifeng, 23
Wareham, Mary, 192
Waymo, 41, 87
Wealth distribution, 121–122, 124
Weapons, AI, 17–19, 163–177
  and arms race, 176–177
  China, 169–170
  diffusion of, 171–173
  drones, 172–175, 191
  fully autonomous, 167, 191–193
  laser, 177, 193
  manufacturers, 172–173
  risks of, 176–177
  Russia, 170–171
  swarming, 174–175
  United States, 165–169, 173–175
WeChat, 158
Whale sharks, 61
WhatsApp, 29
White, Topher, 2, 58
Whittaker, Meredith, 128
Whole Foods, 78
Wilby, Alvin, 175
Wildbook, 61–62
Wildlife, protecting, 59–62, 69. See also
  Animals
Williams, Jody, 192
Williamson, Gavin, 174
Wind power, 80
Winkenbach, Matthias, 79
Winston, Andrew, 78
Winthrop, John, 163
Women
  job loss, 125
  machine bias, 127–128
  in tech, 125–126

Work, Robert, 165, 167
World Resources Institute, 59
World War II, 164

Xcel Energy, 80
Xie Yinan, 154
Xi Jinping, 32, 156–157
Xue Liang project, 154

Yampolskiy, Roman, 7
Y Combinator, 189
Yi-Zheng Lian, 170
YouTube, 6, 25, 42, 61
Yunzhou-Tech, 175

Zavalishina, Jane, 138
Zebras, 61
Zelazny, Frances, 160
Zettabytes, 33
Zhang Guanchao, 153
Zheng Yijiong, 106
Zimbabwe, 156
ZTE Corporation, 155
Zuckerberg, Mark, 25, 27–28, 42, 121